CIVIL PROCEDURE

THIRD EDITION

By

SAMUEL ISSACHAROFF

Bonnie and Richard Reiss Professor of Constitutional Law
New York University School of Law

CONCEPTS AND INSIGHTS SERIES®

FOUNDATION PRESS
2012

THOMSON REUTERS™

© 2005 THOMSON REUTERS/FOUNDATION PRESS
© 2009 By THOMSON REUTERS/FOUNDATION PRESS
© 2012 By THOMSON REUTERS/FOUNDATION PRESS

 1 New York Plaza, 34th Floor

 New York, NY 10004

 Phone Toll Free 1–877–888–1330

 Fax 646–424–5201

 foundation–press.com

Printed in the United States of America

ISBN 978–1–60930–036–4

Mat #41174361

For Cindy.

PREFACE

Students typically enter law school expecting civil procedure to be the most removed topic from their prior experiences with the law. Contracts, property, criminal law, even torts—once they get beyond the name—all correspond to the way we structure our lives and form our expectations of the rules of conduct in our society. Of the traditional first-year courses, only civil procedure seems alien to the lived experiences with the law.

While civil procedure shares with all aspects of law its technical wizardry, one aim of this book is to dispel the sense of distinctiveness of the realm of procedure. No doubt, even in the era of liberal pleading, there are daunting technical issues regarding such matters as preclusion, reconsideration, aggregation, and a host of other exacting lawyer's tools of the trade. But there is also a deep intuitive logic that commands the field, aiming to find a balance between the need for finality and the aspiration for accuracy, weighing the competing considerations of fairness and equity against those of efficiency and cost, and casting legitimacy in outcomes as a function of the integrity of the processes used to arrive at a result.

The book begins with the question of due process. The object of structuring the presentation in this fashion is two-fold. First, there is the inescapable fact that the tools of constitutional balancing, most clearly set forth in *Mathews v. Eldridge*,[1] are now firmly entrenched not only in what are clearly understood as procedural cases, but even in the hardest cases of our times, such as defining the obligations owed enemy combatants, as in *Hamdi v. Rumsfeld*.[2] Second, it is to highlight the centrality of proper procedure in familiar debates about the rule of law. At some point, all societies must reserve to themselves the power to deny goods or benefits, to incarcerate, to seize property, and to otherwise engage in conduct that might be necessary to an ordered life—or might be a sign of tyranny. More often than not, it is the processes underlying the course of conduct, rather than its substance, that determines which side of the liberty versus tyranny divide is invoked.

From this foundation, the book then marches through some of the conventional material in a procedure course, perhaps with a bit more attention to the resolution of disputes than to the familiar mechanisms of adjudication. There is an attention to the economics

1. 424 U.S. 319 (1976).
2. 124 S. Ct. 2633 (2004).

of litigation and the strategic incentives created by rules that might be more direct than in the customary presentation of first-year legal materials. Hopefully, all of these will enrich the understanding of students looking at a civil procedure course largely through the prism of case law and formal rules. The book ends with a more systematic examination of our understanding of the litigation process, drawing initially on economic models of litigation, then challenging those on the basis of a richer understanding of actual human decisionmaking. While this may be less familiar to the customary teaching of procedure, hopefully this too will allow a more coherent presentation of the goals and limitations of our rather intricate world of process.

This book has been several years in the making. I have benefited from comments of colleagues on various parts of this work, particularly David Shapiro and Adrian Zuckerman on the efforts to render comprehensible the questions of preclusion. Throughout this project, I have been assisted by a wonderful group of research assistants at Columbia Law School and New York University School of Law, all of whom struggled through these concepts as my first-year students, then worked hard to recast and develop the classroom presentation for this more systematic account. This book would not exist without the efforts of Camden Hutchison, Dina Lemonik, Todd Lundell, Adam Orford, Olivia Radin, Daniel Suleiman, and Lesley Frieder Wolf of Columbia Law School, as well as Mark Boyko of NYU School of Law, the final addition to the first edition of the book. I was also helped tremendously by Colin Reardon for his careful work on the second edition, and by Nathan Foell on the Third Edition. I should also thank the initial publisher of this series, Steve Errick, for his patience and encouragement in this undertaking. He knew, long before I did, that I wanted to write this book.

Some portions of this book are drawn from work previously appearing in other publications. Chapter 1 owes some debt to an essay on "Due Process" that appeared in the *International Encyclopedia of the Social and Behavioral Sciences*; Chapter 2 contains some material that appeared as "Should There Be Rules of Procedure?," published by Leiden University as part of the *Clifford Chance Distinguished Lecture Series*; Chapter 4 draws on material published as "Governance and Legitimacy in the Law of Class Actions" in the Supreme Court Review; Chapter 8 contains material that has appeared as "The American Law of Repose" in the Civil Justice Quarterly; and parts of Chapter 9 appeared in the Florida State Law Review under the title, "The Content of Our Casebooks: Why Cases Get Litigated."

New York, New York
November 2011

TABLE OF CONTENTS

CIVIL PROCEDURE

Chapter 1

DUE PROCESS

In the American legal system, the term "procedure" refers to two separate bodies of law. The first system of procedure is the constitutional command of due process. The Fifth and Fourteenth Amendments to the Constitution restrict all governmental actors, whether federal, state, or local, from taking actions that impinge upon life, liberty, or property. The scope of these Amendments has been primarily defined by judicial case law, which has given specific form to the open-textured outlines of the Constitution. The second system of procedure is the internal operating commands of courts, which in the federal courts have been embodied since 1938 in the Federal Rules of Civil Procedure. These Federal Rules aim at approximating the ideals of a procedural system: the costless application of substantive law onto specific disputes in the form of judicial decisions. Unlike the broad constitutional command of due process, the Federal Rules are rather detailed, containing a series of commands that propose to govern all circumstances that might present themselves in the judicial system, regardless of the merits of the controversy. The Rules not only attempt to supply specific commands for courts, but in their operation they seek to cover any kind of civil dispute. Thus, in legal jargon, the sweep of the Rules is said to be "transsubstantive."

Despite their different origins and forms, the constitutional command of due process and the specific rule applications of civil procedure not only embody many of the same objectives, they turn out to use the same tools. Both are placeholders for an animating conception of fairness that stands behind any system of process. *Process* assures regularity in the treatment of similarly situated parties. *Process* guarantees against the arbitrariness of either capricious conduct or tyranny. *Process* imposes order and the burden of justification on the exercise of power. In theory, at least, it is *process itself* that constrains the powerful and protects the weak. Procedural order, therefore, can be considered an integral bulwark against the misuse of state authority. And, perhaps ironically, process is also a necessary ingredient of a legal system in which even a state's use of force against its own citizens must comport with the rule of law.

Whenever government acts, some legal process is necessary—or "due," as the Constitution commands—to ensure fairness. The real arguments are about how much, and what kind. Those questions arise not only in the formal constitutional realm, but also when ordinary citizens turn to a court asking that their dispute be resolved and that a remedy be fashioned. Here too, orderliness and predictability are the defining features of a system that may lay claim to being fair and just. Even the conflicts that emerge from the daily interactions of life demand processes that draw from the highest aspirations of our Constitution.

I. The Emergence of Due Process.

The concept of due process emerges from the central paradox in the creation of state authority. As framed in the American Constitution, for example, the due process command is directed as a negative limitation on what the state may do to the citizenry. The underlying question is what is the affirmative role of the state that the constitutional order assumes.

According to Thomas Hobbes in his *Leviathan*,[1] the answer is provided by considering life without government. For Hobbes, this pitiable state of nature allows only a life that is "solitary, poor, nasty, brutish, and short." Each person faces the constant threat of bodily violence, of invasion of the home and of seizure of property, and no man has an incentive to industry because each lacks security in investment, in planning, and in the ability to exchange.[2] The response to this disastrous situation, according to Hobbes, is the creation of the state, a body that can impose order, lift mankind from the pitiable war of all against all, and secure collective benefits.

Paradoxically, in attempting to *escape* from the state of nature, the creation of the governmental state actually magnifies the very threat that was ever-present in the state of nature. The state represents the largest and most powerful entity capable of doing what Hobbes feared most: inflicting bodily violence, invading the home, and seizing property. Indeed, all states reserve to themselves the right to do just that to their citizens, and some (including our own) even claim the right to punish by death. But if this is so, what is it that differentiates the modern state, which claims political legitimacy, from the state of nature? The answer must be an abiding respect for procedural fairness in the imposition of punish-

1. THOMAS HOBBES, LEVIATHAN 88 (Cambridge, 1996) (1651).

2. *Id.* at 89 (noting that in the hypothesized state of nature, "there is no place for industry; because the fruit thereof is uncertain: and consequently no culture of the Earth; no Navigation, nor use of the commodities that may be imported by Sea; no commodious building . . .").

ment and the regulation of the conduct of citizens' lives. The answer, in the terminology of American law, is due process.

This conception of procedural fairness is at the heart of the concept of the rule of law, and of its more technically exigent offshoot, the guarantee of due process. The typical formulation of due process, as that concept has developed in Anglo–American jurisprudence, is derived from the Magna Carta. This basic charter of limited government was issued by King John in 1215, as an exchange with rebellious barons seeking to restrain the exercise of royal prerogatives. The Magna Carta allowed more centralized authority, particularly in the funding of military campaigns, so long as the King's power was legally constrained:

> No free man shall be seized or imprisoned, or stripped of his rights or possessions, or outlawed or exiled, or deprived of his standing in any other way, nor will we proceed with force against him, or send others to do so, except by the lawful judgment of his equals or by the law of the land.[3]

The crux of this original formulation of due process was a limitation on the power of the royal sovereign that granted legal protection to the life, liberty, and property of English freemen. The Magna Carta is significant not because it changed the *substance* of sovereign authority, but because it limited the *forms* in which that authority could be exercised. That is, the document does not attempt to deny the sovereign the capacity to imprison, outlaw, or banish the rights-holding citizenry. Nor does it prevent the sovereign from imposing restraints on the enjoyment of property or other rights held by citizens. Rather, it imposes a condition of procedural regularity in the exercise of the sovereign's power, including orderly trial processes and formal proclamation of the applicable legal standards. This notion of procedural regularity is captured in the actual phrase, "due process of law," which first appeared when the Magna Carta was issued in an English version in 1354 by King Edward III. As recast in statutory form, the guarantee became that, "no man of what estate or condition that he be, shall be put out of land or tenement, nor taken nor imprisoned, nor disinherited, nor put to death, without being brought in answer by due process of the law." The modern vitality of this constraint on the use of sovereign authority derives from the efforts of Sir Edward Coke in the seventeenth century to revive the Magna Carta as a check on the power of the Stuart monarchs.

Not surprisingly, given these origins, due process emerged from medieval Britain primarily as a restraint on the executive power of

---

3. G.R.C. Davis, Magna Carta, (Revised Edition, London: British Museum, 1989).

the sovereign, specifically of the Crown. The concept of due process underwent transformation when the American colonists adapted the Magna Carta as a limiting principle not only on the use of executive power, but also on the scope of the laws that could be passed by the legislature. For colonists lacking the rights of participation in the creation of laws, the insult of arbitrary state power occurred independently of whether power was exercised legislatively or by the sovereign. As recast by the colonists, due process became a limitation that extended beyond simply the power of the Crown, to encompass local assemblies and, by the time of the revolution, Parliament itself.[4] Thus, even as England adopted a system of increasing parliamentary sovereignty, the concept of due process as a constraint on the exercise of governmental power retained its vitality in the colonies. As a result, upon gaining their independence, the Americans established a more limited government than they had had under the British. This is reflected in the Bill of Rights, whose Due Process Clause explicitly limits the use of federal governmental power, including by the legislative branch. As articulated by James Madison, "The legislature, no less than the executive, is under limitations of power," and hence the rights of the people were to be secured "against legislative as well as executive ambition."[5] The source of the limitation was a constitutional command that stood above and apart from the normal operations of state authority. The American focus on legislative power thereby highlights the importance of due process as a restraint not just on the penal powers of the state, but on its civil regulatory powers as well.

II. What Is Due Process?

Due process emerges from this historical origin with two central features. First, it protects substantive rights by requiring procedural regularity in the exercise of all governmental power. Second, the requirement of procedural regularity may not be altered by the normal operations of political power. As a constitutional guarantee, the requirements of due process may not be changed through the customary political processes of legislation or through unilateral executive action. It is these two features—procedural regularity and independence from direct political alteration—that

---

4. Robert E. Riggs, *Substantive Due Process in 1791*, 1990 Wis. L. Rev. 941, 969–71 (1990).

5. JAMES MADISON, REPORT ON THE VIRGINIA RESOLUTIONS (1800), *reprinted in* 4 DEBATES IN THE SEVERAL STATE CONVENTIONS ON THE ADOPTION OF THE FEDERAL CONSTITUTION AS RECOMMENDED BY THE GENERAL CONVENTION AT PHILADELPHIA IN 1787, at 546, 569 (Jonathan Elliot, ed., 2nd ed. 1876).

most clearly define due process as it has emerged in American constitutional law, which long ago described due process as a protection of "those fundamental principles of liberty and justice which lie at the base of all our civil and political institutions."[6] The due process guarantee is the centerpiece of our legal system's "progress from fiat to rationality."[7]

There are five basic elements of due process that may be adduced from American case development, particularly after the post-Civil War amendments to the Constitution extended the due process command to the conduct of the states toward their citizens.[8] The two most prominent are notice and a hearing: "Parties whose rights are to be affected are entitled to be heard; and in order that they may enjoy that right they must first be notified."[9] According to the Supreme Court, these requirements—the opportunity to be heard and its "instrumental corollary, a promise of prior notice"[10]—"seem to be universally prescribed in all systems of law established by civilized countries."[11] The additional elements of due process are, like notice, corollaries necessary to make the right to a hearing meaningful: the right to an impartial arbiter, the right to be represented by counsel, and the right to timely resolution of claims.

It might seem quite satisfying to say that due process consists of five easily articulated elements—hearing, notice, arbiter, counsel, and timeliness—and leave it at that. But to do so is insufficient. The articulation of these elements of due process leaves unanswered a central question dating from the time of the Magna Carta: what is the purpose of these due process rights? That is, we know *what* we are supposed to do, but, without understanding *why* we do it, we still are unable to establish *how much* process is due process.

To determine how much process is due, we need a clearer understanding of the purpose of due process than the necessarily open-ended formulation the Constitution provides. The constitutional due process principle can be understood in two different ways: as a guarantee creating a distinct set of rights among the citizenry, or as a constraint designed to prevent arbitrary govern-

---

6. Hurtado v. California, 110 U.S. 516, 535 (1884).

7. Pacific Mut. Life Ins. Co. v. Haslip, 499 U.S. 1, 40 (1991) (Kennedy, J., concurring).

8. Before the adoption of the Fourteenth Amendment in 1868, the requirement of due process did not extend to state or local governments.

9. Baldwin v. Hale, 68 U.S. (1 Wall.) 223, 233 (1863).

10. Laurence H. Tribe, American Constitutional Law § 10–15, at 732 (2d. ed. 1988).

11. Twining v. New Jersey, 211 U.S. 78, 111 (1908).

mental action. Thus, under the rights-based view, citizens may be thought of as having a right to a hearing and a right to notice, such that they can claim "ownership" of these rights when the government takes any action infringing upon them. Alternatively, due process may be characterized not as vesting the citizens with rights, but as imposing restraints on the state. Seen this way, due process is a check against arbitrary, capricious, or simply misguided state conduct. And in addition, under this view we might recognize the need for gradations in the specific requirements of due process according to the type of governmental action at issue and the likelihood that the government will mistakenly infringe upon the rights to life, liberty, or property of the citizenry. Measured against these two approaches to due process, it is possible to characterize the development of twentieth century due process law as passing through three central phases.

A. *Substantive Due Process.*

Due process entered the American constitutional canon forcefully and controversially with the emergence of the "substantive due process" doctrine in the closing years of the nineteenth century. Using this doctrine, federal courts gave independent *substantive* meaning to the Fourteenth Amendment's prohibition on states' restricting the enjoyment of life, liberty, or property without due process of law. Courts treated state incursions upon the affirmative rights of citizens to be secure in their life, liberty, and property as presumptively invalid, and subjected them to exacting judicial scrutiny. The domain of legitimate state regulatory activity was restricted to ensuring the public health, protecting against inherently hazardous activities, and protecting those who could not fend for themselves at law.[12]

The most controversial feature of substantive due process was its expansive definition of "liberty" to include a broad range of market freedoms, such as the unfettered right to contract. That, in turn, prompted federal courts to strike down state regulatory measures by the dozens. Most famous, no doubt, was the Supreme Court's 1905 ruling in *Lochner v. New York*,[13] a case that held unconstitutional a health regulation that limited the maximum hours bakers could work in a week on the substantive due process ground that the regulation violated the bakers' "liberty of contract." In *Lochner* and many other cases litigated in this era, courts

---

12. In the prose of an earlier time, this last group included "idiots, minors, and married women." Rogers v. Higgins, 48 Ill. 211, 217 (1868).

13. 198 U.S. 45 (1905).

established strong procedural presumptions against the legitimacy of state regulatory initiatives. The period of substantive due process lasted until its repudiation by the Supreme Court in the New Deal period of the 1930s. Nonetheless, the reaction to the perceived hostility of the Court to progressive social legislation earned the "*Lochner* period" notoriety as a constitutional epithet and removed the term "substantive due process" from the constitutional lexicon, until its tentative reemergence at the end of the twentieth century in difficult cases such as the constitutional review of assisted suicide.[14]

B. *Procedural Due Process.*

The second great phase of due process activism came with the Warren Court of the 1960s. Like the *Lochner* Court, the Warren Court viewed due process primarily as a guarantee of specific rights to citizens, not as an instrumental restraint on the potentially mistaken exercise of state power. While the *Lochner* period focused on substantive rights protected by due process, the hallmark of the second phase was a focus on "procedural due process." This era witnessed the dramatic expansion of the process-based requirements that the state had to meet in order to act adversely to the interests of its citizens. In a series of decisions involving legislatively conferred benefits, ranging from driver's licenses to, most famously, welfare benefits, the Court required an elaborate series of processes before such benefits could be withdrawn. Thus, for example, in *Goldberg v. Kelly,* the Court invoked procedural due process when it prevented the cessation of welfare benefits without affording the recipient "the opportunity for an evidentiary hearing prior to termination."[15] The right to a hearing was repeatedly invoked in this period as an affirmative right of all citizens to participate in governmental processes. The Court did not seek to expand the scope of government benefits, which continued to be created by the normal processes of government. Instead, the Court used the Due Process Clause to enforce heightened procedural hurdles that the government had to clear before it could deny a benefit. Instead of the liberty to contract of the early twentieth century, the aggrieved due process claimant of the postwar period would claim a "right to be heard" prior to adverse governmental action.

Critics charged that the elevated procedural steps created a presumption against adverse governmental action almost as certain as that of the substantive due process period. But more problemat-

---

14. Washington v. Glucksberg, 521 U.S. 702 (1997).

15. 397 U.S. 254, 255 (1970).

ic, as evidenced in the ensuing case law, was how to reconcile the elaborate set of processes entailed by procedural due process with emergency situations that required a swift governmental response. Courts struggled to find a mediating principle that would allow police searches, the impounding of goods in flight, the embargo on products or foodstuffs threatening public health or safety, and a range of comparable conduct whose successful implementation could not await notice and an adversarial hearing.

C. Due Process Functionalism.

The difficulties created by the heightened procedures required by the Warren Court prompted a shift from a rights-based view of due process to a more instrumental approach. Where both the substantive due process and procedural due process periods had read the due process command to vest the citizenry with affirmative rights against the state, the functional period beginning in the mid–1970s saw in due process a check against improper or incorrect governmental decisions affecting life, liberty, or property. Thus, in the watershed case of *Mathews v. Eldridge*,[16] the Supreme Court analyzed a challenge to the termination of social security disability benefits not in terms of *whether* due process protections attached, but rather in terms of *how much* process was due. By contrast to cases of the *Goldberg v. Kelly* period, which assumed that process demanded the full panoply of evidentiary protections, *Mathews v. Eldridge* held that the amount of process required prior to adverse governmental conduct would be determined by a three-factor balancing test, heavily weighted toward considerations of cost and likelihood of error:

> [D]ue process generally requires consideration of three distinct factors: First, the private interest that will be affected by the official action; second, the risk of an erroneous deprivation of such interest through the procedures used, and the probable value, if any, of additional or substitute procedural safeguards; and finally, the Government's interest, including the function involved and the fiscal and administrative burdens that the additional or substitute procedural requirement would entail.[17]

Under this view, due process loses the intrinsic value that it held for either the substantive or procedural due process periods. As one American appellate court has expressed it, " '[d]ue process,' unlike some legal rules, is not a technical conception with a fixed content

---

16. 424 U.S. 319 (1976).

17. 424 U.S. at 335.

unrelated to time, place, and circumstances."[18] Thus, the courts could grant radically less process where the deprivation was limited and the likelihood of error was low, as with the lower thresholds of proof for parking tickets or the *ex parte* application of a parking boot to illegally parked cars,[19] and were capable of granting as much as necessary in more extreme cases where denial of essential services was at issue, as in *Goldberg v. Kelly*. Continuing along this spectrum, the court could reserve its most serious procedural protections for situations when incarceration or even death were at issue.

Although *Mathews v. Eldridge*'s focus on the relative interests in accuracy and expediency was a great step forward, it was not as revolutionary as might first appear. It is, in fact, mainly a formalization of preexisting ideas. However, the procedural balancing of *Mathews* performed the valuable service of crystallizing certain intuitions about the role of procedural law that had existed for more than a century. It does not take long to conjure up images of raids on a home in a search for drugs or contraband, as familiarly portrayed in any number of police dramas on television. Surely due process cannot confer the right to prior notice and a hearing in such circumstances, for the illicit goods would be long gone before the police ever arrived. Instead, an elaborate process of warrants and probable cause provides the requisite process under exigent circumstances. Or consider a century-old case concerning whether a state could seize and destroy food deemed "unwholesome" and "unfit for human consumption" *before* any hearing and without notice. Faced with the practical reality that a hearing and other forms of process could not be provided before the seizure without the risk of the potentially tainted food passing into the chain of distribution, the Court in *North American Cold Storage Co. v. Chicago*[20] held that due process would be satisfied by a *post-*deprivation hearing, in which the property owner could recover damages if the seizure proved to have been erroneous. Therefore, even prior to *Mathews*, the Court was struggling to find an appro-

---

18. Hilao v. Estate of Marcos, 103 F.3d 767, 786 (9th Cir. 1996).

19. As Chief Judge Richard Posner of the Seventh Circuit Court of Appeals put it in Van Harken v. City of Chicago, a case upholding the city's new parking ticket plan against the argument that allowing citizens to contest tickets only in front of a part-time judge who would also act as prosecutor did not meet the minimum requirements of procedural due process because it denied citizens a proper hearing, "[t]he test for due process in the sense of procedural minima, as set forth in *Mathews v. Eldridge* . . . requires a comparison of the costs and benefits of whatever procedure the plaintiff contends is required." 103 F.3d 1346, 1351 (1997).

20. 211 U.S. 306 (1908).

priate balance between the risks of acting and not acting, and the costs associated with errors in each direction.

III. Modern Due Process Applied.

We can turn to *United States v. James Daniel Good Real Property,*[21] a case involving the forfeiture of property following a criminal conviction, for a good illustration of the functional balancing test as applied. In 1985, James Daniel Good was found in possession of substantial quantities of marijuana and various drug paraphernalia, and was duly convicted. More than four years later, the federal government brought an *in rem*[22] action for the forfeiture of the house and four-acre site where the drugs had been found. Under the federal forfeiture statute, if the government could establish probable cause to believe that real property had been used in furtherance of a specified list of crimes, the government could obtain an order allowing a seizure of the property in an *ex parte* proceeding. The government seized the property without notice and then proceeded to prosecute its claim for formal title to pass from Good to the United States.

The question before the Supreme Court was simply whether the *ex parte* seizure of Good's home—by definition a seizure without prior notice or an adversarial hearing—satisfied due process. As Chief Justice Rehnquist argued strongly in dissent, there is a long tradition of civil forfeiture in Anglo–American law based on the premise that these proceedings involved only "pecuniary obligations" to the state.[23] The reigning theory in governmental forfeiture cases was that "[w]here only property rights are involved, mere postponement of the judicial enquiry is not a denial of due process, if the opportunity given for the ultimate judicial determination of the liability is adequate."[24] Indeed, the issue had seemed settled by a 1974 Supreme Court case, *Calero–Toledo v. Pearson Yacht Leasing Co.,*[25] upholding the seizure of a yacht used in drug transport under a Puerto Rico variant of the federal forfeiture law.

In *Good,* however, the Court refused to adopt a *per se* rule of any sort governing the *ex parte* seizure of goods subject to forfeiture. While recognizing that the right to prior notice and the

---

21. 510 U.S. 43 (1993).

22. That is, an action against the thing itself. See Chapter 5 for a more detailed discussion of this concept.

23. 510 U.S. at 70 (Rehnquist, J., dissenting) (quoting Phillips v. Commissioner, 283 U.S. 589, 595 (1931)).

24. Phillips, 283 U.S. at 596–97.

25. 416 U.S. 663 (1974).

opportunity for a hearing are central to any constitutional conception of due process, the Court was also attentive to exigencies in the exercise of state authority. Thus the propriety of the yacht seizure in *Calero–Toledo* turned not on a blanket exception for forfeiture cases from the general constraints of due process, but on the particular circumstances which, on balance, made the seizure compelling. In *Good*, the Court revisited *Calero–Toledo* to find it critical that a yacht was the "sort [of property] that could be removed to another jurisdiction, destroyed, or concealed, if advance warning of confiscation were given."[26] This recasting of *Calero–Toledo* allowed far more flexibility in the constitutional examination of the seizure of property. Accordingly, the seizure of real property in *Good* was analyzed as if the Constitution could be read as a series of administrative standards, rather than as a set of rules, as might have been indicated by *Calero–Toledo*:

> The [constitutional] analysis requires us to consider the private interest affected by the official action; the risk of an erroneous deprivation of that interest through the procedures used, as well as the probable value of additional safeguards; and the Government's interest, including the administrative burden that additional procedural requirements would impose.[27]

Under this analysis, the seizure of a home produces a significant deprivation, unjustified by any governmental exigency. Unlike the yacht in *Calero–Toledo*, which could presumably be spirited away, "real property cannot abscond," meaning that "the court's jurisdiction can be preserved without prior seizure."[28] The combination of the lack of exigency, the importance of one's homestead, and the necessarily escalated risk of error in *ex parte* proceedings rendered the seizure unconstitutional.

Although *Good* provides an important example of the operation of *Mathews*-style due process as it is applied to the facts of a particular case, it is only a partial example. At issue in *Good* is the direct action of the state against the citizenry, the same concern that originally animated the Magna Carta. But functional due process has expanded to define appropriate procedures in *all* manner of legal disputes, including those in which the state does not have a direct interest. This is most visible in the Court's handling of prejudgment attachments.

Prejudgment attachment cases involve parties who seek to either seize or place a lien on property or goods held by their

---

26.   510 U.S. at 52 (quoting Calero–Toledo, 416 U.S. at 679).

27.   *Id.* at 53.

28.   *Id.* at 57.

opponents, in anticipation of winning a favorable judgment and thereby acquiring the seized property or the proceeds from its sale as satisfaction for the judgment. By definition, these cases involve a deprivation of property before a full trial and thus raise problems of insufficiency of process. Although the seizure is done on behalf of the interest of an individual, it is the state that is ultimately executing the attachment—the private citizen in effect temporarily wields the power of the state—and therefore due process is implicated. But more significantly, regardless of whether the state is seeking to act on its own behalf or on the behalf of a private third party, once due process is applied to all state functions, then the constitutional commands begin to define all procedural law.

In 1991, the Supreme Court addressed a Connecticut state procedure for prejudgment attachment of real estate in order to provide security for a potential judgment. The question in *Connecticut v. Doehr*[29] was whether the state provided sufficient protection of the defendant's property interest in its procedures for permitting a lien to be placed on his home in a civil action. The case involved an attachment on the home of Brian Doehr to secure a potential judgment from a civil assault and battery claim. The plaintiff in the underlying action claimed that he had been on the losing end of a bar fight in which Doehr was the aggressor. There was no claim of any preexisting interest in Doehr's home or any other basis for the lien besides the prospect of ultimately prevailing at trial, and the plaintiff's desire to secure a source of recovery should he indeed be awarded damages.

The Connecticut statute, however, did not offer any substantial protection to defendants in the event that the plaintiff ultimately lost the suit. The availability of the lien was a pure win for the plaintiff, since it imposed some burden on the defendant (such as disrupting lines of credit, impeding sale of the property, etc.) but demanded nothing of the plaintiff. The statute did not require the plaintiff to post a bond to ensure payment of any damages the defendant might suffer because of the attachment, did not require a showing of "extraordinary circumstances" that would warrant immediate attachment, and did not provide the defendant with prior notice of the seizure or with a preattachment hearing.[30] The statute only required a plaintiff to sign an affidavit (in this case, five one-sentence paragraphs) attesting to the merits of the plaintiff's claim against the defendant. Following Connecticut procedure, and without any further proof, the Superior Court found "probable cause to

29.   501 U.S. 1 (1991).

30.   *Id.* at 4.

sustain the validity of the plaintiff's claim."[31] Only after the property had been attached (and before he had been served with a complaint in the assault case) did Doehr receive notice of the attachment.

Upon appeal, the Supreme Court once again employed a *Mathews*-type standard in declaring the constitutional infirmity of the Connecticut statute. The Court articulated the *Mathews* three-part inquiry and stated that "[h]ere the inquiry is similar but the focus is different."[32] While the first two parts of the test were the same— consideration of the defendant's private interest that would be affected by the state's action as well as the risk of erroneous deprivation of that interest and the probable value of additional safeguards—the focus of the third part shifted from the government's interest to the *plaintiff's* interest in the property. The Court emphasized that the defendant had a significant property interest at stake and that there was a high risk of erroneous deprivation. Further, the Court stressed that a judge "could make no reasonable assessment concerning the likelihood of an action's success based upon these one-sided, self-serving, and conclusory statements" (and nothing more), and that the plaintiff's interest was relatively minimal, as he had no existing interest in the property prior to the attachment.[33] The government's interest was dismissed as being no greater than the plaintiff's, which in this case was "de minimis." Thus, while refusing to say that any *particular* form of process would be due in *all* prejudgment attachment cases, the Court found that the statute lacked adequate due process protections, and that it did not properly address the balancing of the various interests involved.

As with *Good*, the Court's opinion in *Doehr* represented a revisiting of prejudgment seizure law in light of an expansive application of *Mathews*. Under a series of decisions in the 1970s authored by Justice White, the Court had attempted to define the precise contours of what process would substitute for a hearing in cases of a prejudgment seizure. Using this "checklist" approach, certain indicia of reliability—such as a detailed affidavit, a bond, and the participation of a judicial officer in authorizing the seizure—would establish the constitutionality of the seizure. Although Justice White tried to revive portions of this approach in *Doehr*, a majority of the Court rejected any *per se* approaches to the constitutionality or unconstitutionality of a privately-initiated prejudgment seizure. Instead, the indicia of reliability from the pre-*Mathews* case

31. *Id.* at 7.
32. *Id.* at 10.
33. *Id.* at 14.

law were incorporated into the constitutional balancing standard as evidence of the ease with which decisional accuracy could be improved.[34]

In the decades since *Mathews v. Eldridge*, this functional form of due process has come to command this area of constitutional law. All the critical elements of due process, from the right to an evidentiary hearing to the right to counsel, are now subject to a balancing of the magnitude of loss as well as the likelihood of error as well as the governmental interest in swift action. Some of the applications appear inevitable, as with the ability of police to place a boot on illegally parked cars, even in the absence of notice and a prior hearing. Some are far more problematic, as with the denial of the right to have counsel provided to an indigent prisoner facing civil proceedings for termination of parental rights.[35] And some grab at the center of the main concerns of the day, as with the detention of foreign and U.S. citizens in the war on terror.

IV. A Final Example.

Consider one final example: the case of *Hamdi v. Rumsfeld,*[36] concerning an American-born individual taken prisoner in Afghanistan during the American military action in 2002, and subsequently held as an "enemy combatant" in a military prison on United States soil. Like *Good, Hamdi* presents a case of direct government action against a private citizen: the very situation that the Magna Carta was written to control almost 800 years ago. Like *Doehr*, it involves a deprivation—of liberty, rather than property—before a hearing.

The petitioner, Yaser Esam Hamdi, was detained based on government charges that he had "t[aken] up arms" against the U.S. military. The government further took the position that this made Hamdi an enemy combatant, "and that this status justifie[d] holding him in the United States indefinitely—without formal charges or proceedings—unless and until [the government] ma[de] the determination that access to counsel or further process [was] warranted."[37] The government's only evidence supporting Hamdi's classification as an enemy combatant was a signed affidavit by a U.S. official who had never met him, but who was "familiar with

---

34. For further discussion of the use of balancing tests in other areas of constitutional law, see T. Alexander Aleinikoff, *Constitutional Law in the Age of Balancing,* 96 Yale L. J. 943 (1987).

35. Lassiter v. Department of Social Servs. of Durham Cty., 452 U.S. 18 (1981).

36. 542 U.S. 507 (2004).

37. *Id.* at 510–11.

the facts" related to Hamdi's capture, "based on [his] review of relevant records and reports."[38] Under most circumstances, such evidence would be inadmissible as hearsay, but Hamdi was not allowed to challenge it, and was not allowed to speak to a lawyer or contact his family, who themselves had to file a petition of *habeas corpus* on his behalf. The case made its way to the Supreme Court amidst great public attention, and the ultimate question of the case was whether the procedure established for enemy combatants satisfied the due process protections discussed throughout this chapter.

The government insisted that its interest in the detention of uncharged enemy combatants was "preventing those combatants from rejoining the enemy while relieving the military of the burden of litigating the circumstances of wartime captures halfway around the globe,"[39] and that this extraordinary circumstance trumped otherwise important interests, even Hamdi's interest in his freedom. The Supreme Court concluded, however, that the risk of erroneous deprivation of liberty under this approach was "unacceptably high,"[40] and, while conceding that "it is beyond question that substantial interests lie on both sides of the scale in this case,"[41] held that due process demanded certain protections, by now familiar, to assure that "a citizen held in the United States as an enemy combatant be given a meaningful opportunity to contest the factual basis of that detention before a neutral decisionmaker."[42] But, as should also be evident from the discussion of due process functionalism in this chapter, the invocation of due process limitations on governmental action was only the beginning of the inquiry.

Writing the lead opinion of the Court, Justice O'Connor stated, "[i]t is during our most challenging and uncertain moments that our Nation's commitment to due process is most severely tested; and it is in those times that we must preserve our commitment at home to the principles for which we fight abroad."[43] Thus, "a citizen-detainee seeking to challenge his classification as an enemy combatant must receive notice of the factual basis for his classification, and a fair opportunity to rebut the Government's factual assertions before a neutral decisionmaker."[44] However, Justice

---

38. *Id.* at 512.
39. *Id.* at 514.
40. *Id.* at 533.
41. *Id.* at 529.
42. *Id.* at 509.
43. *Id.* at 532.
44. *Id.* at 533.

O'Connor stressed that the fundamental elements of due process—notice, hearing, counsel, arbiter, and timeliness—must be applied in a manner appropriate to the circumstances. How and when such due process rights to challenge governmental conduct should be given effect is therefore the heart of the question.

Invoking *Mathews'* functional approach as the controlling law even in national security cases, the Court conceded that although a hearing was required, it need not, due to the needs of the government during wartime, necessarily include every procedural protection available in, say, a criminal trial. "[T]he exigencies of the circumstances may demand that, aside from [the] core elements, enemy combatant proceedings may be tailored to alleviate their uncommon potential to burden the Executive at a time of ongoing military conflict. Hearsay, for example, may need to be accepted as the most reliable available evidence from the Government in such a proceeding."[45] The exact details of the hearing were left to be developed subsequently, but the Court's message was clear: due process remains a vital protection for U.S. citizens. While it retains flexibility, it may not be discarded altogether when the executive finds its requirements inconvenient. Eight hundred years after the Magna Carta, and presumably for many more to come, due process has been and will remain a conceptual cornerstone in American law.

The *Hamdi* case also serves to elucidate one final point: the reason for beginning this book, a book on civil procedure, with a constitutional topic. In short, this has been done in order to enrich the perspectives of students who, new to law school, often have difficulty seeing civil procedure in its broader context, and, consequently, consider the subject dry, confusing, and technical. While civil procedure *is* complex, and while it does deal with many rules and their oftentimes technical exceptions, at its core are two fundamental ideas about the need for a system of justice to be both equitable and efficient. At the constitutional plane, those ideas have been most fully developed in the *Mathews* line of cases. But to a large extent, even the technical aspects of the formal rules of procedure are themselves simply expressions of these ideas, which, through an enormous and ongoing process of trial and error, have been applied to the realities of dispute resolution.

---

45. *Id.* at 533–34.

Chapter 2
PLEADING

A society premised on liberty will leave individuals largely to their own devices, assuming, in classic liberal fashion, that the unfettered pursuit of individual self-interest will best advance the collective welfare. Even under this classic liberal model, however, individuals must inevitably come into conflict when contractual expectations are dashed, or disputes arise over property, or a lack of due regard for others results in injury. At this point, passions are likely inflamed, civil transactions disrupted, and the orderly workings of society threaten to descend into demands for retribution. As the scale of society expands, as markets grow, and as the mobility of the population increases, these disruptions become not only more common, but must come to be seen as the norm of mass society. What distinguishes a mature society, then, is not the absence of disputes, but the capacity for a just and efficient resolution of these disputes. In practical terms, this means our modern society requires a legal system capable of rendering meaningful justice through dispute resolution, and doing so within reasonable constraints of time and money.

For purposes of bringing all of this to life, let us assume a hypothetical dispute in which a farmer loses a cow, which has apparently wandered off his property. Assume the farmer suspects his neighbor of having either intentionally taken the cow, or else of having profited from the situation by keeping the cow and, in turn, either selling it, consuming it, or infiltrating it into his herd. We will return often in this book to the saga of the wandering cow, for it epitomizes the simplest of disputes that any legal system must be equipped to handle.

From the historic vantage point of Anglo–American law, we may think of the ensuing legal battle over our stray cow as an example of a classic common law dispute of the sort that has been the mainstay of litigation over many centuries. There are defining features of such a dispute that bring it squarely within the ambit of what courts are designed to handle, and indeed what courts are probably best able to handle. As articulated by Abram Chayes:

   (a) The lawsuit is bipolar—it concerns two separate and easily identifiable parties;

   (b) The lawsuit is retrospective—it addresses completed events;

17

(c) The right asserted and the remedy sought are interdependent—the latter flows from the former;

(d) The lawsuit concerns a self-contained episode—the impact of the judgment is confined to the parties to the litigation; and

(e) The process is party-initiated and party-controlled—the issues and facts in the case are developed by the parties and presented by them or their attorneys to the final arbiter.[1]

In such a world, the role of procedure is to encourage the disputants to turn to a public dispute resolution forum rather than to resort to self-help. In particular, the object of a civilized legal system is to offer an alternative to the aggrieved parties taking up arms and trying to seize control of the disputed cow through whatever force they may bring to bear. The need to provide a safe alternative to Hobbesian self-help remedies, in turn, leads to the creation of courts and a system of administration of justice which offers a neutral forum where, among other essentials, neither party is at physical risk. The overriding objective of such a system is the dispensation of justice that will be accepted as such by disputing citizens. Such a system of justice seeks to resolve conflicts based upon the actual facts underlying the dispute, and on the proper application of the law to the particular claims and defenses of the parties. Each disputant must believe that the resolution of the controversy before the court resulted from a set of established practices and law, and must accept that even in defeat, the result was not the product of fraud or corruption. Most often, the defining feature of what it means to be fair is the process by which the case was resolved, particularly since in any claim by two parties to the same good, it is impossible to satisfy each claimant's substantive demand. In turn, the goal of procedure in such a system is to be the efficient medium through which the law may be applied to an accurate factual assessment of the case.

I. From Common Law Pleading to the Present.

The modern system of civil procedure begins with a historical assessment: the common law was only partially successful at implementing procedure to achieve the goals outlined above. While the courts were open and dispensed justice, procedure often served as an obstacle to the determination of the merits of the dispute, rather than as a means to that end.

---

1. Abram Chayes, *The Role of the Judge in Public Law Litigation*, 89 Harv. L. Rev. 1281, 1282–83 (1976).

Let us return to our hypothetical case of the cow wandering into the neighbor's yard. At common law, a remarkably elaborate system of pleading would place a burden on an aggrieved plaintiff to lay out the whole story of the dispute—whether the cow had wandered onto the neighbor's property or been taken, and whether the neighbor continued in possession of the cow or had sold or slaughtered it—at a very high level of specificity, regardless whether the plaintiff had reason to know those details. Through highly technical "writs" with increasingly obscure and now largely forgotten terms, such as *trover, assumpsit,* and *trespass on the case,* the common law demanded that the dispute be framed for presentation to the arbiter prior to the formal involvement of the legal system. The plaintiff had to choose among these writs, and was confined to bringing a maximum of one claim. The defendant was also limited in his options, and was restricted to one of three responses: *demurring* (taking the facts as assumed and challenging their applicability to the law), entering a *dilatory plea* (challenging the jurisdiction of the court), or *pleading in bar* (either denying one or more of the essential allegations or admitting them but justifying the conduct on other grounds). Failure to properly plead by the plaintiff would result in forfeiture of a claim. Therefore, even if the farmer's neighbor had *stolen* the cow and subsequently sold it, the farmer's claim that it had wandered away and that the neighbor had kept it would have occasioned a demurrer and a judgment for the neighbor, and the farmer would not have been allowed to replead. Similarly, the court would hold the defendant to his initial choice of defense. The neighbor's failed challenge to jurisdiction would foreclose even a meritorious alternative challenge, such as a verifiable claim that a third party had stolen the cow. In the unmourned days of old, as one of the leading casebooks explains:

> Each action had to be sustained in terms of the substantive law applicable to that form of action. The inquiry was not whether plaintiff should recover under the law of the land, but whether plaintiff had proved a case *in trespass,* or *in covenant,* or in whatever for the action had been brought. If not, plaintiff lost the case without consideration of the merits.[2]

Though this system might seem excessively rigid, its point was to force the parties to confine their dispute to a single issue of fact or law that could then be resolved by the court. The passive arbiter envisioned in the classic common law formulation of dispute resolution was just that: a Solomonic figure who would pronounce judgment on a fully formed dispute presented by the interested parties.

---

2.   FLEMING JAMES, JR. ET AL., CIVIL PROCEDURE § 1.4, at 12–13 (4th ed. 1992).

But, on this model, how could parties acquire true information through which to contest the actual merits of a claim? Unfortunately, the common law had little to say in this regard. The result was the bizarre world of medieval trials in which "oath-helpers" and other now-forgotten actors would engage in a battle of oaths, oftentimes fairly well divorced from any actual knowledge of the events in question. Unfortunately, as well, the requirement that parties develop information of their own accord did little to dissuade the recourse to self-help that the adjudicative model was supposed to forestall. And, as we have seen, when claims *were* resolved by courts, they were often decided based upon how they were pleaded, rather than on their merits. In short: "The insistence that the decision turn on a single issue, while it produced administrative efficiency with a vengeance, too often did so at the expense of substantive justice."[3]

In the middle of the nineteenth century, numerous American jurisdictions, beginning with New York in 1848 and California in 1850, undertook to reform the arcane common law pleading system and liberalize the pleading requirements. These reform efforts, beginning with the so-called "Field Code" in New York (named after its principal drafter, David Dudley Field), attempted to do away with the common law writ system, requiring instead that plaintiffs put forth in their complaint a "statement of facts constituting the cause of action, in ordinary and concise language." While pleading under the state codes—also called "fact pleading" because it required nothing more than a simple statement of facts, to which a judge could apply the relevant law as he saw fit—succeeded in simplifying the pleading process for both plaintiffs and defendants, it occasioned new problems. For example, it was often unclear what degree of specificity would be required under fact pleading—how detailed the facts had to be, whether there were special situations that required more specificity than others, etc.

But the state codes' most serious shortcoming was a feature they shared with their common law pleading forerunners. By requiring the plaintiff to plead the facts necessary for a legal recovery, the state codes retained the common law's emphasis on possessing knowledge of the actual facts of the dispute. To the extent that relevant facts might be in the possession of the defendant, the plaintiff was systematically disadvantaged. In our cow scenario, under both common law pleading and code pleading, a plaintiff would have difficulty prevailing without actual knowledge of the defendant's conduct with regard to our wandering bovine. Move

---

3. *Id.* at § 3.2, at 141.

beyond this simple claim of misappropriated property and into the more complex world of claims that might turn on the state of mind of the defendant, such as defamation or discrimination, and the difficulty is compounded. Neither common law pleading systems nor the subsequent state codes provided any systematic mechanism for parties to obtain facts not already in their possession. Without the benefit of what we now term the discovery process, it was often difficult to obtain enough facts to make out a cause of action, even under a more relaxed pleading regime.

II.   Pleading Under the Federal Rules.

While some jurisdictions still retain elements of Code-style fact pleading, this nineteenth century innovation has yielded overwhelmingly to the system initiated through the Federal Rules of Civil Procedure, enacted in 1938 under the leadership of Charles Clark, then Dean of Yale Law School. The Federal Rules were designed to bring uniformity to the federal courts, which had previously applied the procedural rules of whatever state a particular federal court happened to sit in. The Rules were also intended to resolve the many problems of the common law and state code approaches to the pleading process.

The Rules begin with Rule 1's stated commitment to "the just, speedy, and inexpensive determination of every action," a goal that clearly had not always been served by the cumbersome common law system. With this end in mind, Rule 7 formally announces the end of the common law system by setting out new, greatly simplified rules for pleadings, and by requiring nothing more than that the pleading of a typical dispute consist of a "complaint" and an "answer." In contrast to the common law system of writs and technical pleading, under Rule 7 specific claims or disputes within the litigation process are raised by "motions" seeking some form of judicial order, and the Rule specifies that "only these pleadings are allowed."

As set out in Rule 7, the starting point for the Rules' liberal system of pleading—also called "notice pleading" because its main purpose is to force the plaintiff to provide enough information to notify the defendant of why she is being haled into court, thus allowing her to prepare a defense—is Rule 8. No longer requiring a detailed allegation of facts, much less a detailed theory of the claim, Rule 8(a)(2) demands only that the plaintiff make "a short and plain statement of the claim showing that the pleader is entitled to relief." In the 1957 case of *Conley v. Gibson*, the Supreme Court advanced a very broad conception of this language, stating that "a complaint should not be dismissed for failure to state a claim unless it appears beyond doubt that the plaintiff can prove *no set of facts in support of his claim which would entitle him to relief.*"[4] As Justice Black, writing for an unanimous Court, concluded: "The Federal Rules reject the approach that pleading is a game of skill in which one misstep by counsel may be decisive to the outcome and accept the principle that the purpose of pleading is to facilitate a proper decision on the merits."

Indeed, the assumption made by the Rules is that the plaintiff does not necessarily know all the relevant facts necessary to establish liability at the time that suit is filed. Such assumptions about access to information are a central insight of the Federal Rules. Unlike the common law, the Rules assume that courts will not only adjudicate disputes, but will also provide a forum for the development of the information necessary to their fair resolution. The Rules reject the critical premise of the common law pleading system that the obligation of the parties was to bring forward completely formed disputes ready for full resolution by a judicial tribunal. Under the modern approach outlined in Rule 8, a plaintiff initiates a lawsuit by stating only the reasons for being in that particular court (the jurisdictional basis of the suit, which will be addressed in Chapters 5 and 6), the nature of the harm claimed by the plaintiff, and the remedy being sought. It is not assumed that the plaintiff has full information about the actions or state of mind of the defendant. Nor is it assumed that the defendant has information about what harms, if any, the plaintiff actually suffered. Just as the plaintiff cannot be presumed to know if the defendant kept, sold, or slaughtered the ill-fated cow, so too it cannot be assumed that the defendant knows whether the plaintiff actually possessed the cow he claims to have lost, whether the cow was diseased or healthy, or whether the plaintiff previously failed to maintain fences around his pasture land.

Our system is premised on the idea that the defendant is more likely to have information about questions of liability, while the plaintiff is more likely to know the facts pertaining to damages. Accordingly, the Rules abandon both the common law demand that the plaintiff set forth a single legal theory of the case, and the common law requirement that the defendant choose only one ground of defense at the outset of the litigation. As most clearly articulated in Rule 8(d)(2), the parties are allowed to "set out 2 or more statements of a claim or defense alternatively or hypothetically." Conceptualized in due process terms, the liberalization of Rule

---

4. 355 U.S. 41, 45–46 (1957) (emphasis added).

8 "operates as a keystone to an entire procedural system where the only function left to be provided by pleadings is notice."[5]

Underlying the liberalization of Rule 8 is a corresponding commitment to the ability of the parties to engage the merits of the claim as quickly and as directly as possible. This is facilitated by the only significant requirement for the form of the complaint: Rule 10's provision that each specific factual or legal claim be set forth in a separately numbered paragraph. This forces the defendant's answer directly to admit or to deny specific claims or factual assertions. The effect of an admission is to remove a potentially contested issue from further development and to allow the parties efficiently to concentrate their efforts on the areas of disagreement.

The liberality of the pleading process is further confirmed by the ease of amendment of the complaint under Rule 15. A plaintiff may amend the complaint as of right before an answer is filed or even afterwards, subject to permission of the court, which "the court should freely give ... when justice so requires." In practice, this means that a plaintiff is generally free to amend the complaint by adding new claims or factual allegations as information about the merits of the case develops, so long as the defendant is given a corresponding opportunity to reply.

Perhaps the most significant aspect of liberalized Rule 15 is subsection (c), as amended in 1991, which addresses the problem of a proposed amendment to a complaint that would name a party or add a claim after the statute of limitations had run. Prior to 1991, courts had generally been quite strict about "relation back" or *nunc pro tunc* ("then as now") amendments that would expand the viability of a claim beyond the statute of limitations. In the leading case of *Schiavone v. Fortune*,[6] for example, the plaintiff in a defamation action arising from an article in Fortune magazine mistakenly named the magazine itself, rather than the owner corporation, Time, Inc., as defendant. When the plaintiff sought to amend the name of the party being sued *after* the time for suit against Time, Inc. had passed, the Supreme Court held that the claim was untimely, and therefore foreclosed. The Court's interpretation was widely criticized as out of keeping with the functional aim of the modern pleading rules, and has now been rejected. As it stands today, Rule 15(c) would permit such an amendment to a complaint, so long as the defendant is *functionally* on notice of the claims within the statute of limitations. In *Schiavone,* Time, Inc.

---

5. Christopher M. Fairman, *Heightened Pleading*, 81 Tex. L. Rev. 551, 556–57 (2002).

6. 477 U.S. 21 (1986).

had been for all practical purposes notified of the claims against it when the plaintiff filed a suit against its subsidiary and served papers on the company's headquarters. Had the new rule been in effect, Time, Inc. could not have escaped suit on a pleading technicality. Once again, the spirit of the Rules is to comport functionally with due process while avoiding, to the extent possible, the formalism of common law pleading that converts process from a means to an impediment.

III.   Heightened Specificity.

Let us posit that, barring private settlement, the ultimate object of a procedural system is to allow the substantive law to be applied to the true facts of a dispute. An indispensable component of such a system is the ability to present the true facts before a tribunal. That immediately raises two critical problems with the factual information relevant to disputes: it is likely to be privately held, and it is likely to be expensive to uncover. The modern pleading system well addresses the first point by relieving the parties of any requirement of comprehensive fact knowledge at the pleading stage. Unfortunately, and perhaps as a consequence, the modern Rules are less attuned to the second problem concerning the costs of fact production. Quite simply, any system that requires parties to provide information imposes costs.

The common law avoided the second-order problem of costs because it was willing to tolerate the first-order problem of insufficient information. It placed the development of the facts of a case outside the supervision of the litigation process, with the result that the cost of the information production system was not part of the litigation calculus. In effect, information costs were off-budget. At the same time, by making it difficult for parties to acquire privately held information, the common law prevented many disputes from being resolved on their merits. As dissatisfaction with this result grew, fact development was brought into the process, and confronting the costs associated with the litigation process could no longer be avoided.

While any procedural system allowing fact development increases costs, liberal pleading can be particularly costly because it permits parties to demand information from each other. It is far cheaper to ask for information than to produce it, which allows parties to impose costs on each other. As might be expected, this system can be the subject of abuse, and mechanisms must exist to prevent anyone from simply demanding information from another party for the sake of harassment or even prurient interest. Later, this chapter will discuss Rule 12, a gatekeeping mechanism that allows the defendant to test the *legal* sufficiency of a plaintiff's complaint. But if the rationale for liberal pleading is that parties are unlikely to be able to develop the information they need themselves, there might also be *fact* specificity requirements that limit liberal pleading when information is likely to be available outside the litigation process.

One of these requirements is Rule 9(b). Per Rule 9(b), a party "alleging fraud or mistake ... must state with particularity the circumstances constituting fraud or mistake." That is, any paragraphs of a complaint that aver instances of either fraud or mistake must set out much more detailed factual allegations. While the import of the word "mistake" in this context is still obscure, allegations of fraud are commonplace, particularly in the financial arena. For example, investors in a business may allege that executives withheld important information regarding the value of the business's products or services, thereby inducing investment when, had the facts been known, there would have been none, or, at the very least, the price paid would have been substantially less. In this instance, courts will require a much higher level of detail in the initial complaint. The plaintiff would be obligated to plead what specific representations were made and, perhaps, how they were false as well. Rule 9(b), therefore, hearkens back to the old common law system, where the initial pleading onus fell squarely on the plaintiff.

Why this departure from the innovative liberal policy of the Rules? Some hint is found in the language of Rule 9(b) itself. While the first sentence requires particularity in pleading the circumstances constituting fraud, the second sentence cautions that "malice, intent, knowledge, and other conditions of a person's mind may be alleged generally." This division between pleading generally and specifically maps directly onto the substance of a fraud claim. The typical claim of fraud is that an incorrect statement was intended to induce reliance by a purchaser on the representation made by the seller. Since the buyer was a party to the transaction, it is reasonable to expect that she will have information about the statement that induced reliance and the reason that it was incorrect when she comes to court as a plaintiff. On the other hand, the buyer cannot be expected to have any direct information about the state of mind of the seller. The pleading burdens under Rule 9(b) are thus premised on the assumption that, at least for certain kinds of facts, the plaintiff and defendant in a fraud case have equal access to relevant information. This state of affairs cannot be presumed to exist in other forms of civil actions, such as our wandering cow hypothetical.

The argument for singling out fraud pushes further. Another traditional defense of Rule 9(b) is that allegations of fraud or mistake are more likely to be brought frivolously than other claims, due to the substantial threat of reputational loss and high *in terrorem* value that they carry. An allegation of fraud can, in many contexts, completely destroy a party's reputation in the community, particularly among financial investors and lenders who might seal that party's future. Since that damage may be done regardless whether the claim has merit, allowing a plaintiff simply to assert that a defendant defrauded him without offering more detail could give opportunistic plaintiffs an incentive to bring meritless claims against innocent defendants. Even a meritless claim would impose the costs of litigation and perhaps far broader costs in reputation. Thus, a claimant might rightly reason that, rather than face whatever costs might be entailed in defending the frivolous suit, the defendant would offer to settle for some portion of those costs. To protect against such abuse, therefore, the Federal Rules require more of parties who would allege fraud or mistake than does Rule 8 on its own. The Private Securities Litigation Reform Act of 1995 (PSLRA) similarly requires that the particulars of fraud in the market for publicly-traded securities be pleaded on the face of the complaint, for the same reasons.

There has been tremendous pressure to expand the scope of Rule 9(b), even though its language is quite clear, and quite narrow. The requirement of heightened specificity does not invite courts to invoke its protections in instances of "fraud, mistake, or any similar situation." Rather the ambit of heightened pleading is strikingly confined. But, despite the narrow language, one ought to question why only fraud should be subject to heightened pleading standards. Can't a person's reputation be harmed just as much by other kinds of suits (defamation, for instance), and aren't other kinds of claims, like complex environmental charges, extremely expensive to defend against, exposing defendants to significant potential liability? The lower federal courts seem to think so, and have continuously attempted to apply heightened pleading requirements outside the fraud and mistake contexts. Reasoning that the same policy justifications that protect against claims of fraud or mistake are applicable elsewhere, these courts have looked to heightened pleading requirements to curtail cases in areas that are deemed particularly subject to frivolous or abusive litigation.

The prime targets have been prisoner lawsuits and other challenges to official conduct that are easy to charge and expensive to defend. But the desire to raise the entry barriers for litigants can be seen in a variety of practices, such as the special "pleading sheets" used for claims brought under RICO, the federal racketeering and corruption statute. In all these cases, courts reason that the threat of reputational harm and the corresponding impulse to settle even nonmeritorious claims allow for the strategic misuse of litigation. Once unleashed, however, the pressure for heightened pleading requirements has not stopped there. In *Cash Energy, Inc. v. Weiner*, for example, building on previous extensions of 9(b) requirements to RICO claims, Judge Keeton reasoned that requiring particularized pleadings for claims brought under CERCLA—a federal environmental protection statute—was appropriate.[7] The effort to expand the heightened pleading requirements of Rule 9(b) has been so widespread, in fact, that the Supreme Court has been moved twice to rein it in. The Court has limited the scope of the Rule to fraud cases narrowly defined, denying its expansion first to civil rights cases alleging municipal liability under 42 U.S.C. § 1983[8] and, subsequently, to claims of employment discrimination.[9]

The Rules do provide some protection to defendants against an empty vessel complaint serving as a vehicle for exploratory discovery. In the first instance, Rule 12(e) gives a defendant the opportunity to move for a "more definite statement," provided the initial pleading is "so vague or ambiguous that a party cannot reasonably prepare a response." Yet, because "notice pleading" is sufficiently liberal, the range of pleadings appropriately subject to 12(e) motions is "quite small."[10]

IV. Sorting Out Claims.

Assuming that a plaintiff has pleaded with enough specificity to put the defendant on notice of the nature of the claim and to overcome any Rule 12(e) and "plausibility" objections (to be discussed in Section VI), we are still a long way from trial. Rule 1's commitment to the "just, speedy, and inexpensive determination of every action" still should not be taken to mean that there is any expectation that every complaint filed will actually culminate in a trial before a judge or jury. In fact, the bulk of cases do not. For as

---

7. 768 F.Supp. 892 (D. Mass. 1991).

8. Leatherman v. Tarrant County Narcotics Intelligence and Coordination Unit, 507 U.S. 163 (1993).

9. Swierkiewicz v. Sorema N.A., 534 U.S. 506 (2002).

10. 5C Charles Alan Wright, Arthur R. Miller & Edward H. Cooper, Federal Practice and Procedure § 1376 (3d ed. 1998).

far back as any tolerably reliable statistics for the Anglo–American legal systems can be obtained, apparently only a scant five percent or so of filed cases actually proceed to trial, and even that percentage is falling at present to the point that barely one percent of the cases filed in federal court are litigated through to trial. Thus, there is some feature of litigation that somehow reduces the total number of claims by more than *95 percent* from the time the case is filed to the time of trial. An important function of the procedural system, it seems, is to winnow down the initial group of claims to those that will eventually arrive at trial.

After the initial pleading—whether by way of Rule 8 or 9—the modern system of civil procedure aims to narrow the area of dispute by forcing parties to converge upon common understandings of the facts and law underlying the dispute. Thus, despite the general liberality of the initial pleading requirement on the plaintiff, each subsequent step in the litigation process is designed to provide an increasingly comprehensive picture of the true facts. It may be helpful to imagine the initial pleading system as the lip of a large funnel system. The liberal pleading regime of Rule 8 allows for easy entry into the system, as does the broad opening of a funnel. Even the heightened requirements of Rule 9(b), while stricter, do not require extensively more. But ease of entry is only half the story. The case as it stands in the initial complaint will almost invariably be dramatically narrowed before trial.

How does the process of winnowing work? It is true that the overwhelming majority of cases filed settle before trial, which helps explain the drop in numbers, but does not address the question of *why* these cases settle, or what it is about the litigation process and the filing of suit that allows these disputes to settle. After all, these cases could have settled prior to filing suit and saved all parties involved the costs of whatever legal processes they invoked.

Rather, the explanation must be derived from three functions performed by the legal system that assist parties to settle disputes—or to proceed to trial should settlement not be possible. First, the litigation process clarifies the law that governs the parties' claims and defenses. Second, unlike the common law system of pleading, the modern procedural system provides for discovery as an organized mechanism for parties to acquire information—what may be thought of as the actual or true facts of the case—that will hopefully permit convergent assessments of what a reasonable resolution would be.[11] Finally, the litigation process itself provides

---

11. The role of discovery and facts will be discussed subsequently in Chapter 3.

not only a means toward a shared consensus about the merits of a case, it also provides strong economic incentives for settlement as opposed to trial.[12] The subject of the following section is the first of these three functions: the initial clarification of the law that governs the parties' claims and defenses.

V. Rule 12(b).

The first gatekeeping mechanism that allows for the testing of the legal sufficiency of the plaintiff's claim is federal civil procedure Rule 12(b). The purpose of Rule 12(b) is to allow the defendant to raise legal, rather than factual, defenses before the factual merits of the case begin to be addressed through the answer to the complaint. Whereas common law pleading required the defendant, like the plaintiff, to choose one theory of the case, Rule 12 allows for alternative challenges, along the lines of what Rule 8 permits the plaintiff. The 12(b) defenses not only serve important screening functions, but Rule 12(b)(6) in particular is a mechanism to actually dismiss unviable claims, thereby commencing and potentially concluding the winnowing function. They also give the defendant the ability to raise these defenses before even answering the complaint, thereby avoiding any disclosure of facts that comes with having to answer specific allegations.

The legal defenses in Rule 12(b) are grouped into three categories. The first may be thought of as the technical defenses that are waivable. These include claims that the matter is in the wrong court, either because of improper venue or a lack of personal jurisdiction over the defendant,[13] or because of a failure to provide service as required by the Rules.[14] These are deemed waived if not raised by way of a Rule 12 motion or if not inserted in the answer to the complaint. But while either a Rule 12 motion or inclusion in the answer will preserve these defenses, only by filing a motion to dismiss may a defendant avoid all engagement with contested facts if the challenge proves to be correct.

The second category consists of the more favored defenses that address in some fashion the merits of the plaintiff's claim. The key examples are the motion to dismiss for failure to state a sufficient legal claim, and the motion to dismiss for failure to join an indispensable party.[15] Both of these defenses may be raised at the

---

12. This is discussed in the final chapter.

13. Rule 12(b)(2)–(3), addressed subsequently in Chapter 5.

14. Rule 12(b)(5).

15. Rule 12(b)(6)–(7).

front-end of the litigation, either as a stand-alone motion or in tandem with an answer, if the issues are sufficiently clear to warrant a challenge to the propriety of suit. More significantly, these defenses are *not* waived if not raised by motion or as part of the answer. Instead, they may be raised at trial as independent defenses not turning on the evidence presented in the trial of the merits of the dispute.

The final, most preferred category of defenses in fact includes only a single motion: the motion to dismiss for lack of subject matter jurisdiction.[16] It may be raised at any point in the litigation—as late as during the appeal of a judgment—and even by the court on its own initiative. This motion is premised on the limited authority enjoyed by federal courts under the dual sovereignty features of our federal system. The implications of federalism for the structure of the court system will be the subject of Chapter 6, but some evidence of the significance of this issue may be garnered from the Rules' unwillingness to foreclose this defense.

VI.   The Legal Basis for Suit: Rule 12(b)(6).

Of all of the Rule 12 defenses, the most important allows the defendant to test the legal premises of a plaintiff's claim right at the threshold stage of litigation. This vehicle is Federal Rule of Civil Procedure 12(b)(6), providing for the motion to dismiss for failure to state a claim for which relief can be granted. Rule 12(b)(6) serves as the modern equivalent of the general demurrer at common law, or an objection to the legal sufficiency of the plaintiff's claim. Rule 12(b)(6) abolished the general demurrer, due in part to the rigidity with which the latter device was applied, and the harsh results it countenanced. As discussed earlier, at common law, if a general demurrer was sustained, the plaintiff's action was thereby terminated and judgment rendered against him. Conversely, if a general demurrer was overruled, the defendant was denied the ability to contest the facts or defend the claim on its merits and judgment was instead rendered against him. Neither party was permitted to amend his pleading or answer. In short, a demurrer foreclosed any further adversarial process and terminated the action, one way or the other.

As the common law general demurrer was incorporated into code pleading, its practice was liberalized to mitigate these harsh consequences. Plaintiffs were given leave to amend their complaints if a demurrer was sustained and defendants were allowed to answer

---

16.   Rule 12(b)(1).

and proceed on the merits if a demurrer was overruled. Code pleading of the demurrer was also expanded to allow dismissal of a complaint for failure to state facts sufficient to constitute a cause of action, for want of proper subject matter jurisdiction, and for deficiencies in the form of the pleading. Code interpretations of the general demurrer, however, produced considerable delay in trials, aggravated by an emphasis on the technicalities of the practice or an unproductive focus on form over substance. Dissatisfaction with the ensuing inefficiencies provoked criticism of the demurrer and its code equivalents:

> In an earlier period, when the ruling on the demurrer termi-nated the action, it was strategic to demur only for clear defects of form or substance. But since the ruling no longer serves to end the litigation but merely postpones the trial, the demurrer is used as a convenient means of delay by counsel with too much business or too little ambition. And where further delay is desired counsel may invoke separately the several motions which exist concurrently with the demurrer: motions to strike, expunge, elect or separate; motions to make more definite and certain or for a bill of particulars. This multiplicity of weapons has inevitably led to a host of tenuous distinctions: whether demurrer or motion is proper, what kind of demurrer, what kind of motion. By the use of successive demurrers and motions, it is possible, then, not only to delay but also to discourage altogether the party whose pleading is subjected to this barrage of objections.[17]

While the use of the general demurrer has disappeared in federal practice, some elements persist. The current Rule 12(b)(6) motion to dismiss assumes, for purposes of the motion, much like its common law predecessor and code equivalents, that all the facts as alleged are true. The key to a 12(b)(6) motion is the assertion that even if the facts are proven to be true, no relief may be granted under governing substantive law. Thus, a 12(b)(6) motion to dismiss, like a demurrer, may neither allege new facts nor contest the facts in the plaintiff's complaint.[18] The motion only challenges the legal sufficiency of the facts the plaintiff has alleged.

---

17. James A. Pike, *Objections to Pleadings Under the New Federal Rules of Civil Procedure*, 47 Yale L.J. 50, 51 (1937).

18. Like its code and common law equivalents, a Rule 12(b)(6) motion to dismiss may not be made on the basis of facts outside those asserted in the pleading, but must rely solely on the facts as alleged in the content of the complaint. The Court in *Neitzke v. Williams* confirmed that "[w]hat Rule 12(b)(6) does not countenance are dismissals based on a judge's disbelief of a complaint's factual allegations." Only those complaints lacking an "arguable basis in law" will be dismissed under Rule 12(b)(6). 490 U.S. 319, 327–28 (1989).

Given this limited burden placed on notice pleading, the Supreme Court has historically cautioned that dismissal of a suit for failure to state a claim is a drastic measure and should be reserved for only the most frivolous cases. As the Supreme Court stated in *Conley v. Gibson*, a case should not be dismissed "unless it appears beyond doubt that the plaintiff can prove no set of facts in support of his claim which would entitle him to relief."[19] Under the traditional *Conley* standard, a court deciding whether or not to dismiss was not supposed to inquire into the possibility that a plaintiff might not be able to prove his factual allegations; rather, faced with a motion to dismiss, federal courts were to construe the claim in the light most favorable for the plaintiff and assume that he will prove them. The classic understanding of the limits of Rule 12(b)(6) is found in *Rennie & Laughlin, Inc. v. Chrysler Corp.*:[20]

> [A] motion to dismiss [is not] the only effective procedural implement for the expeditious handling of legal controversies. Pretrial conference; the discovery procedures; and motions for a more definite statement, judgment on the pleadings and summary judgment, all provide useful tools for the sifting of allegations and the determination of the legal sufficiency of an asserted claim. The salvaged minutes that may accrue from circumventing these procedures can turn to wasted hours if the appellate court feels constrained to reverse the dismissal of the action. That is one of the reasons why a motion to dismiss is viewed with disfavor in the federal courts. Another is the basic precept that the primary objective of the law is to obtain a determination of the merits of any claim; and that a case should be tried on the proofs rather than the pleadings. . . .
> This is not to say or imply that a motion to dismiss should never be granted. It is obvious that there are cases which justify and indeed compel the granting of such motion. The line between the totally unmeritorious claims and the others cannot be drawn by scientific instruments but must be carved out case by case by the sound judgment of trial judges. That judgment should be exercised cautiously on such a motion.[21]

That fairly stable understanding of the motion to dismiss under Rule 12(b)(6) was disrupted in the critical 2007 case of *Bell Atlantic Corp. v. Twombly*.[22] In *Twombly*, the Court returned to the prospect of heightened pleading requirements not by extending

19. 355 U.S. 41, 45–46 (1957).

20. 242 F.2d 208 (9th Cir. 1957).

21. *Id.* at 213 (footnotes omitted).

22. 550 U.S. 544 (2007).

Rule 9(b) as it had previously rejected, but by rereading Rule 8 to require that the facts in a complaint, when assumed to be true, add up to a "plausible" claim. At issue in *Twombly* was an allegation that the regional telephone companies (the so-called "Baby Bells") that had emerged from the break-up of the AT&T telephone monopoly had attempted to recreate local telephone cartels. Originally each of the Baby Bells was a regional monopoly, but in 1996 Congress, seeking to encourage competition, passed legislation requiring the Baby Bells to make their networks available to interested competitors at wholesale rates. The *Twombly* plaintiffs alleged that, in the seven years following deregulation, the Baby Bells conspired to restrain competition in violation of the Sherman Act by, among other things, refusing to try to compete in each other's markets.

The conspiracy claim would require the plaintiffs to prove that there had been a "meeting of the minds," an actual agreement among the defendant phone companies not to try to enter the geographic market controlled by another company. Needless to say, conspirators rarely go around publicizing their misdeeds, making it unlikely that the plaintiffs, even if they had a meritorious claim, would have solid evidence of a conspiratorial agreement at the time they filed suit. Thus, although the plaintiffs claimed a conspiracy existed, they were only able to allege facts suggesting that the defendants *might* have conspired together. Unfortunately for plaintiffs, the Court found that their allegations were equally consistent with an inference that no conspiratorial agreement had ever existed. Following deregulation, the companies had all wanted to preserve their own territory, and each could reasonably have feared that invading a neighbor's region would lead to invasions of their own turf. As a result, it was possible that the observed "parallel conduct" among the defendants was simply the result of each company independently following its self-interest.

Of course, if the plaintiffs had been allowed to conduct discovery, they might have found evidence of a conspiracy. Indeed, the plaintiffs urged the Court to follow the rule of *Conley v. Gibson* and adhere to a broad liberal pleading policy, so that discovery could proceed and a decision on the merits could be reached. But the Court recognized that allowing plaintiffs with little direct evidence supporting their claim to engage in "sprawling, costly, and hugely time-consuming" discovery could unfairly compel "cost-conscious defendants to settle even anemic cases."[23] And so the Court decided to put *Conley's* "no set of facts" standard into "retirement."[24] In

23. *Id.* at 559 & n.6.

24. *Id.* at 563.

its place, the Court announced that a plaintiff in an antitrust case must make allegations "plausibly suggesting" and not "merely consistent with" a conspiratorial agreement.[25] In introducing this "plausibility" standard, the Court placed new emphasis on Rule 8's requirement that a complaint allege facts "showing" that the plaintiff is entitled to relief. In the Court's view, the *Twombly* plaintiffs had "not nudged their claims across the line from conceivable to plausible," with the consequence that "their complaint must be dismissed."[26]

Twombly, together with a companion case in the securities field, *Tellabs, Inc. v. Makor Issues & Rights, Ltd.*,[27] represents a significant retreat from the liberal pleading regime enshrined in *Conley*, at least as it had been interpreted by decades of federal court practice. *Twombly*, and to a lesser extent *Tellabs*, are landmark cases in which the Court began licensing a preliminary assessment of the viability of the plaintiff's case on a motion to dismiss, before the defendant has even answered the complaint. In practice, this means that courts will have to evaluate a claim's plausibility through a preliminary assessment of the positions of each party, even though the only pleading before a district court would be the complaint.

The full import of *Twombly* will be determined by its application. Almost immediately, *Twombly* became one of the most cited Supreme Court cases of all time as literally thousands of district court and appellate decisions began to unravel the relation between the inherited standard of notice pleading and the new demands of plausibility. On one view, *Twombly* could perhaps be more or less limited to its facts in the antitrust context in which fairly reliable evidence of the potential non-conspiratorial reasons for parallel conduct by competitors could be assessed prior to discovery. This view was summarily rejected in *Ashcroft v. Iqbal*,[28] a case involving a claim of governmental misconduct in the aftermath of September 11th. Here the Court made clear that the *Twombly* pleading standard would apply "transsubstantively," meaning uniformly without regard to the area of law at issue in the case:

> Though *Twombly* determined the sufficiency of a complaint
> sounding in antitrust, the decision was based on our interpre-
> tation and application of Rule 8. That Rule in turn governs the
> pleading standard in all civil actions and proceedings in the

25. *Id.* at 557.

26. *Id.* at 570.

27. 551 U.S. 308 (2007).

28. 129 S.Ct. 1937 (2009).

United States district courts. Our decision in *Twombly* expounded the pleading standard for all civil actions, and it applies to antitrust and discrimination suits alike.[29]

As a result, *Twombly* moved the courts away from a strict separation of determinations of law from determinations of fact. The full range of the factual inquiry is addressed in the following Chapter and is still the domain of discovery, summary judgment, and trial. But there is no doubt that at least a preliminary inquiry into the factual underpinnings of a case was introduced at the threshold stages of litigation:

> [A] court considering a motion to dismiss can choose to begin by identifying pleadings that, because they are no more than conclusions, are not entitled to the assumption of truth. While legal conclusions can provide the framework of a complaint, they must be supported by factual allegations. When there are well-pleaded factual allegations, a court should assume their veracity and then determine whether they plausibly give rise to an entitlement to relief.[30]

Exactly what this brave new pleading world will look like in practice is very much still a work in progress. Few doubt that *Twombly* and *Iqbal* introduce an earlier and more forceful judicial intervention into the litigation process. For Professor Arthur Miller the key to the new pleading rules is a retreat from modern procedure's essential commitment to ensuring broad access to civil justice.[31] At particular risk are the areas of law where official misconduct is challenged by lawyers serving as "private attorneys general" in civil rights and similar cases, in which getting to examine the factual underpinnings of institutional conduct is indispensable. Others see *Twombly* as being a practical response to the fact that in the modern world of information access, the premise of exclusive defendant access to the information concerning liability may be inaccurate in broad swaths of the law.[32] Thus, Professor Richard Epstein believes that in the wake of *Twombly* motions to dismiss now operate, and should operate, as anticipatory reviews of factual sufficiency—in effect, an early motion for summary judgment, as will be discussed in Chapter 3—for certain categories of cases where there is an ample public record documenting the

29. 129 S. Ct. at 1953 (internal quotations omitted).

30. *Id.* at 1950.

31. Arthur R. Miller, *From* Conley *to* Twombly *to* Iqbal*: A Double Play on the Federal Rules of Civil Procedure*, 60 Duke L.J. 1 (2010).

32. *See* Colin T. Reardon, *Pleading in the Information Age,* 85 N.Y.U. L. Rev. 2170 (2010).

defendant's conduct even before any litigation-specific discovery.[33] For example, antitrust cases in industries with extensive regulatory reporting requirements, as under the facts of *Twombly*, would be appropriate candidates for a robust motion to dismiss under this approach. By contrast, still using this same approach, a discrimination case turning on private decisionmaking or any case in which the defense asserts privately known reasons for its conduct would demand greater scrutiny through discovery.

However ultimately resolved, the combination of *Twombly* and *Iqbal* represents the single most fundamental transformation of federal practice in many decades. At the very least, the historic understanding of the motion to dismiss is now clearly open to question in light of *Twombly* and *Iqbal*, which give the courts more leeway to examine the factual viability of the plaintiff's claim at the motion to dismiss stage. These cases remove any doubt that the importance of Rule 12(b)(6) and its underlying policies should not be underestimated. The motion's fundamental purpose is to test pure questions of law that must be addressed at the outset of any litigation. It thus provides the first opportunity to purge from an ever-growing caseload those claims lacking legal basis and frees judicial resources to focus on claims that necessarily compel adjudication on their merits. Although Rule 12(b)(6) is not supposed to present too formidable of a barrier to litigation, it does provide a mechanism to eliminate apparently frivolous claims from the system. That a decision on the motion is not fatal to either party is evidence of its policy goal to facilitate access to the legal system: a plaintiff is given the opportunity to replead to remedy any defect and a defendant may continue to defend the claim at trial. At the same time, the fact that a challenge to the legal sufficiency of a pleading is never waived is indicative of its purpose to rid the system of spurious complaints. The logic of the early dismissal is that it is a waste of judicial resources to continue to administer a costly trial based on a claim that, if proved, would have no legal effect in the case. In addition, it is inefficient to force parties to waive a meritorious objection to an insufficient pleading simply because they failed to raise it initially, as this would lead to recovery on imaginary legal claims or the denial of recovery based on imaginary defenses. Rule 12(b)(6) thus provides an effective first guard in a battery of rules designed to increase efficiency and fairness in civil proceedings. The question remains whether the expansive scope of "plausibility" review will sweep in claims whose merit would have been confirmed had discovery been allowed.

---

33. Richard A. Epstein, Bell Atlantic v. Twombly: *How Motions to Dismiss Become (Disguised) Summary Judgments*, 25 Wash. U. J.L. & Pol'y 61 (2007).

VII.   A Word on Method.

Students generally approach a civil procedure class with the expectation of rote learning. The professor assigns them a book entitled *The Federal Rules of Civil Procedure.* The Rules are nicely arrayed numerically from Rule 1 to Rule 86. Together they express an ambition to control the entirety of practices in the federal courts, from the filing of the complaint to the final disposition at trial. There are even Rules of Appellate Procedure for matters pursued beyond the trial court, and rules of Supreme Court practice for the loftiest of cases.

Any expectation of mechanical application should quickly be dashed. The Rules are filled with terms such as "as soon as practicable," or "arising out of the same transaction, occurrence, or series of transactions or occurrences" or "on such terms as are just" or "for good cause shown." Each of these, coupled with the frequent use of "may" rather than "must," indicates that the Rules are intended to be more a guidepost than the final resting ground for procedural disputes. Indeed, almost invariably the obligatory "must" when used in the Rules is directed to ministerial acts taken by the clerk's office, while the discretionary guidance of the term "may" is reserved for the work of the judges themselves.[34]

The difference between "must" and "may" imports to procedural law the distinct regulatory forms that fall under the rubric of *rules* versus *standards.* As a general matter, rules are relatively rigid, fixed regulations that require relatively little interpretation in their administration. Standards, by contrast, tend to be more general in their mandate and require either on-the-spot or afterthe-fact assessments of appropriateness. As formulated by Professor H.L.A. Hart, all systems of regulation must, of necessity, "compromise between two social needs: the need for certain rules which can, over great areas of conduct, safely be applied by private individuals to themselves without fresh official guidance or weighing up of social issues, and the need to leave open, for later settlement by an informed, official choice, issues which can only be properly appreciated and settled when they arise in a concrete case."[35]

Rules aspire to certainty in their application. As Professor Schauer explains, "[i]nstead of allowing decision-makers to scruti-

---

34. Consider the different provisions of Rule 55 as an example. 55(a) and 55(b)(1) are addressed to the clerk, and use "must." Similarly, the first part of 55(b)(2), addressed to litigants, uses "must." The second half of 55(b)(2), however, and 55(c), are addressed to the court and so use "may."

35. H.L.A. HART, THE CONCEPT OF LAW 127 (1993).

nize a large, complex, and variable array of factors, rules substitute decision based on a smaller number of easily identified, easily applied, and easily externally checked factors."[36] Standards, by contrast, are a broad-gauge form of regulation. They outline the general commands to be obeyed without specifying the precise application in any given fact situation. As such, standards are generally easier to formulate, but yield greater uncertainty in their exact requirements. In an economic sense, it may be said that standards defer the cost of factual inquiry to the moment of application, and then require that parties bear the burden of figuring out how the standards are to be implemented.

Perhaps the simplest way to envision this is to think of two roads intersecting and the resulting need for some form of traffic regulation. We can think of a traffic light as a "rule" in this setting. The light at all times directs which cars may proceed and which must stop. There may be some interpretive room when the light is changing, or when the yellow caution appears, but the main contours of desired traffic behavior are fairly clear. On the other hand, the road could remain unregulated except by the general admonition that all drivers be prudent. This would be a very loose standard. It would place all the pressure of interpretation on drivers at the intersection and would force difficult assessments of "prudence" after the fact, should there be an accident. We can then think of firmer directions, such as a yield sign for one of the roads, and perhaps a stop sign, as being a less rigid rules approach.

Given the gain in clarity and ease of administration, why not always have rules? Again, we may think of the two intersecting streets. If they are in the middle of a city, with thousands of cars passing each day, the need for a traffic light is apparent. Not only is the investment in a traffic light worthwhile, but traffic patterns can be studied to know whether one street should have longer green-light periods, whether lights in successive streets should be sequenced, and so forth. But imagine a deserted dirt road in back country. Now, all of a sudden, the investment seems unmerited and any delays caused by a few cars slowing down seem inconsequential. Put simply, there is substantial initial cost and little apparent benefit.

Generalizing a bit from the traffic example, we see that rules require greater initial investment, both in terms of the rules apparatus and the information required to make them work. Rules work best when there are repeat similar experiences likely to

---

36. FREDERICK SCHAUER, PLAYING BY THE RULES: A PHILOSOPHICAL EXAMINATION OF RULE-BASED DECISION-MAKING IN LAW AND IN LIFE 152 (1991).

follow, and when routine application well captures the regulatory environment. The gain is that once in place, rules tend to administer themselves and require little judgment in their application. On the other hand, standards such as admonitions to be prudent or wise require little initial investment, but compel any given actor to assume the burden and expense of interpreting the specific application. Almost inherently, standards will be more difficult to administer and will give rise to disputes that must be resolved after the fact.[37] In turn, rules require bureaucratic administration; standards require discretionary judging. The trade-off is between discretion and predictability.

Viewed in this light, the Federal Rules of Civil Procedure fall more squarely on the "standards" side of the divide than on the "rules" side. This is by no means accidental. One of the animating principles of the Federal Rules, as adopted in 1938, was the move away from the formalism of common law pleading rules. We can return to *Schiavone v. Fortune*, the relation-back amendment case, to illustrate the move toward basic principles of efficiency and equity in procedural law. It would be rather simple to design and administer a fixed-rule approach to pleading. We could require that any suit be brought against the properly denominated party within the statute of limitations and that all claims upon which relief is sought be raised within that period. Any amendment in claims or identified parties not within the statute of limitations would be rejected administratively by a clerk. That system would be rigid, predictable, and a trap for the unwary under situations such as the one in *Schiavone,* where technical issues that prejudiced no party would determine the outcome of the litigation. The result would be a departure from the merits orientation of modern procedure and would value the forms of adjudication over equitable resolution.

But the reason for more standards-based approaches to procedure goes beyond the technicalities of pleading. The common law model of litigation assumed a judge who was a passive arbiter of a dispute fully formed before it came to court. Rules formalism, as reflected in stringent common law pleading practices, ensured that the range of issues presented for the court to decide would be fixed and narrow. The modern rules, by contrast, assume a dynamic process of discovery and engagement across contested issues of law

---

37. For some of the leading academic discussions of rules versus standards, *see* Gillian K. Hadfield, *Weighing the Value of Vagueness: An Economic Perspective on Precision in the Law*, 82 Cal. L. Rev. 541 (1994); Louis Kaplow, *Rules Versus Standards: An Economic Analysis*, 42 Duke L.J. 557 (1992); Kathleen M. Sullivan, *The Justices of Rules and Standards*, 106 Harv. L. Rev. 22 (1992); Jeremy Waldron, *Vagueness in Law and Language: Some Philosophical Issues*, 82 Cal. L. Rev. 509 (1994).

and fact. As we shall see more fully in Chapter 8, the Rules compel more active intervention by the courts and require judges to assume more discretionary and managerial relations to the subject matter of the litigation. The Rules provide form and structure for the process of litigation, but that is only the beginning. The language of the Rules themselves admits of ample opportunity for equitable interpretation, beginning with the admonition in Rule 1 that the object is the just, speedy, and inexpensive determination of each action. In effect, the Rules replicate the balancing approach to process set forth in the constitutional domain by *Mathews v. Eldridge* and its progeny. Liberal pleading is one manifestation of a procedural regime dominated by considerations of equity and efficiency. With the increasing complexity of matters now brought before national judiciaries, it may be that, as Adrian Zuckerman notes, the search for a single global process that can be applied regardless of the nature of the dispute is a romantic notion that is simply unaffordable.[38] In its place emerges a more flexible system, more uncertain in its application, more demanding in its administration, and ultimately to be judged by how well it yields an efficient version of justice.

38. A.A.S. Zuckerman, *Quality and Economy in Civil Procedure: The Case for Commuting Correct Judgments for Timely Judgments,* 14 OXFORD J. OF LEGAL STUDIES 353 (1994).

Chapter 3

FACTS

If the premise of modern American civil procedure were to be expressed in one sentence, it would be as follows: Cases should be resolved on their merits. The discussion of pleading highlights the efforts to move dispute resolution away from technical wizardry and into a more streamlined process that allows parties to address the actual substance of their grievances. Most often the key to the merits of a dispute lies in the facts. Who breached the contract, who ran the red light, who hired or fired for discriminatory reasons, who said what to whom—all the standard sources of disagreement about a perceived injustice start off as matters of fact. It may be that whether the breach of contract was legally justified, or whether running the red light was a sufficiently proximate cause of the accident, or whether the discriminatory reason was within the scope of legal prohibitions, will at the end of the day prove to be questions of law. But, assuming the stated claim is sufficient to survive a motion to dismiss, the hard part is determining whether it is true. This is the world of facts.

Attention to facts permeates the pleading rules. Despite the liberal pleading requirements of Rule 8, the Rules demand attentiveness to factual detail from the parties. As discussed in Chapter 2, the pleading rules require both parties to set forth facts with precision in such a way as to force a convergent set of factual premises about the case, which in turn is presumably a critical inducement to settlement. From the onset of litigation, the parties face corresponding obligations to frame factual statements precisely, to the extent that they are known. Under Rule 10, the plaintiff is required to list all factual statements separately in discrete, numbered paragraphs. That in turn triggers the defendant's obligation under Rule 8 to admit or deny all factual claims, or to state that the defendant is without sufficient information to answer—the functional equivalent of a denial.

The purpose of precise statements of facts and exact admissions or denials is to move the litigation as quickly as possible from the pleading stage to the factual merits. Leaving aside the test for legal sufficiency of a claim under a motion to dismiss and the uncertainty created by the "plausibility" pleading standard introduced in *Bell Atlantic v. Twombly*[1] (topics discussed in Chapter 2),

---

1. 550 U.S. 544 (2007).

the procedural system is designed to force the parties to confront the facts of the case as quickly and as efficiently as possible. As a result, the answer to the complaint is generally held to a higher standard of precision than the complaint itself. The answer is structured to define the ambit of factual disagreement and frame the bounds of pretrial discovery. An admitted claim in the answer serves to remove that factual issue from dispute and allows the parties to focus their attention and resources on matters upon which they disagree or are uncertain. A denial, by contrast, is an invitation to further examination of the basis of the disagreement through the discovery process.

For this process to be effective, the parties must be honest. Thus, as the classic teaching case *Zielinski v. Philadelphia Piers, Inc.*[2] demonstrates, courts tend to react negatively to evasive defendant behavior, even where a plaintiff may also have been sloppy. Under the facts of *Zielinski*, an injured worker sued a firm that he thought was his employer for workplace injuries. In fact, the defendant had spun off its operations to a parallel company with overlapping owners and a joint insurer, presumably for the express purpose of shielding its assets from exposure to liability for workplace injuries. Unaware of this corporate reorganization, the plaintiff sued the firm he believed still responsible for the workplace. When the original defendant coyly skirted admitting that it had indeed ceased operating the loading dock where the accident occurred, the hapless plaintiff found that the statute of limitations had run against his actual employer, thereby foreclosing any remedy. Despite repeated sloppiness by the plaintiff, including in the initial formulation of factual statements in the complaint, the district court ordered a jury instruction that the original defendant was to be deemed the employer, the facts notwithstanding. While an extraordinary remedy, the counterfactual jury instruction was deemed necessary to condemn deceptive behavior contrary to the efficient production of information. The critical lesson is that the answer is part of the production of information, in which exacting conditions of rectitude must prevail. Even though the plaintiff could have avoided much of the harm by clearly framing his factual statements, as required by Rule 10, and despite his failure to follow up on evidence that might have revealed the true owners of the worksite, the obligation of factual forthrightness imposed on the defendant could not be escaped through formalistic evasion.

As evident from *Zielinski*, litigation commences its factual investigation as soon as the defendant answers the complaint.

---

2.   139 F.Supp. 408 (E.D. Pa. 1956).

Outside of matters specifically reserved for factual contestation by a denial, the ambit of factual dispute begins to narrow immediately. The sole exception comes with the capacity to raise what are termed "affirmative defenses" under Rule 8(c). By and large these are issues—such as *res judicata* or the passage of the statute of limitations or prior payment of the damages sought—that do not contest the factual claims in the complaint but rather raise some independent grounds that bar a judgment for the plaintiff. Equally significant, affirmative defenses do not turn on information that is likely to be exclusively in the hands of the opposing party. Instead matters such as whether the statute of limitations has run or whether payment on the judgment has already been made are ascertainable either from the public record or from information held by both parties.

Aside from the affirmative defenses, the passage from mere assertion to the actual merits of the dispute explains the greater requirement of precision on the defendant than on the plaintiff. The complaint is treated as a series of untested statements. The answer, by contrast, either resolves facts conclusively by an admission or, by virtue of a denial, moves the litigation into the fact-gathering stage. As seen in *Zielinski,* sanctions for misanswers may include compelled admission of facts against interest (including, *in extremis,* those not true), preclusion of defenses, and, in the most malodorous cases, even adverse entry of judgment. The entire modern procedural system depends on its ability to resolve disputes on the factual merits, and, in those cases in which the adverse party may be unable to continue asserting claims or defenses, the failure to abide by the obligations of factual production may be dealt with severely.

I. Discovery.

The most distinctive feature of American civil procedure is the adversarial acquisition of information. The ability to compel an opposing party to produce documents, answer written questions, or submit to a sworn oral examination is the core of the litigation process. Few cases go to trial, most cases settle, and yet litigation is an exacting and costly undertaking that focuses overwhelmingly on information. The key to discovery—and what sets it apart from the other rule-based aspects of litigation—is that it is expected to be regulated by the parties themselves, outside the direct supervision of the court. Unlike other aspects of procedure that are triggered by motions and a proposed order, discovery is presumed to be self-executing. The request for information triggers the obligation to provide it, and any party seeking to resist such a request has the burden of initiating motions practice to justify the resistance.

As shown in *Zielinski,* the information acquisition process begins with the answer to the complaint. The formal discovery process begins with Rule 26(f), which mandates a conference between the parties in litigation in part to discuss "a proposed discovery plan." The parties are supposed to endeavor in "good faith" to agree upon discovery issues and the limits on the "subjects on which discovery may be needed." The expectation is that this will limit the open-ended potential scope of discovery. As defined by Rule 26(b), discovery may be had over any matter that is "relevant" to any claim or defense in the case, or the identification of any materials relevant to any claim or defense, regardless whether they would be used at trial or are even admissible at trial. In other words, the scope of potential discovery is exceedingly broad. As stated by the Supreme Court in *Hickman v. Taylor,*[3] a case to which we shall return shortly:

> The various instruments of discovery now serve (1) as a device, along with the pre-trial hearing under Rule 16, to narrow and clarify the basic issues between the parties, and (2) as a device for ascertaining the facts, or information as to the existence or whereabouts of facts, relative to those issues. Thus civil trials in the federal courts no longer need be carried on in the dark. The way is now clear, consistent with recognized privileges, for the parties to obtain the fullest possible knowledge of the issues and facts before trial.[4]

The basic premise of the discovery rules is to arm each side with the tools necessary to secure information. The parties are obligated under the mandatory disclosure provisions of Rule 26(a)(1) to provide each other with the standard materials typically sought in litigation. These include lists of materials to be relied upon in prosecuting or defending the claim, the names of anticipated witnesses, and certain categories of documents, such as underlying insurance agreements, that are conventionally part of any litigated case. These mandatory disclosures are designed to reduce the costs associated with formally requesting information that is sought in most cases. While there are serious questions about the extent to which this process realizes cost savings in most cases, the main effect of the mandatory disclosures is to start the parties down the road of information exchange quickly and on a self-executing basis, as will be further discussed in Chapter 8.

3.   329 U.S. 495 (1947).

4.   *Id.* at 501.

Beyond the required information disclosure in 26(a)(1), the parties have several other methods of gathering information. The easiest way to acquire information is simply to ask for it. Under Rule 33, the parties may submit written questions to the other side in the form of interrogatories. The answers and the information contained in them then form part of the litigation record and may be used to frame the presentation of facts for either further discovery or trial. Similarly, parties are allowed to request the production of documents or the inspection of physical evidence under Rule 34. Both of these Rules serve to create a common factual record, and, in turn, to allow a narrowing of disagreements between the parties.

The parties are then given the opportunity to test the strength of the evidence, primarily by taking the sworn testimony of parties and potential witnesses in the form of depositions. Depositions may be live before a court reporter under Rule 30, or, under Rule 31, upon written questions. Live depositions consist of questions and answers with the witness (termed the "deponent") under oath, as he or she would be if under examination in open court. While written deposition questions, like interrogatories served on parties, are far cheaper, they are also likely to be answered by the opposing attorney—savvier in legal matters than clients—as opposed to the live depositions that are taken directly from parties, witnesses, and experts. The strategic value of the ability to question deponents directly, and to use their videotaped testimony against them should the matter proceed to trial, generally outweighs the cost savings of requesting answers in writing. Finally, the parties are able to remove issues from dispute by serving requests for admissions, pursuant to Rule 36, which allows an admitted fact to be part of the evidentiary record of the case without need for further corroboration.

Backing up the Rules' commitment to the full and efficient exchange of information is Rule 37, which provides for sanctions for litigant misbehavior in discovery. Parties that fail to answer faithfully or that attempt to suppress documents must be dealt with harshly, including by sanctions addressed to the attorneys themselves, to maintain the integrity of a system premised on access to information. Taken as a whole, the discovery rules appear quite neat and tidy. Unfortunately, however, appearances may be deceiving.

There are two distinct problems that plague the discovery system. The first is the absence of controls on cost escalation. It is almost invariably cheaper to ask for materials than to produce them. As a result, parties may be tempted to seek costly information of marginal relevance simply because they do not have to bear the cost burden of producing it—a topic that will be addressed in Chapter 8. At a deeper level, however, the discovery process depends on lawyers faithfully to execute their responsibility to produce all requested information. This often strikes clients, especially those inexperienced in the demands of litigation or more familiar with foreign legal systems, as the lawyer serving almost as the agent of the opposing side, earnestly searching for compromising information to turn over to the adversary.

The discovery process' dependence on lawyers to be faithful agents raises important questions about the limits of discovery. If we return to *Hickman v. Taylor,* a case demanding damages after a fatal tugboat accident, the problem of wide-open discovery becomes more apparent. In that case, appended to a relatively routine discovery request propounded by the plaintiff, was a request for the production of all witness interviews and other notes taken by the defendant's counsel in preparation for the trial of the case. Viewed through the simple prism of the efficient production of information in any particular case, the request would be unobjectionable. Once information is in the possession of a party, no efficiency argument could be advanced for not sharing it with the adversary. Repetition of investigation may guarantee thoroughness; it will rarely be cost efficient.

As the Court recognized, however, allowing counsel to be fully conscripted as an agent of the information gathering process must have its limits. A party that is, in effect, doing the discovery work for two will have little incentive actually to acquire information, thereby paradoxically reducing the total information available in litigation. It may be efficient to disseminate the information broadly once it is in the hands of parties. But the discovery system relies on the incentives operating before the fact that will induce parties to uncover actual information about the merits of the dispute.

The discovery system introduces a further paradox in the lawyer's role as advocate. Discovery ultimately depends on a strong sense of obligation of all attorneys to the courts and the legal system overall, even at the cost of the momentary interests of the clients. Any individual client at any particular point may have a strong incentive in information being suppressed, an incentive that the lawyer must resist. This is generally thought of as the obligation of the lawyer to serve as an officer of the court, accountable not only to the interests of the client but also to the proper functioning of the legal system. But the concept of lawyer as officer of the court must be tempered by the capacity of parties to turn to their lawyers for counsel and confidence, including in fully examining the merits of their case. As the Court concluded in *Hickman*: "Historically, a lawyer is an officer of the court and is bound to work for the advancement of justice while faithfully protecting the rightful interests of his clients. In performing his various duties, however, it is essential that a lawyer work with a certain degree of privacy, free from unnecessary intrusion by opposing parties and their counsel."[5] In a concurring opinion, Justice Jackson put the point more forcefully: "Law-abiding people can go nowhere else to learn the ever changing and constantly multiplying rules by which they must behave and to obtain redress for their wrongs."[6]

Hickman concluded by balancing the competing interests of lawyer as advocate for the client and lawyer as officer of the court. For matters pertaining to client confidences, the inherited common law privilege of attorney-client confidentiality would continue. But the attorney-client privilege was insufficient, standing alone, to protect information acquisition undertaken by the attorney (or his or her agents) at the client's behest. For this a new privilege was created, the attorney work-product exception to full discovery. This new privilege would insulate the lawyer's creative enterprise on behalf of the client from compelled disclosure to the other side. Unlike the attorney-client privilege, however, the newly minted work-product exception to discovery was not absolute. Rather it served as a strong presumption against disclosure that could be overcome where "the [opposing] party shows that it has substantial need for the materials to prepare its case and cannot, without undue hardship, obtain their substantial equivalent by other means," to quote the language of the current form of this privilege, Rule 26(b)(3).

II.　Testing the Factual Record.

So far, the missing party in the fact/information part of a case has been the court. The complaint sets out factual allegations, the answer defines which facts will be in dispute, and the discovery process provides the parties with the tools necessary to create a convergent universe of facts that will define the case. The expectation is that with early recourse to the legal standards governing the case through the motion to dismiss and with a common factual record, the parties will be able to settle the case as their assessments of the claims and defenses begin to converge. While the court may be called upon to rule on the legal issues raised in the motion

---

5.　*Id.* at 510.

6.　*Id.* at 515.

to dismiss, there is not yet any role for the court to play in assessing the factual evidence amassed by the parties.

The missing piece is a form of factual winnowing similar to that of legal testing of claims under Rule 12. The purpose of Rule 12 is to filter out legally untenable claims; a corresponding mechanism should presumably filter out factually untenable claims. Seemingly, therefore, the threshold factual assessment of the case should lie in a form of pretrial judicial screening of the factual merits of a claim, much the way that Rule 12(b)(6) operates in the domain of legal sufficiency of the plaintiff's claim. The difficulty comes with the limited factual role that the federal judiciary may play under the Constitution. By its terms, the Seventh Amendment preserves an autonomous role for the jury in the domain of facts:

> In suits at common law, where the value in controversy shall exceed twenty dollars, the right of trial by jury shall be preserved, and no fact tried by a jury, shall be otherwise re-examined in any Court of the United States, than according to the rules of the common law.[7]

As a result, whatever mechanism allows pretrial screening of the factual basis of the case must not run afoul of the constitutional prerogatives of the jury as the ultimate trier of fact, at least in any case that would have been tried "at common law" under our inherited Anglo–American legal traditions. Since virtually all claims involving a damage remedy or articulating a common law right in tort, contract, or property would have been tried in English courts of law, as opposed to the more limited courts of equity, the prohibitions of the Seventh Amendment are quite sweeping.

Therefore, whatever pretrial factual screen we devise must be attentive to the proper role of the jury as a trier of fact. At the same time, however, the Anglo–American legal tradition has reserved to the judge and not the jury all questions of law governing standards of liability, cognizable defenses, and so forth. Any pretrial screening mechanism must therefore be attentive to the fact/law distinction. In applying this distinction, the key conceptual move is to recognize that courts can use their supervisory powers over questions of law to decide whether certain facts *could* be established on the record before the court, while leaving it to the jury to determine whether they *have* been established. This is necessarily a precarious line.

Under the Federal Rules, there are two possible ways for the court to engage the facts prior to the final jury determination. The

---

7. U.S. Const., 7th Amend.

first, and less significant, is the motion for a directed verdict, now subsumed under a motion for judgment as a matter of law under Rule 50. This is a motion made at the conclusion of the moving party's trial presentation of evidence claiming, as set forth in Rule 50, that there is "no legally sufficient evidentiary basis for a reasonable jury to find for that party on that issue." In effect, this is a defense motion made halfway through a trial when the plaintiff has rested her case. The motion states that the plaintiff has provided so little evidence to support her claim (or at least a critical element of it) that a jury could not possibly find for the plaintiff, or would face reversal by the judge (a "judgment notwithstanding the verdict") were it to so find. Since the plaintiff ultimately has to prove that she is entitled to a favorable verdict, the motion simply asserts that the evidence introduced by the plaintiff was not sufficient to be presented to the jury for ultimate adjudication. Because the motion is directed not to matters of credibility or persuasiveness of the evidence, but to whether there is enough evidence, such matters fall on the "law" side of the fact/law divide.

Alternatively, a party could move for summary judgment under Rule 56. As envisioned by the original Federal Rules in 1938, summary judgment was to serve as a means of testing the legal sufficiency of a factual claim before trial, much as a motion for a directed verdict would operate at trial. Unlike a directed verdict or a judgment as a matter of law, however, the summary judgment motion asks for a factual accounting of a claim before trial, indeed, before a jury has ever been summoned to hear the matter. Thus, by avoiding trial, a summary judgment offers much greater cost savings, but also a potentially much greater affront to the prerogatives of the jury.

The adoption of the Federal Rules made summary judgment available, at least in principle, as a broad-scale tool for the entry of a final decree on the merits of all claims before the federal courts. In reality, from its inception federal judges treated summary judgment warily, perceiving it as threatening a denial of such fundamental guarantees as the right to confront witnesses, the right of the jury to make inferences and determinations of credibility, and the right to have one's cause advocated by counsel before a jury.[8] For example, in 1962 the Supreme Court discouraged the use of summary judgment in antitrust litigation, stating that "[t]rial by affidavit is no substitute for trial by jury which so long has been the hallmark of 'even handed justice.'"[9] Even the reporter for the

---

8. *See, e.g.,* Colby v. Klune, 178 F.2d 872, 873 (2d Cir. 1949) (opinion of Judge Jerome Frank, a leading opponent of summary judgment).

9. Poller v. CBS, Inc., 368 U.S. 464, 473 (1962).

original Federal Rules Committee, Judge Charles Clark, was unable to implement the broad use of summary judgment in his home forum, the Second Circuit.[10] Until 1986 the Second Circuit required denial of summary judgment whenever the "slightest doubt" existed as to whether the nonmovant might persuade a jury of the merits of her case.[11] The "slightest doubt" standard earned the Second Circuit a widespread reputation for hostility to summary judgment motions.

Summary judgment fared little better in other courts. In the Third Circuit, to take another example, summary judgment was denied as a matter of law when the motion was contrary to factual statements that were "well-pleaded," that is, not even a factual matter of record. In effect, the Third Circuit treated the plaintiff's allegations in the complaint as meriting the same weight as factual proof in rebutting the motion for summary judgment. The result was that summary judgment would have little traction beyond the motion to dismiss; each would serve as a pretrial test of the legal sufficiency of the claims asserted in the complaint. The oft-recounted tale of the sign posted in a New Orleans district court, "No Spitting, No Summary Judgments," encapsulates the extreme version of judicial antipathy to summary judgment. Increasingly, therefore, summary judgment became a litigation tool only of the well-heeled litigant who saw in Rule 56 potential strategic value "as a discovery device; to educate the trial judge; in the hope, however faint, of quick victory; and in the expectation, frequently realized, of retarding the progress of a suit and making litigation more expensive."[12] Whatever the strategic gain for a party, summary judgment failed to realize its potential as a pretrial factual filter.

III. The Role of Burden Shifting.

For summary judgment to play a meaningful role in civil procedure, it needed to be reconciled in some manner with the Seventh Amendment's prohibition on judges assuming the role of ultimate fact finder in any case that would have been assigned to a jury at common law. No such reconciliation was necessary on a motion to dismiss, since courts hold plenary power to determine issues of law. Central to permitting a pretrial role for the court on

10. Arnstein v. Porter, 154 F.2d 464, 479 (2d Cir. 1946) (Clark, J., dissenting) (accusing majority of subverting purposes of adoption of Federal Rules by refusing to permit broad use of summary judgment).

11. *See, e.g.,* Dolgow v. Anderson, 438 F.2d 825, 830 (2d Cir. 1970).

12. Professional Managers, Inc. v. Fawer, Brian, Hardy & Zatzkis, 799 F.2d 218, 221–22 (5th Cir. 1986).

questions of fact would be the development of an effective legal screen on the sufficiency of evidence. Much like the motion for a directed verdict at trial, such a screen would shield judges from having to analyze contested factual claims. The language of the summary judgment rule, allowing for judgment to be entered when there is "no genuine issue as to any material fact" in dispute, invites possible court intervention to determine as a matter of law whether disputes are over "material" facts, and whether they are sufficiently presented as to be "genuine."

In order to unleash summary judgment, therefore, there had to be a mechanism permitting factual intervention by the courts that would engage something other than the ultimate disputed issues that were reserved for the jury. The key move comes with distinguishing between the burdens that parties have in the course of litigation. Here it is necessary to be clear on terminology and on the overall structure of the litigation process.

Law is ultimately a conservative enterprise. This means that the law presumes the status quo to be the normal state of affairs. Absent the plaintiff showing an entitlement to some sort of relief, the status quo is the presumed "default" position. The term *"burden of proof"*[13] denotes the responsibility of a party seeking to change the status quo to persuade the ultimate arbiter of facts that a change in the preexisting order is warranted. This includes the ultimate issue of the case—in civil cases, generally whether or not the defendant is liable for harm to the plaintiff—and, therefore, to say that the burden of proof is on the plaintiff means that it is the plaintiff who must show that the defendant is liable. The standard for this ultimate burden of proof in civil cases is "by a preponderance of the evidence," which can be translated roughly as "more likely than not."[14] Thus, if a plaintiff has failed to establish that it is more likely than not that the defendant is liable for her harm, it is said that the plaintiff has failed to discharge her burden of proof in that instance and the law reverts to the *status quo ante:* the defendant owes the plaintiff nothing. While preponderance of the evidence is not a high threshold, it nonetheless signals that the law presumes the natural order that existed before the litigation, absent a showing that the prior state of affairs was legally wrong.

The same principle attaches not just to the ultimate issue in the case, but to intervening procedural issues as well. Thus, a party seeking relief by way of motion bears the burden of proof on the

13. Also variably called the "burden of persuasion," "risk of nonpersuasion," "risk of jury doubt," or the *"onus probandi."* Black's Law Dictionary, 7th edition.

14. Not to be confused with "beyond a reasonable doubt," the common standard in criminal law, which sets a much higher bar for the prosecution to hurdle.

subject of the motion. A defendant seeking relief through a motion to dismiss, or a party seeking to resist discovery as beyond the scope of the dispute, must similarly establish by a preponderance of the evidence her entitlement to the relief sought. In effect, the defendant-movant is seeking to alter the default position of no motion to dismiss or the presumptive responsibility to comply with any discovery request. When a defendant moves for relief, as with a motion to dismiss, the defendant is said to bear the burden of proof on the motion, even though the plaintiff retains the ultimate burden of proof on the litigation as a whole.

While the burden of proof rests on the party seeking to alter the status quo, and while that burden never shifts from the party seeking to alter the status quo, much of the work in litigation is handled through lesser or intermediate burdens. This is the critical issue generally termed either the *"burden of production"* or the *"burden of going forward."* The burden of production is an intermediate burden that orders the presentation of evidentiary proof. The burden of production does not resolve the ultimate issue of liability but is instead a means of structuring what each party must do as the case proceeds. Unlike the burden of proof, which never shifts, the purpose of the burden of production is precisely to shift, to determine who must prove what at a particular stage of litigation. Thus, the concept of burden shifting is a reference to the shifting of the intermediate burden of production as part of the ordering of the presentation of evidence.

Trial lawyers often try to explain the idea of burden shifting in colloquial terms. Imagine, for instance, a parent confronting a child for taking the last piece of cake from the kitchen just before dinner. As the accuser, the parent bears the burden of proof and presumably cannot just demand that the child explain what happened to the cake. It would presumably be wrong just to say, "where's the cake?" With only the information that the cake is not there, it would be unfair to blame the child for the missing cake, as there could be any number of explanations for where it has gone. But there comes a certain point—say, after the parent shows that there is chocolate on the child's hands, that there is no other exit from the kitchen, that the cake was there but five minutes previously, and that nobody else could have eaten the cake—when it is proper to ask the child, "what happened to the cake?" At some point there is so much circumstantial evidence tending to establish the child's guilt that the parent can properly demand an accounting. In legal parlance, one could say that the parent has satisfied the initial burden of production, and that the burden of producing information has shifted to the child. While the parent retains the burden of proof throughout, the failure of the child to rebut the inferences created by the initial presentation will be deemed an admission of the parent's claims.

Stepping back a bit from the colloquial, burden shifting works as follows: A plaintiff bears the burden of proof on her overarching claim at all times. The plaintiff initially also bears the burden of production, meaning that she must present evidence to support her accusations. Once a sufficient quantum of evidence is introduced, however, the *burden of production* shifts to the defendant to establish what facts really are at issue. If the defendant satisfies this shifting of the burden of production, the plaintiff then has one last chance to show that the facts presented by the defendant are immaterial or in some other fashion are not dispositive. The critical question posed in the shifting of the burden of production is how much evidence is required of the movant to demand accountability from the nonmovant.

To return to summary judgment, burden shifting allows a court to interject itself into the process of resolving facts. While resolving disputed issues of fact remains squarely the province of the jury, that is not the end of the story. Determining who must prove what at any given point is considered a question of law reserved to the court. Thus, by deciding whether a party has presented sufficient facts to satisfy a burden of production, a court can decide whether there are any genuine issues of fact that justify having the matter decided by a jury. This is, in effect, what happens in a motion for a directed verdict where the court decides that the plaintiff has not introduced enough evidence to force the defendant to rebut. The decisive legal question at summary judgment is whether the use of intermediate burden shifting can provide a pretrial filter, akin to the use of directed verdict at trial itself. Put a different way, if the plaintiff does not have enough evidence to survive a motion for a directed verdict at trial, why not find that out after discovery and before trial?

IV. Burden Shifting on Summary Judgment.

Prior to a decisive series of cases in 1986, the defining case on summary judgment was *Adickes v. S.H. Kress & Co.*,[15] a civil rights conspiracy case arising from the Freedom Rides of the early 1960s. A white schoolteacher from the North, Sandra Adickes, joined a group of black protesters in a lunch counter sit-in challenging the refusal of the S.H. Kress department store to serve black patrons at

---

15.   398 U.S. 144 (1970).

its store in Hattiesburg, Mississippi. During the course of the protests, Adickes was arrested, and she subsequently sued Kress for violating her civil rights.

In order to prevail on her civil rights claim, under federal laws that governed only the conduct of state officials, Adickes would have had to prove that Kress had acted in concert with the arresting officers, bringing Kress's conduct "under color" of state law. The critical question in the case, therefore, was whether there existed any evidence tying Kress to the offending state conduct. After discovery, Kress sought summary judgment, claiming that "uncontested facts," including the unrebutted affidavits of the store manager and several police officers, repudiated the charge that there had been concerted activity between the store managers or employees and the police, and that the plaintiff had failed to produce any evidence that would have established the existence of the conspiracy.[16] In effect, Kress was seeking to use the summary judgment motion to challenge whether Adickes had any evidence that could tie it to state conduct, a necessary and controlling element of her claim.

There is little doubt that, had Kress challenged this lack of evidence at trial through a motion for a directed verdict, the plaintiff's failure to prove a critical element of her case would have required a defendant's judgment as a matter of law. The question for the Court was whether Kress could anticipate what would happen at trial by claiming, in effect, that even if Adickes were to present all the evidence at trial in the most effective manner possible, there was just not enough evidence to allow the matter to be presented to the jury. In short, could a summary judgment motion at the close of discovery anticipate what would happen at the close of plaintiff's evidence at trial? Or, put in the language of burden shifting, could summary judgment be used to allow Kress to shift the burden of production to Adickes in order to ask, what do you claim to have at trial that would allow you to survive a motion for a directed verdict?

The answer from the Supreme Court was decidedly negative: as the moving party, Kress "had the burden of showing the absence of a genuine issue as to any material fact, and for these purposes the material it lodged must be viewed in the light most favorable to the

---

16. For purposes of comparison, this is the same situation as the parent that presents only the fact that the child was in the same room as the cake, and the precocious child that rebuts it with affidavits from witnesses. Under *Adickes*, the child, as defendant, loses a motion for summary judgment, and the case continues to trial.

opposing party."[17] The motion for summary judgment failed, the Supreme Court held, because the affidavits of record did not *foreclose* a possible inference of a conspiracy by the jury by showing that there was no possible manner in which Kress officials might have communicated with the police. Since such an inference could not be foreclosed from the "factual allegations of [Adickes'] complaint, as well as the material found in the affidavits and depositions presented by Kress ..., [Kress] failed to carry its burden of showing the absence of any genuine issue of fact."[18]

The critical holding in *Adickes* concerned the threshold showing that a movant for summary judgment must make in order to shift the burden of production. For the Court, that burden was essentially indistinguishable from the burden of proof for the motion as a whole: a defendant moving for summary judgment would have "to show *initially* the absence of a genuine issue concerning any material fact."[19] Kress had not discharged this burden because it had failed to establish conclusively that there could not have been concerted conduct. There could always have been some other form of communication, some intermediary who carried the message, some preexisting arrangement, and so forth. Since Kress had failed to prove the negative—a near impossibility—the Court never had occasion to weigh the quality of the plaintiff's evidence, regardless of whether it would have been sufficient to survive a motion for a directed verdict at trial. In effect, the Court rejected any intermediate burden shifting until and unless the movant for summary judgment conclusively discharged its burden of proof on the summary judgment motion.

For all intents and purposes, *Adickes* confirmed that summary judgment would remain unavailable in the great run of cases. Summary judgment would be available in those rare cases in which the parties were able to stipulate to the factual record at the conclusion of discovery. In effect, summary judgment would serve as a mechanism for a court-administered resolution of disputed legal issues when the parties were able to agree to the controlling facts of a dispute. Since almost all cases turn on factual as well as legal disputes, summary judgment could play no significant role as a pretrial screen of cases.

All that changed in 1986, when the Court decided three cases that dramatically altered the operation of summary judgment in

---

17. 398 U.S. at 157. Note that the court uses "burden" in the sense of the burden of proof on a motion.

18. *Id*. at 153.

19. *Id.* at 160 (emphasis added).

federal courts: *Celotex Corp. v. Catrett*,[20] *Matsushita Electrical Industrial Co. v. Zenith Radio Corp.*,[21] and *Anderson v. Liberty Lobby, Inc.*[22] The lead case of this trilogy, *Celotex,* highlighted the shortcomings of the *Adickes* approach. The case involved the widow of an industrial worker exposed to asbestos. A necessary element of proof should the case go to trial would be whether or not the decedent had ever been exposed to asbestos manufactured by the defendant, since without that the critical element of causation liability could not be established. If Mrs. Catrett could not establish that fact she could never survive a motion for a directed verdict. But were Celotex to challenge on that issue prior to trial through a summary judgment motion, its burden would be to establish conclusively that under no set of circumstances could Mr. Catrett ever have been exposed to a Celotex asbestos fiber—an overwhelming and likely impossible task.

Celotex began the process of invigorating summary judgment as what Justice Rehnquist would term an "integral" part of the Federal Rules of Civil Procedure. Although the Court divided into many opinions—all oddly claiming to uphold *Adickes*—all members of the Court rejected the critical holding of *Adickes* that summary judgment would be available only upon a movant's conclusive proof that the nonmovant could not prevail at trial. Instead, all members of the Court ruled that the burden of production on a motion for summary judgment would be conditioned on the ultimate burden of proof that the movant would have at trial.[23] In other words, a defendant moving for summary judgment would bear the burden of proof for the motion, but might be able to shift the burden of production with something less than a showing that under no circumstances could the plaintiff prevail. By allowing a shifting of the intermediate burden of production, the Court allowed for greater judicial oversight of the factual record. Once burden shifting was allowed, judges could determine whether a motion for summary judgment was sufficiently supported to shift the burden of production to the nonmovant and, more critically, whether the nonmovant in turn would be able to satisfy her burden of production or face a summary judgment.

The Court divided over how far to liberalize summary judgment. The dissent, authored by Justice Brennan, feared that if the

---

20. 477 U.S. 317 (1986).

21. 475 U.S. 574 (1986).

22. 477 U.S. 242 (1986).

23. 477 U.S. at 322; see also *id.* at 324 n.5 (citing articles by Professors Louis and Currie urging that summary judgment be recast to reflect the ultimate trial burdens).

burden of production were too low a threshold, defendants might seek strategic gain by simply demanding summary judgment and getting the advantage of forcing the plaintiff to present her entire case—in the same fashion as would occur if the parties were at trial and the defendant sought a directed verdict at the conclusion of the plaintiff's case presentation. The difference is that at trial, if the motion for a directed verdict is denied, the defendant must immediately proceed to the presentation of his case, gaining no strategic benefit from the endeavor. The ability to demand that the plaintiff produce a trial preview at summary judgment does, however, allow the defendant to benefit from the additional time before trial would commence to prepare a rebuttal. Since the defendant is never at risk of an adverse final judgment at the summary judgment stage, there would be no corresponding obligation on the defendant to "preview" its trial presentation to the plaintiff.

Despite this strategic concern, the Court nonetheless held that the burden on a defendant moving for summary judgment would be quite minimal. Rather than prove the negative, the Court held that "a party seeking summary judgment always bears the initial responsibility of informing the district court of the basis for its motion, and identifying those portions of 'the pleadings, depositions, answers to interrogatories, and admissions on file, together with the affidavits, if any,' which it believes demonstrate the absence of a genuine issue of material fact." But that, the Court cautioned, does not constitute an "express or implied requirement in Rule 56 that the moving party support its motion with affidavits or other similar materials *negating* the opponent's claim."[24] The task of "informing" the court of the basis for the summary judgment motion could be as minimal as suggested by the term "inform." Indeed, almost from the outset, courts interpreted *Celotex* to allow the defendant/movant's initial burden of production to be satisfied by the motion itself. Reported decisions on motions for summary judgment after *Celotex* addressed themselves exclusively to what the plaintiff/nonmovant had introduced to show the existence of disputed facts for trial, not what the defendant/movant had introduced initially to support the summary judgment motion.[25] The shift from discussing what the movant had to prove to what the nonmovant had to establish is precisely the doctrinal change from *Adickes* to *Celotex*.

Thus, upon defendant's motion for summary judgment, the burden of production shifts from the defendant to the plaintiff.

---

24. 477 U.S. at 323 (emphasis in original).

25. *See* Samuel Issacharoff & George Loewenstein, *Second Thoughts About Summary Judgment,* 100 Yale L.J. 73, 88–90 (1990).

Celotex still conformed to the normal requirement that a movant bear the ultimate burden for her motion (a trier of fact would still ultimately have to be convinced), but the opinion refocused the critical inquiry from the burden of production that a movant must satisfy to the burden upon the nonmovant to establish *her* right to go to trial. As revealed by the facts of *Celotex*, a moving party may prevail at summary judgment having "made no effort to adduce *any* evidence, in the form of affidavits or otherwise, to support its motion."[26] At bottom, therefore, the significance of *Celotex* lies in the Court's relieving defendants, in their customary posture as the party moving for summary judgment, of *any* significant burden of production to establish initially the absence of material issues of fact in dispute.[27]

V. The Scope of Judicial Fact–Finding.

Celotex began the process of bringing summary judgment into the center of contemporary civil procedure. But *Celotex* focused only on the factual support needed for making a summary judgment motion; it did nothing to alter the limited powers of review of courts over contested issues of fact. Untouched was the traditional view of summary judgment as being "of practical use only in cases in which documentary or circumstantial evidence is dispositive of critical issues. When a case depends on credibility of testimony or a jury's evaluation of a person's conduct, it cannot be determined summarily."[28] Furthermore, "[s]ummary judgment is not intended to resolve issues that are within the traditional province of the trier of fact, but rather to see whether there are such issues."[29] As Judge Jerome Frank of the Second Circuit once famously wrote, in the context of an undoubtedly spurious action in which a frequent (unsuccessful) litigant decided to sue composer Cole Porter for allegedly appropriating his material, a "[p]laintiff must not be deprived the invaluable privilege of cross-examining the defendant—the 'crucial test of credibility'—in the presence of the jury."[30]

---

26. 477 U.S. at 321, quoting Catrett v. Johns–Manville Sales Corp., 756 F.2d 181, 184 (D.C. Cir. 1985) (emphasis in original).

27. The Celotex opinions leave untouched the question of the proper burden of production to be borne by a movant who *would* bear the ultimate burden of proof at trial—i.e., a plaintiff moving for summary judgment. Presumably, the movant under such circumstances is to be held to the *Adickes* standard—that is, the plaintiff (or defendant forwarding an affirmative defense) has to present evidence foreclosing the opposition's arguments.

28. Fleming James, Jr. et al., Civil Procedure § 4.10, at 207 (4th ed. 1992).

29. *Id.* at 4.11, at 209.

30. Arnstein v. Porter, 154 F.2d 464, 469–70 (2d Cir. 1946).

In order to unleash fully summary judgment, there needed to be a corresponding rethinking of the initial determination of what facts are sufficient to require presentation to a jury. Beyond the threshold *Celotex* question of the support required to move for summary judgment, the key case on the scope of review of the summary judgment record is *Matsushita*. The issue in *Matsushita* was a claim by Zenith, the last extant American manufacturer of televisions, that Japanese electronics companies were dumping televisions below cost (referred to in the antitrust literature as "predatory pricing") for the purpose of driving American manufacturers out of business. The district court had entered summary judgment against Zenith, despite the fact that both parties presented extensive factual support for their positions, including well-credentialed expert testimony on both sides of the predatory pricing claim. The existence of significant evidence on both sides would seemingly have precluded summary judgment being upheld, on the simple ground that the record revealed disputed issues of material fact.

Despite the disputed facts, the Court upheld the grant of summary judgment. Zenith could not simply rely on the existence of a factual dispute, but was required to "come forward with more persuasive evidence to support their claim than would otherwise be necessary," because "the claim was one that simply makes no economic sense."[31] The Court found support for this evaluation not from the factual record but from a "consensus among commentators that predatory pricing schemes are rarely tried, and even more rarely successful."[32] Reaching even further into the realm of fact-finding, the Court added, "[t]he alleged conspiracy's failure to achieve its ends in the two decades of its asserted operation is strong evidence that the conspiracy does not in fact exist."[33]

It is certainly possible to challenge the Court's claim that an academic "consensus" regarding predatory pricing existed, drawing as it did from a particular school of thought commonly associated with the law and economics movement at the University of Chicago. And there is the disturbing fact that shortly after the case, Zenith closed down its U.S. television manufacturing business, leaving no standing American manufacturers of televisions. But the significance of *Matsushita* for our purposes is that it gave judges far more latitude to examine the weight of the factual record than had previously existed. Despite the possibility after *Celotex* that the

31. 475 U.S. at 587.
32. *Id.* at 589.
33. *Id.* at 592.

defendant might move for summary judgment with no support simply for strategic advantage, the far greater inducement was to present the trial court with an ample record supporting a motion for summary judgment—then securing a ruling at summary judgment rather than trial.

The final step in moving the first review of facts from trial to summary judgment comes with the third case of the trilogy, *Anderson v. Liberty Lobby.* In the context of a defamation action, the Court expressly invited the greater use of summary judgment as a way of forestalling the potential chilling effect on the press that ready access to juries might have. Here the Court added that what constitutes sufficient evidence to present a "genuine issue" under the terms of Rule 56 would be conditioned by the evidentiary burdens the parties shouldered at trial and by the nature of the claim. Thus, under appropriate trial burdens, a nonmovant could survive summary judgment if and only if "the evidence is such that a reasonable jury could return a verdict for the nonmoving party."[34] The issue is "whether reasonable jurors could find by a preponderance of the evidence that the plaintiff was entitled to a verdict. . . ."[35] The Court then capped this off by making clear that the standard would be the same as under a directed verdict at trial: Rule 56, like Rule 50, requires that a court "direct a verdict if, under governing law, there can be but one reasonable conclusion as to the verdict."[36]

As a consequence of the trilogy, the Court transformed summary judgment. From its original purpose to ensure a modicum of genuine dispute in cases set for trial, summary judgment has become a full dress-rehearsal for trial with legal burdens and evidentiary standards to match those that would apply at trial. Indeed, the trilogy can be read to "endorse summary judgment as a substitute for trial."[37] The effect of the trilogy is aptly summarized by Professor Arthur Miller: "*Celotex* has made it easier to make the [summary judgment] motion, *Anderson* and *Matsushita* have increased the chances that it will be granted."[38] Neither the dress-rehearsal analogy nor the trial analogy should obscure the critical difference between summary judgment and trial: there is no jury

34.   477 U.S. at 248.

35.   *Id.* at 252.

36.   *Id.* at 250.

37.   Richard Marcus, *Completing Equity's Conquest? Reflections on the Future of Trial Under the Federal Rules of Civil Procedure,* 50 U. Pitt. L. Rev. 725, 740 (1989).

38.   Arthur R. Miller, *The Pretrial Rush to Judgment: Are the "Litigation Explosion," "Liability Crisis," and Efficiency Cliches Eroding Our Day in Court and Jury Trial Commitments?,* 78 N.Y.U. L. Rev. 982, 1041 (2003).

sitting as trier of fact and only plaintiffs are at risk of adverse final judgment.

The remaining question after the summary judgment trilogy is the scope of potential judicial review of facts in determining that there are no issues to be resolved at trial. At some point, the Court would have to confront more directly the remaining force of the Seventh Amendment's guarantee of trial by jury. While this issue has not yet been revisited in the context of summary judgment, the Court has significantly revised its interpretation of the Seventh Amendment in the distinct context of patent claims in *Markman v. Westview Instruments*.[39] At issue in *Markman* were the intellectual property rights for a computerized system that relied on barcodes to track clothes left at dry cleaners. Markman's patent covered the "means to maintain an inventory total" that could "detect and localize spurious additions to inventory as well as spurious deletions therefrom." Westview had created a similar computerized tracking system that relied on infrared scanners, but its system, unlike Markman's, could not track articles of clothing throughout the cleaning process and could not generate reports on their status and location. Markman sued for patent infringement and Westview subsequently moved for summary judgment. The precise issue was whether the patent's use of the term "inventory" should be read to include item management systems that arguably could not track inventory. The dispositive issue in the case would likely be the exact meaning of the word "inventory."

In a significant departure from prior Seventh Amendment law, the Court in *Markman* did not try to reconstruct what would have been the historic practices governing whether a jury would have heard such cases. Rather than looking back to 1791, the date of adoption of the Seventh Amendment, to determine whether patent claims would be handled as a matter of law or equity, the Court resorted to "functional considerations" to decide "the choice between judge and jury to define terms of art."[40] The question was whether one or another "judicial actor" was better positioned to decide the issue. According to the Court, the "construction of written instruments is one of those things that judges often do and are likely to do better than jurors unburdened by training in exegesis."[41] The application to the facts of *Markman* is slightly peculiar. A judge may be more expert in the construction of documents, but is not likely to have any particular expertise in the

39.   517 U.S. 370 (1996).

40.   *Id.* at 388.

41.   *Id.*

interpretation of the term "inventory" in the dry cleaning business. Whether decided by a judge or jury, the trade meaning of inventory was going to turn on expert testimony or some form of reference to trade usage, not to any specialized set of skills of a trial judge.

Regardless of the soundness of the application in the case of a trade-specific use of a term, *Markman* opened up a new area for judicial intervention into the fact-finding process. The Court buttressed its holding by pointing to the importance of uniformity in the interpretation of terms in patents, an argument that is no doubt correct. But the functional account of jury trial rights introduces a significant limitation on the role of the civil jury. Nearly all contract cases require the trier of fact to interpret a document, preferably by parties benefited by "training in exegesis," as the Court characterized the added benefit of having a judge rather than a jury interpret an ambiguous term. Antitrust cases or complex product liability cases might require the trier of fact to examine complicated expert analyses, presumably also an area where training in document analysis might be at the forefront of the necessary fact-finding. Were *Markman* to invite a view of the Seventh Amendment that required a trial by jury only where the functional balance indicated that a determination of credibility was at issue—a classic "he said/she said" fact dispute—the role of the jury would be dramatically circumscribed and the prospect for judicial resolution of fact greatly expanded.

Thus far, *Markman* has been confined to the world of patent disputes, although *Twombly* (also written by Justice Souter) does introduce some elements of factual inquiry to the motion to dismiss stage. Nonetheless, the Supreme Court has not accepted invitations to extend the logic of judicial expertise on factual matters into other domains of law.[42] But *Markman* is consistent with the desire to expand the ambit of judicial intervention into the process of resolving facts, clearly evidenced by the trajectory of summary judgment law. This is still an area of law under development.

VI. The Disappearing Trial.

Missing thus far from the account of how a fact record is developed is the question of trial. In the popular imagination, the trial is the final crucible for the battle between truth and falsehood. More than anything else, it is the drama of courtroom confrontation that drives the popular image of the law. And yet, both the

---

42. *See, e.g.,* City of Monterey v. Del Monte Dunes at Monterey, Ltd., 526 U.S. 687 (1999).

expansion of summary judgment and the increasing role of judges as managers of private dispute resolution (the subject of Chapter 8) have rendered trials increasingly unlikely, even rare. As a result, I have left the actual mechanisms of trial and appeal out of the present review of civil procedure. This may seem a stunning omission, but the federal civil jury trial is a declining institution, and there is significant evidence that state court trials are diminishing in frequency as well.[43] The actual practices of trial deserve independent treatment apart from this review of modern civil procedure.

The primary purpose of the civil trial was to ascertain facts through the confrontation of witnesses and evidence. That process of winnowing facts has moved decisively upstream to the summary judgment stage, and may move even more fully there depending on the ultimate evolution of cases such as *Markman*. Under current federal practice, the premise is increasingly that facts will get worked out through discovery and tested at some level well before trial. As stated by former Chief Judge Patricia Wald of the United States Court of Appeals for the District of Columbia Circuit, "Federal jurisprudence is largely the product of summary judgment in civil cases."[44] Put more graphically, the litigation of a case through trial may be sufficiently infrequent as to be seen as a "pathological event."[45]

Consider the following data on trial trends over a 27-year period:

	1983	1993	2003	2010
Federal Civil Trials[46]	11,625	7,740	4,206	3,309
% Cases Reaching Trial[47]	5.4%	3.4%	1.7%	1.1%
Federal District Judges[48]	658	784	926	946
Avg. No. Trials / Judge	17–18	9–10	4–5	3–4

A little over five percent of the civil cases filed in federal court in 1983 would ultimately be resolved by trial, with some fraction of

43. *See, e.g.,* Brian J. Ostrom, Shauna M. Strickland, and Paula L. Hannaford–Agor, *Examining Trial Trends in State Courts: 1976–2002*, 1 J. Empirical Legal Stud. 755 (2004).

44. Patricia M. Wald, *Summary Judgment at Sixty*, 76 Tex. L. Rev. 1897 (1998).

45. Judith Resnik, *Many Doors? Closing Doors? Alternative Dispute Resolution and Adjudication*, 10 Ohio St. J. on Disp. Resol. 211, 261 & n.200 (1995) (quoting Edward H. Cooper, Reporter, Minutes of the Advisory Committee of the Federal Rules of Civil Procedure 17 (Oct. 21–23, 1993)).

46. Judicial Business of the United States Courts, Table C–4.

47. *Id.*

48. Annual Report of the Director of the Office of Administration of the United States Courts. Number represents total authorized judgeships, less vacancies, plus senior judges.

those then going on to appeal. The five percent figure is more or less the best estimate of 1983 trial rates not only for the federal system, but for state systems as well. By 2003, that figure had been reduced to less than two percent in the federal system, and by 2010, it had been reduced to 1.1 percent. Over the same period of time, the number of federal judges went up over 40 percent. Thus, the average number of cases tried by an individual federal judge fell by over two-thirds in less than 30 years.

Another way to consider the phenomenon of the disappearing trial is to examine how issues in the federal courts are preserved for appeal. One illustrative study simply looked at the federal appellate reporters over a 25–year period to assess how many appeals from trial were getting to the courts of appeals. In 1973, an average volume of the federal appellate reporter contained opinions on 52 appeals from a trial and only 14 appeals from a summary judgment ruling. By 1997–98 that ratio had been reversed, to an average of 20 trial and 47 summary judgment appeals per volume.[49]

The upshot is that while American civil procedure remains highly fact-attentive, trials are no longer the presumed venue for the resolution of fact disputes. And, while the bulk of costs associated with litigation involve fact production during discovery, the goal is not trial but either informed settlement or summary disposition.

49. Paul W. Mollica, *Federal Summary Judgment at High Tide*, 84 Marq. L. Rev. 141, 144 (2000).

Chapter 4

PARTIES

Perhaps no area of procedural law marks the boundary between the common law of old and the modern era as clearly as the concept of parties to the litigation. The common law assumed a world of bipolar disputes in which all individuals with a legal interest in a proceeding would themselves be parties to the litigation. A dispute over a wandering cow, to return to a recurring hypothetical, would presumably involve the two neighbors claiming an ownership interest in the cherished bovine. The common law presumption was that the rights and remedies—and hence the interest—would be limited to the two parties to the dispute, and that they would control all facets of the case.

Even in this simple case, however, it is not difficult to see that others may have a stake in how the dispute is resolved. The rights of other parties may be affected, either directly or indirectly, by the outcome of this particular case. Other neighbors could come forward to claim ownership of the cow after the court had resolved the dispute between the first two parties. In effect, these neighbors would be seeking to contest the presumed exclusivity of interest of the original parties in how the rights to the cow were to be assigned. Alternatively, other effects may be less direct but nonetheless far-reaching and significant. The court in the dispute over the cow might develop a rule of law ordering that all livestock found on one's property could be immediately consumed, or a court could develop a presumption of treble damages as a remedy for erroneous holding of chattels. The precedential effects of each of these decisions could well extend far beyond the two parties involved in the original dispute, yet the common law would have excluded all of those additional interests and left the disagreement in the hands of the primary disputants.

The common law conception of parties flowed directly from the limited, bipolar conception of dispute resolution. Not only were third-party effects not considered in the framing of a legal action, but a case could only be brought by a person with legal title to the right being asserted. Thus, if the owner of the wandering cow had assigned an interest in the cow—for example, pledging part of his herd as collateral for a loan—the assignee could assert no claim of his own against the party now thought to be in wrongful possession of the cow. Similarly, had the original owner insured the cow and recovered in whole or in part from his insurer, the insurance company could assert no claim of its own for the loss—what we now term the "subrogation rights" of the insurer to assert claims for recovery of payments made under an insurance policy held by an injured party. The interests of assignees or subrogees at common law would have been considered equitable rather than legal, meaning that they would not be considered parties for purposes of asserting the common law claim for loss of property.

It is difficult to justify a formal rule that excludes parties, such as assignees or subrogees, who have suffered tangible harms, from seeking some form of legal redress. That in itself puts great pressure on the narrow common law conception of proper parties to a dispute. But the pressure on the narrow definition of parties emerged not only from the spreading web of contractually-related parties, but from the types of cases that were being presented to the courts. Procedural systems are under constant strain as the range of substantive law moves beyond the narrow common law view of dispute resolution. As courts have become increasingly involved in matters like school desegregation cases, administrative law proceedings, reapportionment claims, and environmental tort actions, the narrow common law definition of interested parties has become strained beyond its breaking point.

As with many of the evolutionary pressures on the procedural system, the response to the specific pressures on the definition of appropriate parties to a lawsuit turns on the competing considerations of equity and efficiency. The demands of equity are realized through the expansion of parties able to overcome barriers to participation, either by being recognized as "real parties in interest" or by being offered some kind of access to judicial proceedings even if not granted full status as a party to the proceeding, as with the process of intervention. Efficiency concerns push the concept of proper or necessary parties to a litigation even further. The result is a broad system of aggregation of similarly situated parties to maximize the legal resolution possible from any particular adjudication.

I. Proper Parties.

At the heart of the modern treatment of parties in the pleading system is Rule 20, providing for the permissive joinder of parties. This Rule allows modern litigation to be structured to bring in as many similarly situated parties as are deemed necessary to a fair and complete adjudication. The Rule allows the plaintiff, as the master of the complaint, to initially join as plaintiffs as many other persons as necessary. These additional plaintiffs may be joined as long as (1) their claims arise out of the same transaction or occurrence, or even out of the same "series of transactions or occurrences," and (2) "any question of law or fact common to all plaintiffs will arise in the action." Correspondingly, the plaintiff is allowed to name as many defendants as will meet a comparably ample definition of appropriate parties to the litigation. While strikingly expansive, this initial definition of proper parties is in reality simply a broader recognition of persons that the common law system would have recognized as having claims or defenses against each other, even if the joint litigation format is somewhat more extended.

The current Rules make their first inroad into the restrictive common law definition of parties with Rules 17 and 19, reflecting the idea of "a real party in interest" and "required" parties. The real party in interest rule is an innovation of the nineteenth century, particularly the Field Code in New York, which attempted to move law away from formalism in pleading. As originally designed, allowing a case to be prosecuted in the name of any party with a legally cognizable claim accomplished two things. First, it streamlined litigation by, for example, allowing trustees to sue in their individual capacity rather than through the formalism of the beneficiaries of a trust or permitting parties with a stake in contract completion to sue on their own behalf, rather than standing behind the party nominally harmed. By allowing a broader class of interested parties to sue, the Rule also had the effect of facilitating the final resolution of disputes. As will be discussed more fully in Chapter 7, freeing parties who might have a legal claim to sue in their own name, regardless of the immediate procedural posture of the case, introduced a "use it or lose it" quality to the initial resolution of related legal claims. Liberalizing access to the courts allowed adjudicated outcomes to have greater binding effects across the entire universe of affected parties, even if the common law would not have recognized their capacity to sue in their own names.

In practice, Rule 17 no longer has much effect. Indeed, it has derisively been called a "barnacle on the federal practice ship"[1] by both academics and courts. The reason is that the Rule was designed to bring pleading practice into conformity with a broader range of claims than would have been recognized through narrow common law concepts such as privity. In the meantime, however, other aspects of court practice have evolved to recognize the "standing" of third-party beneficiaries, trustees, insurance subrogees, and other such interested parties to initiate actions to vindi-

---

1. John E. Kennedy, *Federal Rule 17(a): Will the Real Party in Interest Please Stand?,* 51 Minn. L. Rev. 675, 724 (1967).

cate their specific and perhaps partial interests. As a result, the first clause of Rule 17, permitting an action to be brought in the name of the real party in interest, does not provide much beyond what the law of standing has independently moved to recognize.

More significant to the real world of litigation is the second clause which refers to controlling substantive law to determine the capacity of an individual or entity to sue. Once in place, this rule is virtually self-executing since it allows a claim to be brought by anyone who can identify a basis in substantive law sufficient to withstand a Rule 12(b)(6) motion to dismiss. But the simplicity of the Rule obscures the difficult problem that it overcame. So long as the capacity to sue was restricted to the parties with common law privity to the claim, additional parties claiming injury faced the prospect of the claimholder acting as a gatekeeper—in effect, able to demand payment from either the injured to allow the claim to go forward, or from the defendant to stand as a shield against those claiming harm. The effect was to force parties to contract for protection ahead of time against unknown contingencies, or face the possibility of being held up by a well-positioned claimholder. The gatekeeper always demands a toll, as it were. The liberalization of standing and pleading rules eliminated this transactional barrier to confronting legal claims on their merits.

The flip side of Rule 17 is the ability of a defendant under Rule 19 to seek to realign the litigation. Rule 19 gives the defendant the ability to make sure that claims are properly presented by the real claimholders, and by all the ones "required" to guarantee a complete adjudication. Rule 19 is an especially cumbersome and confusing attempt to bring common law concepts of interested parties into alignment with the modern demands of litigation. The Rule begins by identifying persons to be joined if feasible, and characterizing them as required if either complete relief cannot be granted in their absence or if the practical effect of an adjudication would be to implicate their rights or interests. The critical provision of the Rule is 19(b), which allows a defendant to seek dismissal or some protective order in case a court is unable to join a needed party, as, for example, when the court would not have jurisdiction over the additional party. In effect, Rule 19(a) only identifies the parties that are of concern to the court; Rule 19(b) provides some operational remedy. Rule 19(b) reads as a familiar balancing test that asks about the amount of prejudice to all parties if the case does or does not go forward, the systemic interests in ensuring that some forum is available to provide a remedy, and the equitable tools that the court might use to protect the interests of all affected parties.

Viewed in this fashion, Rule 19 is intended to allow both parties to secure the participation of all parties necessary for a just and final adjudication. This is rarely of concern to the plaintiff, who, by fashioning the complaint, creates the scope of dispute best suited to her interests. But it is a source of concern to a defendant who may fear conflicting injunctive orders or some strategic disadvantage from some but not all the interested parties in a case being before the court. For all practical purposes, Rule 19 serves as a second motion to dismiss by a defendant claiming some unfairness from how the case is structured.

The Rule is, however, plagued by two defects. The first results from the Rule's clumsy language. Prior to 2007, Rule 19(a) referred to "necessary" parties, while 19(b) concerned "indispensable" parties. This "confusing terminology" prompted criticism from the Supreme Court: "the decision to proceed is a decision that the absent person is merely 'necessary' while the decision to dismiss is a decision that he is 'indispensable.' "[2] In the 2007 stylistic revisions to the Federal Rules, which were intended to improve the Rules' clarity without changing their meaning, Rule 19 was amended to refer to "required" parties. Unfortunately, this formulation is not much clearer. As the Supreme Court has recently noted, persons "required" for purposes of Rule 19(a) "may turn out not to be required for the action to proceed after all" under Rule 19(b).[3]

The second defect is that the Rule allows for a conventional balancing of interests under 19(b), but only if the narrow gatekeeping of 19(a) has first been satisfied. This structural obstacle to the full use of Rule 19 puts modern courts in the unfamiliar posture of having to first conduct a highly formal assessment of the parties whose joinder might be necessary, rather than proceed immediately to a more conventional balancing of interests to manage equitably the litigation process. Here too the Supreme Court, in a case decided under the old version of Rule 19, has recognized the difficulty of the inquiry: "To say that a court 'must' dismiss in the absence of an indispensable party and that it 'cannot proceed' without him puts the matter the wrong way around: a court does not know whether a particular person is 'indispensable' until it had examined the situation to determine whether it can proceed without him."[4] This problem remains even after the 2007 stylistic revisions to Rule 19, which changed one of the Rule's key terms, but did nothing to fix its underlying structural flaws.

---

2. Provident Tradesmens Bank & Trust Co. v. Patterson, 390 U.S. 102, 118 (1968).

3. Republic of Philippines v. Pimentel, 553 U.S. 851 (2008).

4. *Provident Tradesmens Bank*, 390 U.S. at 119.

Nonetheless, Rules 17 and 19, despite the difficulty in their actual implementation, represent the first recognition that the appropriate scope of litigation will often push beyond the narrow common law vision of two independent parties mired in a dispute over finite resources that only they care about.

II. Necessary and Interested Parties.

A. *The Demands of Complete Resolution.*

Even at common law, courts recognized that sometimes it was impossible to resolve a claim in its entirety without expanding the limited bipolar characterization of the prototypical dispute. English courts utilized exceptional equity powers to realign a dispute so as to bring in all "necessary parties," an early recognition of the steps taken in part in modern Rules 17 and 19. The equitable "necessary parties rule" mandated that "all persons materially interested, either as plaintiffs or defendants in the subject matter of the bill ought to be made parties to the suit, however numerous they may be."[5] The idea of necessary parties is directly tied into the idea of litigation providing a "bill of peace" by which litigants are offered final resolution of disputes through adjudication.

In some circumstances, however, it is not simply that strangers to the immediate dispute might have an interest in the outcome; instead, the particulars of the case might make it impossible for the actual litigants to achieve peace without the participation of additional parties. Let's return once again to our hypothetically-taxed wandering cow. Expanding the definitions of the real party in interest or of necessary parties, per Rules 17 and 19, allows the litigation to include insurers, creditors and other such individuals contractually linked to the primary disputants. But imagine the plight of the landholder who awakens to find a cow in his yard and one of his neighbors demanding that the cow be returned. How does the landowner know that the cow belongs to the red-faced neighbor, assuming no telling brands or other information being volunteered by the disputed cow? If the cow were to be simply turned over, what protects the landholder from being in turn confronted by other neighbors similarly claiming ownership and threatening legal retaliation if their demands are not satisfied? And, given that there is only one cow at issue, no decision by the landholder, even a Solomonic butchering, could possibly satisfy all the neighbors who might want to claim the cow as their own, whether justified or not.

---

5. West v. Randall, 29 F. Cas. 718, 721 (C.C.D.R.I. 1820) (No. 17, 424).

What distinguishes the multiparty dispute from the earlier bilateral claims is not just that more potential parties have been added. Rather, the introduction of additional potential claimants to ownership of the cow yields an inability to resolve the simple bilateral dispute between the cow's temporary custodian and the putative owner as between them. In this case, legal uncertainty over whether ownership resides with either of them means that they need a determination of not only their legal claims, but those of all other potentially interested persons before they can be sure of how to resolve their dispute. The puzzle, therefore, is to fashion a procedure that recognizes that all contested legal claims have to be resolved before any subset can be satisfied.

The answer reaching back centuries has been an action in interpleader, in effect letting the bewildered landowner bring suit as plaintiff against anyone who might have an interest in the cow. Upon notice to all potential claimants, the interpleader plaintiff (in our case, the temporary custodian of the cow) could require that they appear in court and make their case for return of the cow, or forever abandon their claim to ownership. Then, in a single proceeding, the court would be able to adjudicate ownership of the cow, once and for all. The condition for the action in interpleader was that the custodian deposit the contested goods or property with the court and foreswear any personal interest in them.

Modern civil procedure has carried forward interpleader in two forms, through Rule 22 of the Federal Rules and under 28 U.S.C. § 1335, what is termed statutory interpleader. Although the two forms have different jurisdictional requirements, they are both faithful to the central intuition of common law interpleader that the impossibility of satisfying all claims to limited resources may require conclusive disposition of all potential claims before any one of them may be satisfied. At the same time, modern procedure has altered interpleader in two ways. First, the stakeholder need not physically place the goods in the hands of the court—an eminently salutary development given the inability of most courthouses to attend to warehoused goods, let alone livestock. Second, and more significantly, modern interpleader allows the stakeholder to remain a claimant himself. This transforms interpleader from a form of renunciation into an efficient, aggregate resolution of conflicting claims to finite goods in which no property interest may be recognized conclusively until all claims are resolved.

A more modern version of the wandering cow problem is illustrated by *State Farm Fire & Casualty Co. v. Tashire.*[6] The case

---

6.   386 U.S. 523 (1967).

stemmed from a collision between a truck and a bus in which numerous bus passengers were injured and several killed; these individuals or their estates, in turn, sued various defendants, including the bus line, the bus driver, the driver of the truck, and the owner of the truck. State Farm was a minor actor in the case, having issued an insurance policy in the amount of $20,000 per incident to the driver of the truck. Since the accident constituted an incident for purposes of insurance coverage, the most that State Farm could pay out was $20,000, although it could end up paying a great deal more to defend the truck driver, who was likely indigent, in repeated actions. State Farm reasoned that its $20,000 could not possibly cover the total amount of harm caused were its insured, the truck driver, to have been the culpable party. Thus, State Farm was able to consolidate all claims against the truck driver in one forum, and, under modern interpleader, contest whether there was any liability at all.

While *State Farm v. Tashire* shows the streamlined use of modern interpleader, it also shows its limitations. Even if State Farm's potential liability for its insured were removed from the case, there still remained dozens of individual actions all arising from the same factual circumstances. In potentially dozens of trials, juries could be asked to assess the culpability of Greyhound, the bus company at issue, or any of the other actors in the fatal incident. To the extent that State Farm was seeking a unified, consistent, and efficient determination of its liability for the accident, that logic would extend as well to other defendants in the various personal injury lawsuits, most notably Greyhound. Perhaps not surprisingly, Greyhound came to see that State Farm's interpleader action could ease its litigation burden too, and sought unitary resolution of all claims against it as well. This, however, was rejected by the Supreme Court, which held that interpleader was not intended so "that the tail be allowed to wag the dog in this fashion," and refused to allow a minor player in the litigation, here the insurer on a relatively small policy, to dictate the venue and proceeding of the entire case.[7]

State Farm therefore limited the reach of interpleader to those defendants who have a clear fixed pot or defined asset that is incapable of satisfying all claimants. Interpleader, thus construed, addressed only the circumstances in which it is impossible for a party to satisfy competing claims against it because of a fixed legal limit to its ability to comply with competing obligations—as if our custodian of the wandering cow had been ordered to turn it over to

---

7. 386 U.S. at 535.

different neighboring farmers in successive lawsuits. Interpleader is not intended for the defendant who may simply not have enough money to survive all claims—that is the role of bankruptcy. Nor is it intended to serve as the unifying mechanism for disparate lawsuits that are related transactionally to each other and whose common resolution might well serve the aim of efficiency. These limitations were apparent to the Court:

> We recognize, of course, that our view of interpleader means that it cannot be used to solve all the vexing problems of multiparty litigation arising out of a mass tort. But interpleader was never intended to perform such a function, to be an all-purpose 'bill of peace.' Had it been so intended, careful provision would necessarily have been made to insure that a party with little or no interest in the outcome of a complex controversy should not strip truly interested parties of substantial rights—such as the right to choose the forum in which to establish their claims, subject to generally applicable rules of jurisdiction, venue, service of process, removal, and change of venue. None of the legislative and academic sponsors of a modern federal interpleader device viewed their accomplishment as a 'bill of peace,' capable of sweeping dozens of lawsuits out of the various state and federal courts in which they were brought and into a single interpleader proceeding.[8]

With interpleader restricted to addressing cases of a fixed, limited fund, the multiparty, mass harm would have to await its own procedural developments.

B.   *The Expanding Realm of Interested Parties.*

The idea of a non-party to litigation, one from whom nothing is demanded and who is in turn not directly a claimant, having a "right" to participate is a stunning departure from common law principles of party autonomy. Yet that is exactly what intervention under Rule 24 provides. Simply put, intervention allows an outside party to enter into a lawsuit, though not joined from the beginning by the original parties to the litigation, and often over their objections. Unlike interpleader, intervention has no common law antecedent. By its very terms, intervention imposes an additional, unwanted party, with some shared and some unique interests in the outcome of the litigation. Application of the Rule therefore must attempt to balance the interests of the original parties against the efficiency, equity, and finality interests in allowing other parties to join the litigation.

---

8. *Id.* at 535–36.

Rule 24 provides for intervention in either of two ways. First, under Rule 24(a)(2), if a party can demonstrate (1) a sufficient interest in the litigation, (2) a risk of impairment of that interest without intervention, and (3) an inability of the original parties to the litigation to adequately represent that interest, then there is what is termed a "right" of intervention. On the other hand, a party raising a common question of law or fact at issue in the primary litigation may petition to intervene "permissively" pursuant to 24(b), and will be allowed to do so if there is some gain from that participation that outweighs any potential prejudice to the original parties to the case.

For the purposes of Rule 24(a)(2), a prospective intervenor's first hurdle is to confront the imprecision of what it means to have an "interest" in litigation between other parties. What constitutes an interest is not at all self-evident. A conservation group may have an "interest" in the outcome of the application of new environmental regulations, a creditor might have an "interest" in an action affecting the property of a debtor, and a recipient of state funds might have an "interest" in any litigation which could reduce or eliminate them, but none of these interests is equal. In fact, matters of "interest" to everyone are decided in the courts on a daily basis, as the very premise of published decisional law is to inform nonparties of their potential rights and obligations. Nonetheless, it should be fairly clear that mere concern for the outcome of particular litigation is not enough to justify a party's self-imposition into it. But beyond that, what is?

Posed in this fashion, Rule 24 risks circularity because its premise of interest is also what it seeks to resolve. The original phrasing of Rule 24 required that a party had to be "bound by a judgment in the action," rather than simply that his interest be potentially impaired, in order to have a right to intervene. The Supreme Court, in *Sam Fox Publishing Co. v. United States*,[9] determined that this meant that in order to intervene, a party had to prove that, lacking intervention, it would risk being barred from bringing its own suit under the doctrine of *res judicata*—an area of law that we shall return to in Chapter 7. However, this reasoning was flawed in at least one major respect. Because the question in any future *res judicata* determination would be whether or not the party could have joined the lawsuit before, and the question in intervention is whether the party can join, using *res judicata* as a measure for intervention essentially became self-fulfilling: if the party were allowed to intervene (purportedly because it was at risk

---

9.   366 U.S. 683 (1961).

of being bound), then it would be bound. If the party were not allowed to intervene (purportedly because it was not at risk of being bound), then it would not be bound. Thus tying intervention solely to *res judicata* became either unhelpfully tautological or unworkable. As a result, in 1966, the Rule was revised to the form it takes today, which focuses on "impairment," a more flexible and practical standard.

In practice, the critical concept of "interest" became a mechanism for assessing the nature of the dispute and the claim of the original parties to the case to retain a private preserve against the outside world. This mechanism, in turn, requires that lines be drawn focusing on the private versus public quality of the dispute, and allowing the rule-based inquiry into "interest" to be calibrated accordingly. In critical cases such as *Natural Resources Defense Council v. U.S. Nuclear Regulatory Commission*,[10] for example, the question was whether private parties seeking to mine uranium could participate in a challenge to the way the Nuclear Regulatory Commission interpreted environmental impact assessments of proposed mining. In such a case, it makes little sense to think that a challenge between a public interest organization and a federal agency retains much of the self-contained character of the idealized common law dispute of old. At the same time, there are still legions of other cases that remain essentially disputes between neighbors or within families or between two parties to a contract that do retain the classic form of a bipolar disagreement in which the resolution is overwhelmingly of interest to the litigants, and virtually to them alone.

The problem is that on its face, Rule 24 does little to capture the distinction between public-regarding litigation and a more conventional dispute between individuals seeking simply a bill of peace between themselves. Rule 24 speaks broadly of an undefined "interest" on the part of the would-be intervenor, without tying the concept to the lawsuit directly or explicating how it is to be measured. What constitutes an interest, however, is best gauged not in the abstract but by reference to the type of lawsuit in which intervention is sought. The more private the dispute, the less outsiders have any claim to participate. Conversely, the claim to intervention forces courts to confront how far they have moved from private dispute resolution to a world now identified as "public law." As well captured by Professor Tobias:

Public law litigation comprises lawsuits that vindicate significant social values affecting large numbers of people. Many

10. 578 F.2d 1341 (10th Cir. 1978).

aspects of this litigation are unlike traditional private, two-party cases. For instance, the subject matter of public law litigation may be the practices or policies of enormous units of government or multinational corporations, while the cases can be exceedingly complex, involving hundreds of issues and thousands of parties....

When resolving public law suits, judges assume different roles than in private litigation. Perhaps most important, they give substantive content to public norms in constitutional or statutory provisions that underlie the cases and attempt to prevent or correct inappropriate governmental behavior. Judges also manage the litigation more closely in several ways. In institutional reform cases, for example, courts may undertake major responsibility for fact-gathering, even appointing adjuncts such as special masters, to fulfill what essentially are "quasi-legislative" or "quasi-administrative" decisional duties.[11]

This concern, perhaps, is the impetus behind an identifiable trend towards relaxation of the "interest" standard when issues of public law are the reason for a party's request for intervention. The Supreme Court first took this approach in *Cascade Natural Gas Corp. v. El Paso Natural Gas Co.*,[12] and the inclination to lower the bar has since been followed by most lower courts as well, though not without some ongoing debate.[13]

C. Related Parties.

Although not generally thought of in conjunction with interpleader and the party joinder rules, Rule 42 concerns the same problem of related interests and efficient adjudication. Rule 42 gives courts the power either to join or separate claims pending within a particular judicial district. Under Rule 42(a), a court can join claims for a particular hearing or an entire trial with regard to any or all issues involved in particular cases for the purpose of avoiding "unnecessary costs or delay." Consolidation allows the court to avoid duplicative discovery or presentations of evidence in cases that raise overlapping factual or legal issues.

Taken collectively, the joinder and consolidation rules allow courts to bring together the parties that must be present to ensure

---

11. Carl Tobias, *Standing to Intervene*, 1991 Wis. L. Rev. 415, 420.

12. 386 U.S. 129 (1967).

13. *See, e.g.,* Keith v. Daley, 764 F.2d 1265, 1268–69 (7th Cir. 1985) (holding that in the Seventh Circuit "no special broad definition of 'interest' applies to suits involving public law cases").

an equitable resolution of claims, while seeking to realize the efficiency gains of streamlined factual presentations of evidence. But, as with interpleader, the actual gain from consolidation is limited. Only pending cases in the same venue can be consolidated and no additional parties may be added. Nothing in Rule 42 allows courts to reach beyond cases already pending in the same judicial district, and nothing allows a court to reach the claims of those who have not yet filed cases. While the overall efficiency gains are limited, the requirements for consolidation are not at all onerous. For a consolidated proceeding, the party seeking consolidation need only convince the court of efficiency gains, some common issue or identity of the parties, and that a jury will not be confused by the multiple actions before it.

Two statutory additions mildly expand the reach of consolidation. First, under 28 U.S.C. § 1404, a federal court may order a change of venue, thereby allowing a case pending before one federal court to be transferred to another federal judicial district. Among the reasons for transfer is the pendency of related cases in the transferee jurisdiction. Of broader scope is 28 U.S.C. § 1407, which provides for the transfer and consolidation of related proceedings from around the country, what is referred to as multidistrict litigation (MDL). Under the MDL statute, a special panel of federal judges may order all related proceedings in the federal courts consolidated for purposes of pretrial discovery and other common features of the cases. Both transfer and MDL joinder build on the basic model of consolidation of like cases to realize efficiency gains in court management of overlapping factual and legal issues. The gain from both transfers and MDL joinders is the expanded geographic reach of cases that are subject to consolidation.

But the similarity to consolidation also highlights the limitations of the transfer and MDL mechanisms. Each can only reach cases that are in the federal court system at the same time. Thus, in *State Farm v. Tashire*, for example, there is no procedure for cross-jurisdictional consolidation or transfer between state and federal courts, even for cases arising from the same bus accident. Cases filed in different court systems, or in different state courts, are beyond the reach of any single judicial authority, and thus must proceed independently. Moreover, in *Lexecon Inc. v. Milberg Weiss Bershad Hynes & Lerach*,[14] the Supreme Court held that the MDL pretrial transfer mechanism applies only to the pretrial period. At the conclusion of discovery and other pretrial matters, MDL courts must return cases to their courts of origin for individual adjudica-

---

14.   523 U.S. 26 (1998).

tion. There is no mechanism for trials originating from multiple jurisdictions to be consolidated in front of one judge, even if there would be great efficiency gains from common resolution.

State Farm v. Tashire also exposes another critical shortcoming in the consolidation mechanisms. As the Court recognized, a multiple casualty bus accident is the modern rendition of a simple tort accident, only compounded procedurally by the fact of mass transportation. But many mass harms, ranging from consumers confronted with a malfunctioning product to toxic exposures to industrial contaminants or pollutants, do not arise all at once, as with a sudden road accident. In such situations, not only are the cases likely to be dispersed geographically across multiple jurisdictions, they are also likely to be dispersed in time. Some harms may accrue immediately, some may mature only over the long latency period of a toxic exposure. Some potential claimants may be aware of the potential harm even before the consequences are manifest; some may go for years unaware of what may befall them. Consolidation, in any of its guises, can only reach cases in the same court system at the same time. It has no anticipatory powers, even where tremendous efficiencies could be realized and where common treatment would promote the equitable aims of treating similarly situated persons in similar fashion.

III. Aggregated Parties.
A. *Representative Litigation.*

Both efficiency and equity often require expanding the scope of litigation beyond that afforded by consolidation. In effect, there must be some mechanism to compel similarly situated potential claimants to come together in one proceeding and to achieve finality beyond those who have already filed suit individually. There are many mechanisms that can perform this function, such as bankruptcy which creates a common forum for the resolution of all creditor actions against an insolvent debtor. But the most common in the civil procedure context is the class action, a sweeping and oftentimes controversial joinder rule that allows comprehensive resolution of related claims through a *representative action* that will bind even those who do not directly participate in the litigation.

The historic antecedents of class actions were directed to some familiar problems from days gone by, variants of the problem posed by interpleader. For example, the orderly transmission of property rights from one generation to the next has been a central concern of the law for as long as the common law system has existed. In any proceeding to settle an estate, no claim can be finalized without a conclusive legal proceeding binding on all potential heirs. If a decedent has left each of four children a 25 percent stake in his estate, it would be impossible to have a different calculation of the size of the estate in four different proceedings. No one individual can claim his or her proportionate share of the estate unless there is a binding determination as to both the size of the estate and what each inheritor stands to acquire. Or take the problem presented by the substantial financing of the British Navy by war booty seized from enemy vessels. As popularized in the novels of Patrick O'Brian—and as portrayed in film by Russell Crowe—a ship returning to port would distribute the benefits of its maritime success according to a carefully dictated formula apportioning interests by rank, from the Crown through the officers through the deckhands. Once these ships returned to port, there were strict conventions governing the distribution of booty, and the seamen could claim a legal entitlement to an accurate distribution. The courts of equity were called upon to act as the final arbiters of the accuracy of the distribution of booty and did so in a binding representative proceeding. "Non-participating crew members were not allowed to challenge the final decree's determination of the total crewshare fund or the proportion to which fellow crew members were entitled."[15] As with probate proceedings to settle an estate, the needs of finality overwhelmed any claim to hold out for a private individual action.

At other times, aggregation through incipient forms of class actions corresponded to the existence of rights that were already held in the collective or to political representation that existed independently of the issues in dispute. Thus, for example, in one famous case, the mayor of York assumed the role of representative agent on behalf of the residents of his city in a dispute with citizens of other towns concerning fishing rights in a local river.[16] For a court to recognize this representative role for the mayor did nothing more than extend an already existing political authority into the jural realm. Other similar cases recognize the propriety of an unincorporated association assuming the role of protector of the interests of its members, as with the members of a freemasons' lodge suing on behalf of all lodge members in an action over legal title to the lodge's possessions.[17]

15. Robert G. Bone, *Personal and Impersonal Litigative Forms: Reconceiving the History of Adjudicative Representation*, 70 B.U. L. Rev. 213, 267 (1990).

16. Mayor of York v. Pilkington, 25 Eng. Rep. 946 (Ch. 1737).

17. Lloyd v. Loaring, 31 Eng. Rep. 1302 (Ch. 1802); *see generally* Geoffrey C. Hazard, Jr. et al., *An Historical Analysis of the Binding Effect of Class Suits,* 146 U. Pa. L. Rev. 1849, 1874–76 (1998).

In all these cases involving similarly situated claimants, the nominal plaintiff invoked the court's jurisdiction for a ruling that would be applicable to all represented parties, who were in turn defined by being similarly situated to the nominal plaintiff. However, in the premodern class actions, the litigation was truly a representative action. The claims of the class representatives were put forward as they would be if the case were adjudicated individually. In the event of a plaintiff's victory, the absent class members could, in effect, join into the lawsuit—what in modern parlance would be termed an "opt in" class action, but only after the fact, and only if the nominal plaintiff had prevailed. This procedure avoids any issue about the legitimacy of the representative party's role, since the class representative does not assume any capacity to impart anything but a costless victory upon the absent class members. Should the named plaintiff prevail, each class member retains the individual option of joining in the judgment; should the named plaintiff fail, the rights of the absent class members are unaffected. But this legitimacy for the role of the named representative is bought at a tremendous cost for the defendant in the class action. In reality, in any such class litigation, the defendant is able to prevail only as to the named plaintiff, but can lose to the entire class. Should the defendant prevail, there is the potential for demoralization of potential future plaintiffs, but no prohibition on multiple suits. Indeed, subsequent cases may be benefited by lessons learned in the first case, and from the second, and the third, and so on.[18] But, for the defendant, a loss is potentially conclusive as to all class members.

Since the 1921 decision in *Supreme Tribe of Ben–Hur v. Cauble*,[19] the Supreme Court has made clear that the object of class actions must be to bind absent class members and consequently achieve finality—thereby equalizing the stakes in the litigation. The challenge of the modern class action is therefore to find mechanisms that confer legitimacy under two conditions that were relatively absent from historic class action practice: first, that there is no preexisting political or organizational vehicle that can claim an independent source of authority to speak for the collective, and, second, that modern conceptions of fairness and finality require that the nonparticipating class members be bound to the outcome of the litigation as if they were parties, and be bound regardless

---

18. *See* Jack Ratliff, *Offensive Collateral Estoppel and the Option Effect*, 67 Tex. L. Rev. 63, 77, 79 (1988) ("The basic unfairness lies in the disparate risks taken by plaintiffs as a class and the defendant in the first case.... The option effect forces the first-case defendant to play for low stakes if he wins, but for high stakes if he loses.").

19. 255 U.S. 356 (1921).

whether the class wins or loses. So until the modern class actions with these two features arose, there was no need to worry about potential abuses in the use of class actions or to police independently the adequacy of representation. As a result, the modern class action requires a new concept of "adequate representation" as a prerequisite for binding individuals to the outcome of a case, and this in turn requires that the class representatives "fairly represent them with respect to the matters as to which the judgment is subsequently involved."[20]

Legitimacy as a threshold concept, therefore, comes to dominate the class action in a manner unlike that of the other joinder devices we have surveyed. This is because the question of the propriety or the fairness of representation does not arise in ordinary litigation, in which parties are presumed to have the authority to represent their own interests, even if their individual cases might be bound up procedurally with those of other individuals whose claims are transactionally related. None of these other joinder devices compromises the longstanding "principle of general application in Anglo–American jurisprudence that one is not bound by a judgment in personam in a litigation in which he is not designated as a party or to which he has not been made a party by service of process."[21] But class actions are necessarily the exception to this general principle. Ever since at least *Ben–Hur*, courts have recognized that the purpose of the class action is to resolve conclusively matters in such fashion as to bind those who have not individually been designated parties or been served with individual service of process. The class action device creates what David Shapiro has called an "entity" comprised of absent class members with representatives standing in their place.[22] The question for class actions, therefore, is what permits "members of a class not present as parties to the litigation" to be bound by the conduct of representatives claiming the right to "stand in judgment" on their behalf.[23]

The authority for a claimed representative to bind others is squarely presented in the classic case of *Hansberry v. Lee*.[24] At issue in *Hansberry* was an attempt by white homeowners in south

---

20. Restatement (Second) of Judgments § 42(1)(d) (1982).

21. Hansberry v. Lee, 311 U.S. 32, 40 (1940), *quoting* Pennoyer v. Neff, 95 U.S. 714 (1877).

22. David L. Shapiro, *Class Actions: The Class as Party and Client,* 73 Notre Dame L. Rev. 913 (1998); *see also* Samuel Issacharoff, *Governance and Legitimacy in the Law of Class Actions,* 1999 Sup. Ct. Rev. 337.

23. *Hansberry,* 311 U.S. at 42–43.

24. 311 U.S. 32 (1940).

Chicago to prevent a black family from buying a home in their neighborhood. The white homeowners invoked a racially restrictive covenant to bar the sale of the home—in the days before the U.S. Supreme Court found such forms of racial exclusion to be constitutionally unenforceable. The covenant forbade the sale or rental of homes in the neighborhood to black families. But the restrictive covenant could only take effect if 95 percent of the homeowners approved it, a highly questionable factual precondition that was likely not met. The objecting homeowners, however, invoked an earlier state court action, *Burke v. Kleiman*,[25] that had found the covenant effective in blocking an earlier attempt to rent a home in the same neighborhood to a black family. The critical issue in *Hansberry v. Lee* was the effect of the prior ruling that the covenant was indeed in effect and did control the disposition of real estate in the area. Because *Burke v. Kleiman* had been a class action—as opposed to an individual suit—the parties who were bound by its earlier rulings included not only Burke and Kleiman, the objecting homeowner and the would-be landlord, but the entire group of homeowners as to whom the restrictions could apply.

Although the trial court in *Hansberry v. Lee* recognized that the covenant had probably never garnered the requisite signatures to be made effective, as the Hansberrys asserted, the court nonetheless found its hands tied by the outcome in *Burke*, which presumably bound all future potential home sellers as successors in interest to the original absent parties in the earlier class action. In other words, if *Burke v. Kleiman* were allowed to stand as a class action, then all future homeowners in the area would be bound by the outcome of that case, until and unless a change in substantive law made the covenants unenforceable.

Ultimately, the Supreme Court reversed and found the prior litigation not binding on the Hansberrys and their would-be sellers. The Court focused on the adequacy of the representation offered in the prior litigation, particularly since the Hansberrys, a black family, were to be bound as potential successor homeowners to the outcome of a case among only white families. But in order to free the Hansberrys from the effects of the prior litigation, the Court had to extricate the hopeful sellers from any binding effects of the prior case, in which they were part of the class of affected homeowners. The key question became whether the decision in *Burke v. Kleiman* to certify a class provided sufficient assurances of adequacy and fairness in representation so as to allow the earlier ruling to have prospective effects on the absent class members. Framed this

25.   Burke v. Kleiman, 277 Ill. App. 519 (1934).

way, the Supreme Court found that the first state court decision did not have enough procedural protections in place and that, as a result, it could not bind the absent class members to the judgment.[26] The state court had relied on an informal mechanism, the local court rules of equity, to allow the class to be formed, without subjecting the representation offered to the absent class members to any particular scrutiny. The Supreme Court found the informal procedures of the Illinois state courts to be an insufficient guarantee of proper representation for absent class members and voided any binding effect the Illinois state decision might have as a class action.

Hansberry leaves two legacies. Most notably, the Hansberry daughter, Lorraine Hansberry, wrote a poignant account of her childhood in the oft reprised play, *A Raisin in the Sun*. More prosaically, but more central to our purposes, *Hansberry* places tremendous due process pressure on the procedural mechanisms necessary to provide what the Court would later term the "structural assurance of fair and adequate representation."[27]

B.   *Modern Rule 23.*

In 1966, Rule 23 of the Federal Rules of Civil Procedure was amended to yield the current form of the class action. In many ways, modern Rule 23 may be seen as the Rules response to the problem in *Hansberry*. The modern class action rule requires a trial court to justify the extraordinary step of allowing nonparticipating parties to be bound to a judgment and to inquire directly at the threshold stages of the litigation as to the adequacy of representation that will be afforded the absent class members. The two principal provisions of Rule 23 set out the critical determinations that a court must make in deciding whether or not to certify a class: why a class is being certified; who is going to be bound by the class outcome; and what kind of class is going to be certified— including what sorts of protections must be afforded to class members.

Rule 23(a) imposes four preliminary requirements on all class actions. These requirements are referred to in short form as: (1) numerosity, (2) commonality, (3) typicality, and (4) adequacy of representation.[28] There is a logical consistency to these require-

---

26. For a fuller account of *Hansberry,* see Richard A. Nagareda, *Administering Adequacy in Class Representation,* 82 Tex. L. Rev. 287 (2003).

27. Amchem Products, Inc. v. Windsor, 521 U.S. 591, 627 (1997).

28. *See* Fed. R. Civ. P. 23(a).

ments. First they ask whether there is any justification for treating the case through the extraordinary mechanism of representative litigation. Second these prerequisites attempt to ensure that the aims of efficient resolution will be advanced by collective treatment. In simple terms, they ask if the questions to be resolved by the proposed class action are of the sort that, "if as to one, then as to all." In other words, does the case really appear to be controlled by a common core that will resolve all or much of the dispute not only for the named class representative, but for all class members?

Thus, the typical class action will ask one central question of the following sort: was the product defective? did the employer discriminate? was the securities offering fraudulent? did the manufacturer engage in anticompetitive behavior? did the chemical plant discharge toxins into the stream?—all of these are questions that if true or false as to one class member are likely to be true or false as to all. Put another way, much of the issue on class certification turns on whether there are any individual specific issues that define the case proposed for class treatment, or whether the individuals are likely to be more or less passive subjects of alleged wrongdoing that treats them in an undifferentiated fashion. One way of thinking about this is to consider class actions as an efficiency driven device for cases that focus "upstream" on the initial conduct of the defendant in creating a defective product, or embarking on a set of discriminatory practices, or perpetuating a fraud in the securities markets, and so on. By contrast, a case that focuses on the "downstream" events of what happened to an individual or how a product was utilized, or the subjective understanding of a financial transaction, is unlikely to be a suitable candidate for efficient class treatment. It is hard in such "downstream" inquiries to pose a question that can be answered in the "if as to one, then as to all" framework.

The first three prerequisites in Rule 23(a) get at this basic structure. Rule 23(a)(1) requires that the proposed class be sufficiently numerous to make joinder impracticable. The basic idea is that there be some sufficient efficiency gain to justify class treatment over simpler forms of joinder. Class actions have been certified with just 20 class members, on rare occasion even fewer, and as many as several million members, though a number greater than 20 by no means assures certification. Rule 23(a)(2) then asks whether the efficiency gains will indeed be realized by resolving questions of law or fact that are common to the class. For example, if all members of the class were victimized by the same claimed discriminatory employment practice or all suffered harms as a result of a security suddenly depreciating in value, a court would likely find that the commonality requirement has been met. The combination of 23(a)(1) and 23(a)(2) in effect asks if there are a lot of people in the same boat, and if their claims were litigated together, would the result approximate the "if as to one, then as to all" ideal by yielding answers to key questions in the litigation that would be the same for the class as a whole. Finally, 23(a)(3) asks whether the proposed named plaintiff is "typical" of the class, a non-exacting inquiry that seeks to ensure that the class has a titular head with an actual grievance against the defendant.

Adequacy of representation, the requirement of Rule 23(a)(4), presents a more challenging standard for litigants to meet. Originally this requirement focused on the named class representative and asked about the legitimacy of that person speaking for the entire class. This requirement made some sense when classes arose primarily out of preexisting relations or obligations among people, as when the mayor of York claimed to speak for the citizens of that city. But when classes are far removed from any preexisting relation among class members, and when the stakes for any particular class member are low, the reality is that the class representative is the class lawyer. It is the lawyer who likely puts together the claim. It is the lawyer who funds the investigation. It is the lawyer who likely makes all the decisions relevant to the case. And in such circumstances, class members are "rationally indifferent"[29] to the day-to-day decisions in the litigation, perhaps even to the outcome.

The Supreme Court has recognized this vicarious representation feature of class actions, and has imparted increasing significance to the adequacy-of-representation prong of class actions, particularly in the relatively recent form of the settlement class: an action filed with an agreed upon settlement between class counsel and the defendant, in which the reviewing court and class members are first presented with a case in the form of a proposed settlement. As the Court noted in the leading proposed settlement case, *Amchem Products v. Windsor*:

> The policy at the very core of the class action mechanism is to overcome the problem that small recoveries do not provide the incentive for any individual to bring a solo action prosecuting his or her rights. A class action solves this problem by aggregating the relatively paltry potential recoveries into something worth someone's (usually an attorney's) labor.[30]

---

29. John C. Coffee, Jr., *Conflicts, Consent, And Allocation After* Amchem Products—*Or, Why Attorneys Still Need Consent To Give Away Their Clients' Money*, 84 Va. L. Rev. 1541, 1558 (1998).

30. *Amchem Products*, 521 U.S. at 617 (1997), *quoting* Mace v. Van Ru Credit Corp., 109 F.3d 338, 344 (7th Cir. 1997).

The mechanics of how courts review class actions, how they decide to approve or disapprove settlements, and the conflicting incentives operating on counsel in class actions are all matters that take us beyond this introductory treatment of an extraordinarily complicated and controversial body of law. But *Amchem* carries the central lesson from *Hansberry* forward in the law of class actions: ultimately class actions offer an efficient mechanism to resolve comparably situated claims in one aggregate proceeding by testing the claims of the representative parties. For those whose rights are to be decided *in absentia* the critical due process issue is the quality of the representation that was afforded. It is the adequacy of that representation that allows this extraordinary departure from the conventional rule that each individual is entitled to his or her own opportunity to control any litigation that threatens to impose liability or terminate a claim.

C. Types of Class Actions.

As the name would imply, the Rule 23(a) prerequisites for class certification are just that: prerequisites. Rule 23(b) requires that once a court finds that the prerequisites are met, the court must then determine which of the three primary sorts of class action is to be created. The distinct class action types correspond to familiar problems in the joinder rules: responding to competing demands for insufficient resources; the indivisibility of the remedies sought by the class; or the simple efficiency commands of aggregate treatment of small claims that would not merit prosecution on their own.

1. Limited Fund Class Actions.

Rule 23(b)(1) is generally referred to as the limited fund class action. It is, in effect, the plaintiffs' equivalent of an interpleader action that might be filed by a stakeholder. Interpleader places responsibility for the collective resolution on the stakeholder, the party that might have the least interest in the equitable allocation of scarce assets. For example, the insurance company in *State Farm v. Tashire* could just as easily have paid the limited insurance proceeds to the first successful plaintiff from the bus accident, and then told any future claimants that the pot was empty. By contrast, the limited fund class action allows the claimants to protect their own interests by directly seeking unified distribution of insufficient assets. Accordingly, a class may be certified when individual pursuit of claims "as a practical matter, would be dispositive of the interests of other members not parties to the individual adjudications.''[31] The effect of a limited fund class action is to avoid a run on the bank in which competing plaintiffs try to press their claim—or settle on the cheap—before some other litigant exhausts the limited resources of the defendant. Returning to the fact pattern of *State Farm v. Tashire*, for instance, a limited fund class action allows the plaintiffs directly to claim common control over the limited insurance proceeds, rather than hoping that the insurer seeks collective resolution. While an individual plaintiff may fare worse under the class action, collectively the plaintiffs are better off under this regime, as it ensures that everyone gets at least an equitable slice of the pie.

In order for a limited fund class action to work, it must necessarily encompass all possible claimants. Accordingly, it is deemed mandatory and, once certified as a class, extinguishes all claims without any individual ability to opt out of the class. The mandatory feature of the limited fund class could serve as an invitation to mischief should parties attempt to "cram down" an insufficient settlement under the guise of a mandatory class action. The attention of the Supreme Court was drawn to the mandatory quality of a 23(b)(1) class action in *Ortiz v. Fibreboard Corp.*,[32] an attempted sweeping settlement of asbestos liabilities as a limited fund class action. The Court, echoing its concerns in *State Farm*, restricted the use of 23(b)(1) to cases in which the fund is limited by its very terms (as with a fixed pot insurance pool), and not by the potentially devastating spiral of litigated claims. The Court rejected the proposed settlement in *Ortiz* because, despite the manifest inability of the Fibreboard company to satisfy all asbestos claims against it, there was not a preexisting limited fund that marked the outer bounds of the controversy. The limited fund proved not to be an available bill of peace for mass tort cases, just as interpleader had failed in that charge. The result for the Fibreboard company was that the claims were eventually addressed in bankruptcy, where the company collapsed under the weight of claims for harms from asbestos exposure.

2. *Injunctive Classes.*

Rule 23(b)(2) provides for certification of classes where a defendant is alleged to have "acted or refused to act on grounds that apply generally to the class, so that final injunctive relief or corresponding declaratory relief is appropriate respecting the class

---

31.   Fed. R. Civ. P. 23(b)(1)(B).

32.   527 U.S. 815 (1999).

as a whole." As with the limited fund class action, the premise of the 23(b)(2) class is that there is no way to disaggregate the claims for relief for the entire class. In the limited fund context, what draws the class together is that the claims are ultimately rivalrous over a stake that is insufficient to satisfy all claimants. In the 23(b)(2) context, what unifies the class is that the relief cannot meaningfully be given to one without giving it to all.

The indivisibility of the remedy is clearest in the paradigmatic (b)(2) class action. The 1966 amendments to Rule 23, which created the current typology of class actions, held out the civil rights claim to end discrimination as the prototype of a (b)(2) class action. If we were to imagine a classic case such as *Brown v. Board of Education*,[33] there is no ability to isolate individual claims for relief. Either the segregated public schools of Topeka, Kansas violated the Constitution, or they did not. If they did, then some remedy had to be fashioned; if the dual school system was not unconstitutional, then there would be no remedial order. But in either case, it was impossible for the schools to be unconstitutional as to some black schoolchildren, but not others. Similarly, it makes no sense to think that if the schools were unconstitutionally segregated, some black schoolchildren, but not others, would be entitled to relief.

Because claims for injunctive or declaratory relief may not be disaggregated, there is little sense in giving individual class members an ability to remove themselves from being represented by the class action. As a result, there is no requirement in a (b)(2) class that individual class members be provided with direct notice or given the opportunity to opt out of the class action proceeding and pursue their claims independently. While courts sometimes impose these additional requirements in extraordinary circumstances, the (b)(2) class is generally a neat and clean way to adjudicate the rights of numerous plaintiffs without sacrificing fairness or finality.

Rule 23(b)(2) operates optimally in the context of injunctive and declaratory relief, to which the rule speaks explicitly. However, the mandatory features of (b)(2), as with the (b)(1) class action, provide inducements for creative litigants to test the boundaries in order to obtain more conclusive resolution of cases. The boundaries of a permissible (b)(2) class action are most directly tested when parties assert not only their rights to various forms of equitable relief, but also to monetary damages. For the most part, this issue arises in cases involving civil rights claims over employment discrimination, in which the demand for injunctive relief triggers accompanying claims for backpay and other individual relief. The

---

33. 349 U.S. 294 (1955).

advisory committee notes accompanying the rules provide only a partial answer to this challenge by stating that (b)(2) certification is not appropriate where the relief sought is "predominately" money damages.[34] Unfortunately, the text fails to define "predominately," leaving courts to do so on their own. Some courts had allowed such hybrid cases so long as the monetary recovery was "incidental" to the requested injunctive or declaratory relief. The Supreme Court's recent decision in *Wal–Mart v. Dukes*[35] narrowed the area of uncertainty by limiting the 23(b)(2) class action to cases that were shaped around a common claim for injunctive relief:

> The key to the (b)(2) class is "the indivisible nature of the injunctive or declaratory remedy warranted—the notion that the conduct is such that it can be enjoined or declared unlawful only as to all of the class members or as to none of them." In other words, Rule 23(b)(2) applies only when a single injunction or declaratory judgment would provide relief to each member of the class. It does not authorize class certification when each individual class member would be entitled to a *different* injunction or declaratory judgment against the defendant. Similarly, it does not authorize class certification when each class member would be entitled to an individualized award of monetary damages.[36]

More succinctly put, the Court declared: "we think it clear that individualized monetary claims belong in Rule 23(b)(3)."[37]

3.   *Damages Classes.*

The final provision of Rule 23(b), the (b)(3) class action, acts as a catch-all for cases that do not fit precisely within the definition of the first two provisions, but where courts would still find it expedient to have the claims presented in an aggregate setting. Rule 23(b)(3) permits certification of a class upon a determination that "questions of law or fact common to class members predominate over any questions affecting only individual members, and that a class action is superior to other available methods for fairly and efficiently adjudicating the controversy." The requirements of "predominance" and "superiority" confirm that what holds the 23(b)(3)

---

34.   Fed. R. Civ. P. 23(b)(2) advisory committee's notes.

35.   131 S.Ct. 2541 (2011).

36.   *Id.* at 2557, *quoting* Richard Nagareda, *Class Certification in the Age of Aggregate Proof*, 84 N.Y.U. L. Rev. 97, 132 (2009); *see also* PRINCIPLES OF THE LAW OF AGGREGATE LITIG. § 2.04 (2010).

37.   *Id.* at 2558.

class together is not the inability to grant justice to one without affecting all, as in the (b)(1) limited fund, nor the integral nature of the remedy across the class, as in the (b)(2) injunctive action. Rather, it is the demand of efficient resolution that drives the (b)(3) class action and unifies claims that, but for the transactions costs of individual prosecution, could just as well proceed on their own.

With the introduction of the 23(b)(3) class action in 1966, the Rules for the first time addressed themselves openly to the problems of mass society. Permitting cases to be grouped together for the sake of efficiency enabled common resolution of similar claims, and even allowed for rulings that would bind non-participants. In this sense, the 23(b)(3) class action allowed courts to use a joinder device that reached beyond litigants who had actually filed suit, and held out the promise of perhaps even addressing the individual harm case arising from a common event, as with the bus accident in *State Farm v. Tashire*. Even the drafters of the initial Rule were uncertain how far its reach should be, and the advisory notes accompanying the original introduction of Rule 23(b)(3) indicated that the provision should not be used to resolve mass torts.[38] The fuller reaches of Rule 23(b)(3) are beyond the scope of this volume; indeed that is a primary focus in the companion volume on complex litigation in this series.[39] But the 1966 reforms to Rule 23 brought to life a range of economic harm cases that were almost unimaginable previously, such as securities class actions.

Rule 23(b)(3) posed a greater constitutional due process challenge than did (b)(1) or (b)(2) class actions. Because (b)(3) was driven by the efficiencies of aggregate treatment, rather than the inextricably interwoven remedial claims, there had to be a greater measure of protection for the independent rights held by the absent class members. In effect, absent class members were being asked to yield a private rights claim, what the common law termed a *chose in action*, a protected right to bring suit.[40] As a result, a 23(b)(3) class action must provide notice to the absent class members alerting them to the fact that their legal rights are at issue in the case and that they may opt out of the proceedings altogether. The Supreme Court has held that individualized notice and the ability to choose to proceed independently rises to the level of a due process constitutional requirement.[41] Any (b)(3) class therefore

38. Fed. R. Civ. P. 23(b)(3) advisory committee's notes.

39. *See* Jay Tidmarsh & Roger H. Transgrud, Complex Litigation: Problems in Advanced Civil Procedure (2002).

40. *See* Patrick Woolley, *Rethinking The Adequacy of Adequate Representation,* 75 Tex. L. Rev. 571 (1997).

41. *See* Mullane v. Central Hanover Bank & Trust Co., 339 U.S. 306 (1950). While *Mullane* did not involve a class action, it did involve numerous plaintiffs living

must provide the most effective notice possible, given the circumstances. Where plaintiffs are known, putative class counsel must make sure that they are provided with individual notice, regardless of their number and the expense of doing so.[42] The utility of such a costly expenditure is often of questionable value as class claimants may be inclined to disregard or just throw away hard-to-follow class notices. Yet the demands of fairness and the finality stakes linked to notice are thought to outweigh the cost, particularly since notice establishes clearly who is bound by the judgment—a problem we already confronted in *Hansberry v. Lee.*

IV. Conclusion.

The development of modern procedure's treatment of parties has been a process of grudging accommodation of the reality of mass society. The common law assumption of disputes limited in parties and scope has broken down across innumerable areas of substantive law. The move from the expansion of interested parties to the use of representative litigation through the class action is in many ways the story of the increasingly complex role that courts are expected to play in modern society. In the final form of expansion, the class action, the rules emerge as both complex and controversial. Contested issues include the rival jurisdiction of state and federal courts, the relation between litigation classes and those constructed only for purposes of settlement, the conflicts that often arise in class representation, the compensation of class counsel, and many more. For our purposes, the main contribution of the class action is to highlight the break from the narrow common law view of parties. The world is far too complex and interdependent to entertain the fiction, even if comforting, that the civil procedure system is about nothing more than resolving the common law disputes of two private citizens locked in their own world. The modern joinder rules are a steady progression in the rejection of the limited bipolar world of dispute resolution. Class actions are a significant marker in the development of modern procedural law.

in various states and the Court refused to bind a plaintiff to the judgment where he had had no notice of the proceeding.

42. *See* Eisen v. Carlisle & Jacquelin, 417 U.S. 156 (1974) (requiring that individual notice be sent to all 2 million class members whose names and addresses were easily discoverable).

Chapter 5
JURISDICTION

Ultimately, the aim of any procedural system is the resolution of disputes. As we shall see in Chapter 7, the resolution of disputes requires finality in the litigation process and the ability to enforce judgments so as to provide the disputants with closure. Our attention thus far has been on the mechanisms by which parties engage the court system and on the expanding definition of who are proper parties to a dispute. Thus, we may think of the Federal Rules as comprising the nuts and bolts of the litigation process, providing the requirements for a complaint, instructions for service of process, and the many rules of discovery, class action, summary judgment, joinder, default, and so on, all precisely detailed and constantly reviewed and revised to more closely conform to the changing ideals of the American procedural system.

At the end of the day, however, for any dispute that is litigated to conclusion, there must be a judgment and the capacity to enforce the court's decrees. That leads inescapably to the question of power. In order to render a meaningful judgment in a case, courts must have the ability to command parties to appear before them and to enforce their decrees. Since courts are famously endowed with neither the purse nor the sword, the source of their power must be derived externally. The ability to enforce a judicial decree turns ultimately on the authority that judges can invoke to coerce recalcitrant parties to appear before them and abide by their commands, as the need may arise. That authority is termed the jurisdiction of the court, a concept that is defined by the governmental authority on whose behalf the court ultimately acts.

The Federal Rules of Civil Procedure are themselves silent on the source of a court's jurisdiction. Rule 82 expressly provides that the Rules are not intended to define, let alone alter, the jurisdictional authority of federal courts. So the source of a court's power must be found elsewhere and must answer a fundamental question: over whom may courts exercise their authority to hear and adjudicate a lawsuit? As with much of procedure, American law on the jurisdictional authority for the enforcement of a court's decree draws from its British antecedents. As is also true of much American law that builds on the British common law, the prior rules tend to be instructive in both their application and their limitations.

In Britain of old, all courts ultimately derived their power from the Crown. The King's courts could exercise their dominion either upon the citizenry, who were the Crown's subjects, or upon the land holdings within the kingdom, which were also deemed to be subject to the power of the ruling monarch. Jurisdiction that required a decree over a person was termed *in personam,* while jurisdiction to settle title to real property was termed *in rem.* In either case, the power of the court to have its decrees enforced drew from the sovereign power of the Crown over both persons and landholdings in the kingdom. The courts served, in effect, as the agents of the Crown, acting to resolve disputes in the name of the kingdom through powers delegated by the Crown or by Parliament.

The key to such early theories of jurisdiction was the idea of undisputed sovereignty. The concept of sovereignty is that of a supreme legal authority, conceived to encompass a particular geographic area, such that, for example, the King of England was sovereign over one domain, England, and the King of France was sovereign over another, France, and the two spheres of influence could not, by definition, overlap. Within defined territorial boundaries, all law was the responsibility of the sovereign, and judgment on disputes was one essential legal function. As a necessary result of the delegated source of their authority, the reach of the English courts could not exceed that of the sovereign. Since the sovereign's authority was limited geographically, geography similarly limited the jurisdiction of English courts. If a person were in France, English courts could not control him, but if that person entered England, he was accountable to its courts.

This territorial model of jurisdiction was perfectly adequate for a premodern society such as medieval England. On an island nation with a single sovereign, and moreover in a society in which citizens lived in the same small communities their entire lives and rarely, if ever, traveled, it was usually quite clear which courts had jurisdiction over which people. Since medieval society defined citizens by status in relation to land, in conditions ranging from serf to lord, a legal order that presumed a single sovereign power made perfect sense. Even the rudimentary forms of commerce that did exist were mostly small and local, such that a territorial basis for judicial authority would provoke little confusion about who was accountable to whom. Perhaps even more central in a medieval world in which status entailed obligations, the power of the Crown's courts was an extension of the duty of the Crown to provide for the security and welfare of the population.

The development of American society conspired to undermine the neat application of the inherited territorial models of jurisdiction. The first development was in place even at the time of the founding: the United States, going back even to the colonial period, never operated under a single sovereign. While the Crown reigned supreme until the Revolution, local authority was divided between the various colonies. Following the Revolution, both during the Articles of Confederation and ultimately under the modern American state, the federal government was expressly granted power over certain areas (most notably interstate commerce), while each American state retained sovereignty over most affairs occurring within its borders. Consequently, following the English territorial model of jurisdiction, the courts of the various American governments were to attend only to the issues that were within their power to control. But the fact of multiple sovereigns created a problem of potentially overlapping jurisdiction over commerce or over individuals moving from one state to another. Although a general sense of cooperation between the states was facilitated by the Full Faith and Credit Clause,[1] which commanded state courts to respect each others' judgments, the idea persisted that it was an unacceptable abuse of power for one state's courts to attempt to exercise their jurisdiction beyond the state's border.

Two other features of developing American society further compromised a narrow territorial basis for jurisdiction. First, the increased mobility of the population and the constitutional commitment to freedom of travel among the states further eroded the clear hierarchical relations between subjects and sovereign. This trend became all the more apparent as changes in technology allowed for routine travel and even commuting between the territories of the erstwhile sovereigns. Second, large corporations came to increasingly dominate commerce. Their size provided them with the ability to contract or commit harms across great distances without any corporeal presence in jurisdictions where they might need to be held judicially accountable. In recent years, their reach has been extended by new forms of communication, most notably the Internet.

I. Limits of Territorial Jurisdiction.

The Supreme Court's first great confrontation with questions of jurisdiction came in the landmark case of *Pennoyer v. Neff*[2] in 1877. At that time, there were already 38 state governments and a federal government, court systems accountable to all of them, and a booming, dynamic nation that had spread its territories to the

---

1. U.S. CONST. art. IV, § 1, cl. 1.

2. 95 U.S. 714 (1877).

Pacific. The facts of the case advertised how far the country had come from the simple assumption of unified territorial sovereignty under one reigning monarch.

Pennoyer begins simply enough with a dispute involving the illiterate and indigent Neff, who contracts for legal services in Oregon from a lawyer named Mitchell. Neff ends up moving to California, leaving behind unpaid bills to Mitchell, but also leaving a piece of property in Oregon. Mitchell would prove to be a bit of a rogue, a man who had come West to escape the reach of the law for various crimes, including bigamy, but who would ultimately find his calling as a United States Senator from Oregon. But for purposes of the dispute at hand, there is no gainsaying the legitimate interest of the state of Oregon in providing its citizens, including Mitchell, with legal recourse for the claimed breach of a contract for services entered into and performed in Oregon. The difficulty lay with the fact that, despite Neff's having contracted for services in Oregon, he was no longer in the state and was no longer a subject of the sovereign state of Oregon. Indeed, Neff was now a subject of the equally sovereign state of California, which could be thought to have its own sovereign interest in protecting its citizens from being hauled before the courts of some other sovereign power. But, to the extent that California claimed its sovereign due of having complete dominion over the affairs of its subjects, Oregon would to that extent be precluded from its sovereign prerogative, indeed its obligation, to make legal redress available to its citizens for harms suffered within its dominion. Mobility of persons thus made jurisdiction a zero sum game: the exercise of jurisdiction by one sovereign state in order to protect its citizens from harms caused by citizens of another state in turn diminished the other state's ability to protect its own citizens from being subjected to outside demands.

Mitchell attempted to recover in contract, as he was undoubtedly entitled to do. He filed suit and proceeded as if Neff's departure from the state were of no consequence—indeed, it is not clear that Mitchell had any knowledge of Neff's precise whereabouts. In this, he was aided fully by Oregon law, which treated Mitchell's claim for contract remedies no differently than any other claim in the Oregon courts. In order to initiate suit and properly establish the court's jurisdiction over Neff, Mitchell was required by Oregon law to serve Neff with notification and details of the lawsuit. This presented Mitchell with a problem, since he could not find Neff to serve him. But Oregon law allowed for alternative notice in those circumstances in which a defendant could not be located, and permitted service of process to be satisfied by posting notice of the suit on property belonging to the defendant, along with publishing copies of this notice in the local newspaper for six weeks.

Mitchell did just this, but Neff of course never saw either notice and so never appeared in court. A default judgment was therefore entered against him *in absentia*. Mitchell then laid claim to Neff's land to satisfy the judgment and Neff's land was duly seized and sold at auction to Pennoyer, the proceeds covering Mitchell's contract judgment for his unpaid fees. Upon a subsequent visit to Oregon, Neff discovered his land in the possession of Pennoyer and brought suit to void the sale of his land. Neff's claim was simply that since he was not a domiciliary of Oregon, Oregon had no personal jurisdiction over him and could not enforce a judicial decree against him. Since a judgment entered without proper jurisdiction over the parties is a legal nullity, the forced sale of his land should therefore be found invalid.

The Supreme Court agreed with Neff that personal jurisdiction could only reach as far as the territorial sovereignty of the state. According to the majority in *Pennoyer*, "[E]very State possesses exclusive jurisdiction and sovereignty over persons and property within its territory," and consequently, "no State can exercise direct jurisdiction and authority over persons or property without its territory."[3] The Court held that a state court could obtain proper *in personam* jurisdiction only under one of three conditions, which may be termed the *Pennoyer* requirements. These conditions were: 1) if service of process were made in the state, thereby establishing the physical presence of the defendant within the territory; or 2) if the defendant were a domiciliary of the state and hence a subject of the sovereign power of the state; or 3) if the defendant consented to the exercise of jurisdiction. Each of these conditions had its roots in the concept of territoriality. The Court found that none of these requirements had been met in Neff's case. Since Neff was living in California, had not been served notice of the lawsuit in Oregon, and certainly hadn't consented to Oregon's jurisdiction over him, he was not required to answer suit in Oregon. If Mitchell had wanted to sue him, the Court held that he ought to have done so in California. Therefore, the sale of land to Pennoyer had been improper, and Neff got his land back.

The *Pennoyer* requirements, based on territorial definitions of sovereignty, would command the question of personal jurisdiction for the next 70 years. However, the lynchpin of *Pennoyer* is the method by which the Court applied the concept of territorial limitations on jurisdiction to the states. Not authorized to simply

---

3. *Id.* at 722.

invent jurisdictional rules for the states, the Supreme Court rested its holding on the federal Constitution: "proceedings in a court of justice to determine the personal rights and obligations of parties over whom that court has no jurisdiction do not constitute *due process of law*."[4] This phrase should be familiar from Chapter 1. The Fourteenth Amendment, which had been ratified nine years earlier in 1868, was not yet in effect at the time of the original litigation between Mitchell and Neff. Nonetheless, the passage of the Fourteenth Amendment after the Civil War provided a significant tool for federal limitations on the use of state power. By including jurisdiction under the aegis of due process, the court perhaps unknowingly ensured that, as the due process jurisprudence advanced, so would its command of the field of personal jurisdiction. However, it would be some time before due process theory was advanced enough to contest the continued application of the *Pennoyer* doctrine.

Before moving to the breakdown of the *Pennoyer* model, it is worth exploring one example of the difficulties inherent in narrow territorial notions of sovereignty as the mobility of the population grew. In particular, the invention and popularization of the automobile provided the perfect medium for Americans to cross state lines routinely, engage in tortious activity, and scurry home to the welcoming protection of their own sovereign.

The Court faced this problem squarely in *Hess v. Pawloski*.[5] Hess, a Pennsylvanian, was involved in a car accident with Pawloski, a Massachusetts resident, while driving in Massachusetts. Hess did not wait around to be served in the state, as would have satisfied the first *Pennoyer* condition, but returned to Pennsylvania before Pawloski could sue him in Massachusetts. Although, under a straightforward reading of *Pennoyer,* the Massachusetts courts could not touch Hess, the state had an unmistakable sovereign interest in protecting its citizens and encouraging safety on its roadways. Massachusetts had tried to solve this somewhat irksome dilemma by passing a law which provided that, in accordance with *Pennoyer*, any individual who drove into Massachusetts would be deemed to have *consented* to the jurisdiction of Massachusetts courts for any accidents occurring in that state. As if this weren't enough, the statute covered its *Pennoyer* bases by appointing the state's registrar as the legal agent of anyone who drove there, and implying consent to that appointment by all those who drove a car in the state, regardless whether they were citizens of Massachu-

---

4. *Id.* at 733 (emphasis added).

5. 274 U.S. 352 (1927).

setts. Since a legal agent may receive service of process in the place of a principal, in-state service upon the registrar would then be just as good as service upon the driver himself.

This attempt to square the need for personal jurisdiction over out-of-state defendants with the *Pennoyer* framework does not stand up to much analysis: the consent to both the jurisdiction and the appointment of an agent was completely fictional. It is impossible to reconcile this unknowing implied consent with the fixed territorial conception of jurisdiction under *Pennoyer*. More significantly, the two requirements made no practical sense since individuals could not reasonably be presumed to have read the Massachusetts code before entering the state, or to have actually consented to the appointment of an "agent" in the state bureaucracy. This purported agent had no contact with out-of-state individuals, such as Pawloski, and would surely not be adequate to represent them at trial. Yet the Court still held the application of jurisdiction in Massachusetts constitutional and, in so doing, foreshadowed the development of modern personal jurisdiction law.

The key move in anticipation of modern law was that the Massachusetts law in question did not *only* construct consent where there was none and appoint a fictional agent. It also mandated one other very important action: the plaintiff was required to mail formal notice to the defendant, and the requirement for notification was not satisfied until a record of the receipt was given to the court. Thus, the defendant was guaranteed to be notified of the suit. The reader will recall, again from Chapter 1, that notice is one of the fundamental underpinnings of procedural due process. In essence, the Court upheld the Massachusetts statute not because it conformed to the *Pennoyer* doctrine, but because it satisfied a separate due process command: notice. Further, the fact that Pawloski had driven into Massachusetts and that the lawsuit arose from activities in that state made the jurisdiction fundamentally fair.

Other states enacted similar attempts to construct consent by creating what are generically termed "long-arm statutes." These follow the approach endorsed by the Court in *Hess* in providing a defendant with "notice" of potential liability in the forum, typically by asserting that jurisdiction may follow from the commission of a tortious act within the State. The conduct of business creating the opportunity to commit a tortious act, as with the shipment of a defective product into the forum state,[6] brought the defendant

6. This is the fact pattern from a leading Illinois Supreme Court case on jurisdiction based on long-arm statutes. Gray v. American Radiator & Standard Sanitary Corp., 22 Ill.2d 432, 176 N.E.2d 761 (1961).

within the scope of the notice and presumably constituted consent to suit, although local practices coupled this formal consent with the type of notice seen in *Hess*. The problem remained that such long-arm statutes often failed to anticipate the type of conduct that the forum state might legitimately seek to regulate. As judgments based upon long-arm statutes became more accepted and their reach was deemed constitutional, states began to expand the conduct encompassed within their long-arm statutes. The result was that states rewrote their statutes to provide for long-arm jurisdiction on any basis that would not offend due process, with California providing the typical formulation: "A court of this state may exercise jurisdiction on any basis not inconsistent with the Constitution of this state or of the United States."[7] While this provided great flexibility in asserting jurisdiction, it reduced the notice component to hollow formalism.

Despite the formalistic steps of *Hess* and the reliance on long-arm statutes, a new understanding of jurisdiction was nonetheless emerging separately from the territorial *Pennoyer* doctrine. *Hess* began the process of inquiring into the "reasonableness," or "fairness," of the exercise of jurisdiction, and enforced these through the Due Process Clause. In effect, although the *Hess* Court did not use these precise terms, the propriety of personal jurisdiction increasingly turned on whether its imposition was fair. The Court in *Hess* set off down the path of due process balancing to determine whether the Constitution was offended by the exercise of personal jurisdiction. While *Hess* was still saddled with the idiom of *Pennoyer,* the beginnings of modern due process analysis were upon us.

II.   The Emergence of the Transactional Approach.

With the emergence of the due process era, the law of personal jurisdiction changed from a focus on status—in practice, the relation of a citizen to a state—to a focus on the underlying conduct giving rise to suit. In particular, the rise of the modern corporation required states to confront actors who were legally incorporated elsewhere, but who engaged in conduct affecting their citizens on a daily basis. Rather than a fictional imputation of consent to jurisdiction or an equally fictional assumption that corporations were domiciliaries of any state in which they conducted business, what was needed was a transactional approach that would allow states to assert jurisdiction over disputes that arose from specific in-state

---

7.   Cal. Code Civ. Proc. § 410.10.

activities. Over time, this came to be known as the doctrine of "specific *in personam* jurisdiction."

The defining case proved to be *International Shoe v. Washington*.[8] The International Shoe Company was a Delaware corporation whose headquarters were in St. Louis, and which employed itinerant salesmen to sell shoes door-to-door during the Depression. The state of Washington sought to enforce the state labor code against the company, but under *Pennoyer* it appeared untouchable before the courts of Washington. The state of Washington tried to manufacture jurisdiction by serving subpoenas on some of the company's salesmen, a particularly unstable workforce that the company entrusted only with one-shoe samples—for fear of the employees literally walking off with the goods. But the real notice was provided through the mailing of a subpoena to company headquarters in St. Louis, thereby posing squarely the question whether meaningful notice and a reasonable basis for suit could serve as the constitutional touchstone for the exercise of personal jurisdiction.

The Supreme Court rejected the narrow territorial command of *Pennoyer* in favor of a transactional assessment of whether the defendant's conduct was sufficient to expose it to suit. Sufficient economic activity within the state would establish the defendant's presence there for purposes of suit related to that same activity. The defendant could be deemed present in the forum not by virtue of where notice happened to be served, or by being considered a permanent domiciliary of the forum, but based on its conduct. As explained by the Court, "the terms 'present' or 'presence' are used merely to symbolize those activities of the corporation's agent within the state which courts will deem to be sufficient to satisfy the demands of due process." For corporations, " '[p]resence' in the state in this sense has never been doubted when the activities of the corporation there have not only been continuous and systematic, but also given rise to the liabilities sued on, *even though no consent to be sued or authorization to an agent to accept service of process has been given*."[9] Rather than focus on sovereign authority over territory, as in *Pennoyer,* the test of adequate presence turned on two factors: whether the defendant had "minimum contacts" in the forum to justify the state courts' jurisdiction over it, and, if met, whether the exercise of jurisdiction would "offend traditional notions of fair play and substantial justice."[10] This was the culmination of inquiries into "fairness" that the court had been trying to

---

8.   326 U.S. 310 (1945).

9.   *Id.* at 316–17 (emphasis added).

10.   *Id.*, at 314 (internal quotations omitted).

implement within the territorial confines of *Pennoyer* for the previous 70 years.

With *International Shoe,* the law of personal jurisdiction shed both the restrictions and the certainty of *Pennoyer's* formalism. The two-part test brought the law closer to the real issue of how to ensure accountability for wrongful *acts,* regardless of the formalities of citizenship or form of service. At the same time, the determination of what would constitute minimum contacts or what would be the boundaries of fair play and substantial justice were difficult to predict ahead of time. As the cases developed, minimum contacts came to include virtually any commercial transaction within the forum, thereby incorporating the sale of shoes in Washington, or any tort committed while present in the state, the problem from *Hess.* In its most far-reaching application, the Court in *McGee v. International Life Insurance Company*[11] found adequate contacts in a single insurance contract with an insured in a state where the company had no offices, no ongoing business, and no other clients. Whereas the Court in *International Shoe* had tread carefully and examined the ongoing and routine contacts of the defendant with the state before finding them to meet the required minimum, here a *single* interaction between the parties was found to suffice: International Life had mailed the life insurance contract to and had received premium payments from a deceased insured in California. By upholding minimum contacts based on one interaction, and finding that due process was satisfied by suit in California, the Court had removed all protections of out-of-state defendants possibly afforded by the minimum contacts prong of the *International Shoe* test. Thereafter, at least until the most recent iteration of the personal jurisdiction drama, any defendant with any contact with a forum could only resist personal jurisdiction based on the imprecise inquiry into whether the exercise of jurisdiction would comport with fair play and substantial justice.

The new focus on the transactions giving rise to a claim in a particular forum helped courts sort out claims that had proved troublesome under *Pennoyer.* Going back to *Hess,* for example, the balance of considerations compelled that a driver who had voluntarily entered Massachusetts and had an accident there should be accountable before the courts of that state. Any other rule would deny the state the ability to secure the safety of its citizens, and also deny the injured Massachusetts driver the ability to seek redress in his own courts. But the imprecision of the boundaries of fair play and substantial justice was itself troubling. Justice Black,

---

11.   355 U.S. 220 (1957).

for example, wrote separately in *International Shoe* to express his fear that fair play and substantial justice would end up denying states the ability to police conduct within their own borders, since by definition the second prong of *International Shoe* would only be triggered in those cases in which courts had already found that there were transactionally-related minimum contacts. Again, returning to *Hess*, since the driving of a car in Massachusetts was the predicate for finding minimum contacts, there was no basis, for Justice Black, in even contemplating that Massachusetts could not exercise power over the dispute.

In practice, however, the *International Shoe* test served to widen dramatically the jurisdictional reach of the states, as evident in the *McGee* case where just one contact was sufficient to expose a company to suit. The reason for the pressure to expand jurisdictional reach is largely strategic. Cases against out-of-state defendants are often brought in state court. Although out-of-state defendants may wish to "remove" the case to federal court[12] by claiming diversity jurisdiction (discussed in Chapter 6), that can often be frustrated by adding as a nominal party an in-state defendant. The presence of the in-state defendant defeats the basis for removal of the case to federal court and leaves the question of personal jurisdiction over the out-of-state defendant to be resolved in state court. Such a dispute will thus often pit a local injured party against a relatively distant large corporation and will play out before a judge drawn from the same community as the plaintiff, often elected by voters of that jurisdiction. The judge's incentive is to err on the side of expanding jurisdiction. If a defendant wishes to challenge the exercise of jurisdiction, the appeal will be before appellate courts (who are also often elected) that not only possess the same inclination to protect in-state parties, but also may be reluctant to reverse a jury determination that those parties suffered an injury meriting compensation.

III. The Search for Limits.

In the aftermath of *McGee*, courts readily expanded jurisdiction in cases that added a laundry list of factors to balance in assessing

---

12. Under 28 U.S.C. § 1446, a defendant may force a case from state court into federal court if the state court proceeding is between diverse parties or asserts a federal law basis for suit. The act of transferring the case from state to federal court is called removal. When removal is sought on the basis of diversity of citizenship of the parties, there must be "perfect diversity" in that all parties on one side of the "v." must be from states different from all parties on the other side of the "v." The concept of perfect diversity is discussed more fully in the next chapter. The addition of an in-state defendant, even where the expectation of recovery from that defendant is remote at best, may serve to prevent removal by destroying perfect diversity.

the ultimate fairness of compelling an out-of-state defendant to appear before a state's tribunals. The same pressures existed even in federal courts whose jurisdictional reach in a diversity case is basically that of the highest state court in the same jurisdiction. As courts inquired into the foreseeability of suit in the forum, or the balance of conveniences between the parties, or the interest of the forum state in providing a remedy to its citizens, it appeared that the scales would tip decisively in favor of wide-open jurisdictional accountability. Further spurring the expansion of jurisdictional reach was the fact that courts had no mechanism to weigh the comparative claims of different fora to adjudge a particular dispute. The jurisdictional issue was always presented as a question of whether the forum state had a cognizable interest in trying the case, never as the question whether the forum state was the best jurisdiction to handle the dispute.

In a federal system, the exclusive focus on whether the forum state has an interest yielded some paradoxical results. Consider, for example, the case that ended up in the Supreme Court as *Keeton v. Hustler Magazine, Inc.*[13] There a plaintiff chose to bring a defamation action over a rather lurid portrayal in Hustler under the relatively favorable defamation laws of New Hampshire. The plaintiff had no contact with New Hampshire and the defendant sold a small percentage of its magazines there. But defamation law recognizes the situs of a harm as any place where publication occurs, and sales or other distribution count as publication. There was little doubt the magazine had minimum contacts in New Hampshire and that there was a credible claim of injury under the substantive terms of defamation law, and the Supreme Court duly upheld the exercise of jurisdiction in New Hampshire. Yet the definition of the defamation turned heavily on community norms, such that, in effect, a local jury in New Hampshire was in the position of dictating what would be considered prurient for the entire nation. That is, unless Hustler wanted to produce a special edition solely for New Hampshire—an impractical solution—it would have no choice but to limit its content to the standards of the most rigorous state's law, or accept the risk of liability in that most unwelcoming state. As Hustler is sold nationally, one particularly unwelcoming state could determine acceptable reading material for the whole nation.

The outcome in *Keeton* and countless other cases involving the application of local standards to national—or even international— products reveals the paradox of liberal jurisdictional rules. Under

13.   465 U.S. 770 (1984).

the old *Pennoyer* regime, restrictive territorial jurisdiction prevented Oregon from legitimately exercising its sovereign powers to
enforce the integrity of contracts entered into in that state. The
narrower the jurisdictional reach of the states, the more compromised the capacity of states to protect their own citizens. However,
expanding jurisdiction frustrated the claimed sovereign powers of
the states no less. The more expansive the jurisdictional reach, as
in cases like *Keeton,* the more it denies other states the ability to
set independent standards. Liability for Hustler in New Hampshire,
like stringent emissions or safety standards in one state but not
others, have the effect of defining a national market, without the
participation of the citizens of other states or, presumably, the
political legitimacy of a national debate or national consensus.

Additionally, this attempt at expanding jurisdiction placed the
heaviest burdens on those least able to bear them—the small
defendants. A national company such as Hustler magazine could
afford to defend itself anywhere in the country because, in all
likelihood, it already had representatives nationwide or had significant legal services at its command. Indeed, given the salacious
nature of its business, we might speculate that Hustler was not
unfamiliar with the legal systems in many jurisdictions. But a
small, local company would not likely have those connections and
could legitimately fear that its exposure to suit would follow its
products around the country. It also might not have the capital to
engage in protracted litigation in a distant jurisdiction. Thus, the
post-*International Shoe* expansion of jurisdiction threatened to put
even the smallest enterprises at the greatest peril, forcing those
defendants least able to internalize the costs of cross-country litigation to defend law suits anywhere or limit their business ventures
for fear of potential exposure to distant and expensive litigation.

Seen from the vantage point of potential defendants, the open-
ended quality of jurisdiction created uncertainty, a risk of significant costs, and, at the very least, a need to insure against being
unable to afford far-reaching litigation. In 1980, the Supreme Court
began to stem the tide of expanding jurisdiction by focusing on the
expectations of the out-of-state defendant, rather than the interests
of the plaintiff and the forum state. The critical case was *World–
Wide Volkswagen v. Woodson,*[14] a suit brought in Oklahoma by New
York residents who had been injured by the claimed malfunction of
their automobile while driving through Oklahoma. The plaintiffs
sued not only the manufacturers of their car, who no doubt had
contact with Oklahoma through the sale of other automobiles there,

---

14. 444 U.S. 286 (1980).

but the New York car dealership from whom they had purchased the car. The jurisdictional question was whether the New York dealership could be held accountable in an Oklahoma state court solely on the basis of the happenstance of its customer's presence there at the time of the accident. This is what is known in the jurisdiction trade as chattel-driven entry into the forum, here more literally than in most cases. Nonetheless, arguably consistently with *McGee*, the Oklahoma court held that it was foreseeable in a modern, mobile society that the car would end up in Oklahoma and therefore that minimum contacts were established and Oklahoma's exercise of jurisdiction over the New York dealership did not offend due process notions of what is fair and just. In effect, this meant that anyone selling a car to anyone in the United States would have to foresee the possibility of being sued anywhere that car might end up.

On appeal, however, the Supreme Court reversed, holding that the foreseeability of the car ending up in Oklahoma was an insufficient basis for minimum contacts. The Court first distinguished commercial activity that was still part of the stream of commerce, the initial efforts to sell goods or services, from chattel-driven commercial activities, with the former much more likely to satisfy minimum contacts. The automobile had not been brought to Oklahoma as part of a stream of commerce—shipped there to be sold by a retailer—but rather, by customers after the final sales contract was concluded. In other words, it was the sold car that came into Oklahoma and not the deal for the car. To find that this alone satisfied jurisdiction was to say that "[e]very seller of chattels would in effect appoint the chattel his agent for service of process. His amenability to suit would travel with the chattel."[15] Instead of the loose balancing factors that had emerged after *McGee,* the propriety of personal jurisdiction would turn on the defendant's conduct, and determining whether the defendant had "purposefully availed" itself of the benefits and burdens of activity in the forum state. Absent such purposeful availment, the *International Shoe* requirement of minimum contacts would not be satisfied and jurisdiction could not attach. Under the facts presented, since the dealership in New York had not advertised in Oklahoma, had not engaged in any transactions there, had no physical presence there, and reaped no benefits from Oklahoma's business climate, the dealership could not be said to have purposefully availed itself of the forum and the state's exercise of jurisdiction was improper.

15. *Id.* at 296.

Three different problems quickly emerged from the "purposeful availment" standard for personal jurisdiction. First, there was the problem of defining what contacts were foreseeable. It may seem readily apparent that the New York dealership did not purposefully avail itself of anything in the quite distant state of Oklahoma. But *World–Wide Volkswagen* does not tell us the geographical point at which the car would have been close enough to New York that the defendant may be thought to have purposefully availed itself of the forum state. Even under the purposeful availment test, a distinct factual inquiry would have to be made about the number of customers a business might draw from other states, as well as the effective diffusion of its advertising. So nearby New England? Halfway through Vermont perhaps? Although the Court identified several factors to determine the existence of purposeful availment, foreseeability remained factually imprecise.

Second, the Court's decision looked only at the defendant's side of the equation. Under the facts of *World–Wide Volkswagen*, the plaintiff was a New York resident who wished to sue in Oklahoma for strategic reasons (Oklahoma state court juries in that part of the state were thought to be plaintiff-friendly). Plaintiffs had added the dealership in order to keep the true targets of suit (the manufacturers Audi and Volkswagen—the genuinely "world-wide" entities) from trying to remove the case to federal court. It thus was not too disconcerting to say that these particular plaintiffs could choose between suing the manufacturers in Oklahoma federal court or suing all the defendants back in New York, where the assertedly defective car had been purchased. But the minimum contacts test, as refined in *World–Wide Volkswagen,* would have yielded the same conclusion even if the plaintiff had been an Oklahoma resident innocently walking down the street when she was injured as a result of a dangerous defect in the car. By focusing solely on the anticipated economic benefits of the defendant in the forum, the Court cut off all inquiry into other factors that might make the exercise of jurisdiction more compelling. Returning to the paradox of jurisdiction, protecting the New York resident dealership may have had the unintended effect of denying to Oklahoma the ability to control its own highways and protect its own citizens.

Third, by abruptly shifting from the fair-play-and-substantial-justice prong to a narrow focus on the defendant's conduct giving rise to minimum contacts, the Court inadvertently left open a possible expansion of jurisdiction where a bare minimum of contacts had indeed occurred. The leading example is *Burger King v.*

Rudzewicz,[16] a case involving a large corporate *plaintiff*. Burger King, headquartered in Florida, sued two small Michigan franchisees at the site of its corporate headquarters, rather than at the site of the Michigan franchise that underlay the dispute. Although the franchisees had contracted with a Florida-based conglomerate and sent their franchise payments to Florida, there was little doubt that the entire case was about contractual obligations for the operation of a Burger King franchise in Michigan, a decidedly local operation. Whatever minimum contacts there may have been with Florida, there is little doubt that allowing the corporate entity to force the franchisees to Florida was both unfair and an affront to Michigan's ability to police commercial activity within its borders. The Court, however, stood the minimum contacts analysis on its head by making the "purposeful availment" inquiry the stand-alone test for jurisdiction. Writing for the majority, Justice Brennan, the Court's strongest proponent of expansive state jurisdiction, took that which had been necessary and made it sufficient. Since the Michigan franchisees had had some minimum contacts with Florida, and had an ongoing commercial relationship with a Florida entity, that alone was sufficient for the exercise of personal jurisdiction in Florida. Again, the inquiry was plagued by an inability to entertain a comparative judgment as to the superiority of the Michigan versus Florida forum. Instead the Court inquired only whether Florida, standing alone, was a constitutionally conceivable jurisdiction. After *Burger King*, it appeared that if minimum contacts were satisfied, then a court had jurisdiction, an inquiry perhaps more concrete than during the era of expansive jurisdiction, but no less arbitrary or unfair in practice.

IV.   The Rise of Due Process Balancing.

The attempt to define the necessary elements for the exercise of jurisdiction hearkens back to the formalist era of due process prior to *Mathews v. Eldridge,* as discussed in Chapter 1. Trying to catalogue the requirements for the constitutional reach of a state's courts runs into the same problems that had bedeviled similar efforts to define as necessary the components of notice or the right to a hearing across the broad expanse of state interaction with the citizenry. It should therefore come as no surprise that the formalist enterprise would ultimately yield to a due process balancing approach, very much analogous to the well-traveled *Mathews v. Eldridge* approach.

16.   471 U.S. 462 (1985).

The triumph, and high-water mark, of the modern due process analysis of personal jurisdiction came about in *Asahi Metal Industry v. Superior Court of California*,[17] which presented a far more complex problem of jurisdiction than any examined thus far. A California plaintiff named Gary Zurcher was injured in a motorcycle accident in California apparently caused by a tire blow-out. Zurcher sued various parties in California state court, including the manufacturer of the tire's tube, a Taiwanese company called Cheng Shin. Cheng Shin in turn brought a claim for indemnification against the Japanese manufacturer of the tire tube's valves, a corporation called Asahi Metal Industry. The original plaintiff eventually settled his claims, leaving only the secondary issue of each defendant's comparative liability in a derivative suit between Cheng Shin and Asahi over their relative shares.

In many ways, *Asahi* exposed the deficiencies of prior jurisdictional rules. Under the strict "purposeful availment" standard, it was unlikely that subpart manufacturers such as either Asahi or Cheng Shin could be liable in the state where their products caused harm. Subpart manufacturers are unlikely to advertise directly in the forum, unlikely to market for the forum, and most likely to direct their commercial efforts only to the ultimate manufacturer. Under the "purposeful availment" standard, neither California nor Zurcher would be able to hold subpart manufacturers accountable in the California courts even for dangerous acts of negligence. At the same time, expanding the concept of minimum contacts to include any commercial contact, as in *Burger King*, would hold a commercial dispute between Cheng Shin and Asahi amenable to suit in California, even after Zurcher had settled out. Under *Burger King*, the stream of commerce was still flowing when the subparts reached California, establishing the minimally necessary contacts. Neither the inherited tests from *World–Wide Volkswagen* nor *Burger King* could untangle the complicated fact pattern in *Asahi*.

The Court in *Asahi* tried to resolve this complicated jurisdictional puzzle in two ways. First, Justice O'Connor, writing for a plurality, tried to stiffen the purposeful availment test inherited from *World–Wide Volkswagen* to focus on overt acts taken by the defendant to secure commercial or other benefits in the forum. The higher minimum contacts threshold would ask whether the defendant had engaged in conduct such as marketing within the forum, offering service in the forum, designing parts specifically for the forum, or soliciting business within the forum. A subparts manufacturer would be unlikely to meet this threshold even though, in the

17. 480 U.S. 102 (1987).

era of the global economy, it would be entirely foreseeable that a tire valve made in Japan and sold to a company in Taiwan could become part of a motorcycle sold in California that crashed and caused injury, because such is the nature of worldwide manufacturing and distribution. The practical consequence of Justice O'Connor's approach would have been effectively to limit suit to the ultimate manufacturer of the motorcycle, Honda, which would in turn be held vicariously liable for any defects in the product it ultimately sold. While restrictive, this would have invited Honda to establish contractually the liability of its subparts manufacturers through indemnification agreements. But it would limit the redress of injured consumers to the parties with whom they had some measure of direct contractual privity, which might be problematic if the final manufacturer had become insolvent, to give but one example of a potential problem. This restrictive definition of minimum contacts was rejected by five members of the Court, who found that, at the very least, ongoing sales within the stream of commerce were sufficient to satisfy the baseline constitutional requirement of minimum contacts. So long as the product had not yet been delivered to its ultimate consumer—as in the final sale of the car in *World–Wide Volkswagen*—minimum contacts would follow the chain of sale.

Thus, although the opinion is less than clear, a majority of the Court found that there were sufficient minimum contacts between Asahi and California, or at least that the volume of valves that Asahi shipped each year, a number of which would enter the California market, satisfied the minimum-contacts prong of the due process inquiry. However, the Court deemed the exercise of jurisdiction to be unconstitutional based on the second inquiry into fair play and substantial justice.

Writing here for a clear majority of the Court, Justice O'Connor abandoned the unwieldy multifactor test that had emerged in the post-*McGee* era. In its place, she set out a more streamlined balancing test that would guide future courts in determining the propriety of personal jurisdiction under the fair-play-and-substantial-justice prong of *International Shoe*. She pointed to four key factors that courts should weigh: the interest of the plaintiff in proceeding in the forum, the burden on the defendant of having to defend in the forum, the interest of the forum state in the subject matter of the lawsuit, and the overall interests of the legal system in the efficient resolution of the dispute in the chosen forum. Rather than apply a checklist, the Court invited a streamlined inquiry into the competing equities of having the lawsuit in the plaintiff's chosen jurisdiction and the systemic efficiency interests in finding the most suitable forum. In other words, the Court subjected personal jurisdiction to the typical due process balancing approach that we have seen throughout civil procedure, beginning with *Mathews v. Eldridge.*

Applying this analysis to the facts of *Asahi*, the Court found that due process would not permit a California court to exercise jurisdiction over the Japanese subpart manufacturer in its dispute with a Taiwanese company for contractual indemnification. The burden on the foreign defendant was very high and, since the original Californian plaintiff had already settled out and been compensated for his injuries, the interests of the Taiwanese tire manufacturer in having the case heard in California were at best questionable. Furthermore, California had no reason to protect either party, no real interest in the case, and no one had demonstrated that the legal system at large would benefit from adjudicating a foreign law claim for indemnification in California. Thus, even those justices who found that minimum contacts were met agreed that fair play and substantial justice demanded that jurisdiction be found lacking. Forty years after *International Shoe*, Justice Black's concern about the operation of the two-prong *International Shoe* test was finally realized: fair play and substantial justice could in fact defeat minimum contacts if the burdens sufficiently outweighed the interests.

The *Asahi* analysis rejects formalism in favor of the familiar balancing test, viewing jurisdiction as simply another due process problem and therefore not amenable to hard and fast rules. At the same time, it does not entirely eliminate consideration of the formalistic minimum contacts factors developed first in *World–Wide Volkswagen.* Rather, it subsumes those elements into a determination of the burden on the defendant, a move first suggested by *International Shoe*, which looked back at the activities of the defendant to determine the fairness of asserting jurisdiction. By focusing the inquiry on a balance among competing burdens and interests, *Asahi* takes into account the totality of the circumstances to determine which is the best forum for the dispute. This approach was lacking both in *Burger King*, which focused only on minimum contacts, and in *World–Wide Volkswagen*, which asked only whether jurisdiction was reasonable to the defendant. By combining all of the due process factors, the *Asahi* test is able to hold both that it would be proper under some circumstances to hold a Taiwanese manufacturer responsible in a California court and that an exercise of jurisdiction would be improper under the particular facts of that case.

After *Asahi*, courts could finally distinguish between the New York driver in Oklahoma and the Oklahoman bystander on the side of the road, under the problem presented in *World–Wide Volkswagen*. *Asahi* therefore offers the level of sensitivity found throughout other areas of civil procedure and that was so sorely lacking in the complex arena of personal jurisdiction.

What is lost in this modern due process approach to personal jurisdiction is predictability. In a global economy, foreign subpart manufacturers or even foreign manufacturers themselves might look with dismay upon an American jurisdictional system that exposes them to liability wherever the stream of commerce might sweep their products. As the Supreme Court has noted in a different context, "the point of due process—of the law in general—is to allow citizens to order their behavior."[18] Unpredictability in the application of law forces parties to contract for their protection from those further up the distribution ladder and closer to the ultimate consumers. What is gained in doctrinal flexibility is also lost in terms of orderly application of law and the costs that this imposes on unwitting parties scattered around the globe.

V. Looking Backward: The Unresolved Legacy of Pennoyer v. Neff.

While *Asahi* may seem the logical end point of the evolution of due process analysis in the law of personal jurisdiction, much remains unresolved. Recall that the case developments discussed thus far have all arisen from specific *in personam* jurisdiction. But that is not the full scope of jurisdictional regimes. At common law of old, jurisdiction could be based on the Crown's authority over the person or over real property, the latter designated *in rem* jurisdiction. One mechanism that allowed for greater state jurisdiction, even under *Pennoyer,* was the emerging doctrine of *quasi in rem* jurisdiction. Unlike a classic action brought *in rem* to settle a dispute as to the ownership of land, a *quasi in rem* action sued the land as a placeholder for a claim against the owner for matters unrelated to the land. Imagine, for example, that in *Hess v. Pawloski* the defendant were beyond the jurisdictional reach of Massachusetts, yet owned land in that state. Hess might well bring a *quasi in rem* action against Pawloski's landholdings in the state, seeking to recover from the liquidation value of the land for the injuries he had suffered in the accident. The claim would be unrelated to the ownership of the land, but were Hess to prevail, he

---

18. State Farm v. Campbell, 538 U.S. 408, 418 (2003).

might seize from a forced sale of the land as much as a jury would award for his personal injuries.

With the expansion of property to include all manner of holdings and entitlements, the ability to sue *quasi in rem* grew as well. The extreme manifestation was presented in *Shaffer v. Heitner,*[19] in which the plaintiff perfected jurisdiction against out-of-state defendants by attaching stock certificates that were held in deposit in Delaware. Since virtually all stock transactions in the U.S. are electronic, with the official certificates held in depositories in Delaware, the fact of shareholding would expose anyone in the U.S. who owned stock to being sued in Delaware up to the value of the underlying shares. This would lead to absurd results, in effect turning Delaware into a magnet forum for anyone who wished to sue there. Nonetheless, *International Shoe* and its progeny did not cover this particular scenario because the exercise of jurisdiction was based not on power over the person, but on the state's sovereign authority over all property within its dominion.

The Supreme Court in *Shaffer* stuck down this assertion of jurisdiction by Delaware courts. In examining the relation between the post-*International Shoe* cases and other bases for jurisdiction, the Court could find no principle that would distinguish the due process concerns in the *in personam* cases. As a result, the Court not only struck down the broad-scale use of *quasi in rem* to circumvent the limits on *in personam* jurisdiction, but it stated that all claims of personal jurisdiction, regardless whether *in personam* or *in rem* or *quasi in rem,* would be held to the *International Shoe* standards of minimum contacts and fair play and substantial justice.

Seemingly, *Shaffer* should have settled the issue for jurisdiction after *Asahi.* If all claims of personal jurisdiction were to be held to the same due process standards, and if *Asahi* were the most evolved exposition of the due process command, the law of personal jurisdiction should fall in line behind the new due process balance. As we shall see, though, this is not the case, as signaled by the fact that Justice Scalia did not join the due process section of Justice O'Connor's *Asahi* opinion, indicating at least lingering resistance to the broad due process sweep of jurisdictional law. In at least three critical areas somewhat outside the core concern of the *International Shoe* line of cases, the picture is not quite so neat, and reflects a lingering attachment to clearer if more formalistic lines of jurisdictional authority. Most recently, and most significantly, the Court fractured in a case squarely within the central legacy of *Interna-*

---

19.   433 U.S. 186 (1977).

tional Shoe, one dealing with the importation of dangerous machinery into a state for the routine and ordinary use of that machinery.

A.   *In–State Service: Burnham v. Superior Court.*

The first break with the due process approach came in *Burnham v. Superior Court of California,*[20] the unfortunate story of a broken marriage between two highly mobile individuals. After marrying in West Virginia, the Burnham couple moved to New Jersey and raised their children there. However, the marriage fell apart and the couple agreed on terms of child support and on how to proceed with the divorce. The husband filed suit for divorce in New Jersey, but did not serve his wife with a subpoena while she was in New Jersey. In the meantime, she moved with the children to California, where she sued for divorce and child support under California law. In a display of tactical "gotcha" or "tag" jurisdiction, the husband was served with a subpoena while in California on business. The actual service of the subpoena occurred while he was visiting with his children at his wife's home.

Under the old common law principle of *capias ad respondendum*, meaning roughly that you answer where your body is found, being subject to service within a jurisdiction was a sufficient basis for the exercise of personal jurisdiction. *Pennoyer* kept alive the historical practice of permitting in-state service as a basis for jurisdiction. But not only had the Court in *World–Wide Volkswagen* derisively spoken of *Pennoyer* as a "shibboleth," in *Shaffer* it had also seemingly brought all exercises of jurisdiction within due process scrutiny. The question for the Court was whether this kind of jurisdictional claim survived due process scrutiny, or whether it was even subject to due process review.

Faced with the question of the propriety of California jurisdiction in this case, the Court could have, and arguably should have, applied the *Asahi* due process balancing test to determine whether burdens outweighed interests or vice versa. The husband would have had a strong due process argument that he did not have minimum contacts with California relative to the dispute, and that even if he did, the burden on him was too high to render jurisdiction fair. Both the wife and California might well have countered that the interests of providing for the welfare of the children, now resident in California, created the basis for jurisdiction. The case would have been difficult under the *Asahi* balancing test, but the balance likely would have tipped in favor of jurisdiction, on the

20.   495 U.S. 604 (1990).

ground that the state's interest in providing for the best interests of the children trumped all other considerations. But this was not the basis for decision. None of the Justices faithfully applied the balancing test set out in Asahi; they instead turned to formalistic analyses reminiscent either of the 1877 *Pennoyer* ruling that in-state service alone sufficed for a state to assert jurisdiction, or of *Burger King's* mechanical application of the minimum contacts test.

The court fractured and there was no controlling opinion. Justice Scalia's effort would have recast the law of personal jurisdiction most aggressively. For Justice Scalia, the one Justice who had refused the due process gambit in *Asahi,* the entire *International Shoe* line of cases addressed only exceptional circumstances, such as the need to perfect service on out-of-state corporations doing business in the forum state, while leaving the bulk of sovereignty-based territorial jurisdiction intact. Since in-state service was expressly addressed in *Pennoyer* as having common law roots, and since according to Justice Scalia constitutional commands should be read to lock in legal norms and rules in existence at the time of their ratification, this renders subsequent evolution irrelevant. Accordingly, he argued that in the case of personal jurisdiction, the courts must look at whatever was accepted as the proper norm of due process at the time the Fourteenth Amendment was ratified. Along this line of thought, *Pennoyer* is seen as the first and final word on personal jurisdiction, with *International Shoe* merely filling a gap created by the problem of the out-of-state defendant typically associated with the automobile and the corporation. In *Burnham*, the *Pennoyer* framework was sufficient to decide the issue of jurisdiction, and, according to Justice Scalia, the Court should go no further than that analysis.

Writing in the alternative, but reaching the same conclusion, was Justice Brennan, who would have applied a due process approach, but found jurisdiction proper all the same. In his view, jurisdictional questions boil down to a *quid pro quo*; if a party reaps the benefits of a state, then it is only fair that he or she pay the jurisdictional price of accountability in that state's courts. While perhaps reasonable, the definition of the benefits and costs would amount to little more than the *Burger King* holding that minimum contacts are always a sufficient basis for jurisdiction. For Justice Brennan, mere presence in a state was sufficient to say that a party received benefits. As examples, he pointed to the benefits of police protection, use of state roads, and purchase of goods and services, which essentially makes in-state presence a proxy for high benefit to the defendant. Moreover, in analyzing the burdens of California exercising jurisdiction, Justice Brennan maintained that it could not be too difficult for the defendant to litigate in California, because the defendant had already shown his ability to travel to California when he had, after all, been served in-state. In Justice Brennan's view, therefore, whenever in-state service exists, due process will be satisfied.

After decades of developing a modern due process analysis for the problems of a mobile population, the Court's retreat to formalism was quite troubling. Allowing tag jurisdiction to hold up, virtually regardless of the contacts with the forum, invites gamesmanship in litigation and dictates that parties exercise caution in where they travel for fear of being served in an inconvenient or inhospitable forum. This unfortunate outcome is another example of *Pennoyer's* inapplicability in a mobile society, which every case from *International Shoe* to *Asahi* had attempted to resolve.

B.   Consent–Based Jurisdiction: *Carnival Cruise Lines, Inc. v. Shute.*

Stepping back for a moment from the technical issues of jurisdiction permits us to revisit the real source of concern in a case such as *International Shoe*. The problem with the modern corporation having its "personhood" defined in one jurisdiction, but its affairs conducted in many others, is not a matter of the difficulty of service of process. Rather, it is that the legal form of the corporation may create a shield between the conduct the firm undertakes in many jurisdictions and its legal responsibility for the consequences of its conduct. The move away from formalism in the post-*International Shoe* line of cases may be seen as an attempt to accommodate the need for effective legal redress for aggrieved parties where their harms may have been suffered, regardless of the technical citizenship or domicile of the party claimed to be at fault.

Unfortunately, incorporation or simply being outside the state are not the exclusive mechanisms for erecting a legal barrier to accountability. In *Carnival Cruise Lines, Inc. v. Shute*,[21] the Court confronted a jurisdictional barrier created through a contract of adhesion—a form contract created by a seller for many buyers—rather than through the citizenship of the defendant. The case arose out of a shipboard accident involving a woman who, along with her husband, had bought cruise tickets from the couple's home in Washington, boarded the ship in California, and was

21.   499 U.S. 585 (1991).

injured along the coast of Mexico. The initial transaction was only for payment in exchange for the cruise. The tickets themselves were not available to the Shutes until they had traveled from Washington to California to board the ship. Not until the Shutes received the tickets, which were nonrefundable, would they have discovered that, in addition to some odd points such as the limited liability of the shipboard barber, the tickets obligated the Shutes to a forum selection clause requiring that all litigation relating to the cruise be tried in Florida.

Prior to *International Shoe*, Carnival Cruise might have claimed that it could not be sued in Washington because it was not domiciled there, did not consent, and could not be served there. But the effect of the contract was to raise the exact same geographic barriers to suit that had been undone by the due process reformulation of personal jurisdiction. Perhaps pursuant to *International Shoe*, the Court should have carefully considered the need to protect the weaker party—in this case the plaintiffs—from being haled into a distant forum. But, as with *Burnham*, the Court in *Carnival Cruise Lines* did not look to *International Shoe* and *Asahi*. Instead it focused on the existence of implied consent in an analysis reminiscent of the highly problematic formalism of *Burger King*. The majority opinion, per Justice Stevens, pointed to the benefits that the Shutes had purportedly derived from the forum selection clause, particularly Carnival Cruise's presumed ability to offer a lower cruise fare because of the reduced costs from limiting its liability to Florida alone. In the Court's opinion, that was a sufficient *quid pro quo* to foreclose the home forum where the transaction occurred, or even California, where the fateful cruise began. But the same argument could as easily have been made in *International Shoe* or any other case where the claimed savings from limiting liability could presumably be passed on to the ultimate consumer. For the Court, however, the due process line of cases did not amount to home forum access, only to some kind of reasonable forum in light of the totality of circumstances.

Carnival Cruise Lines is especially disturbing in the age of the computer. Anyone who has bought software has seen, and most likely disregarded, the user agreements contained in shrink-wrapped packages which, once opened, cannot be returned, or has clicked through a series of dreary web pages before buying goods on-line, which often arrive with similar click-through processes. Generally one of the elements in the software agreements or on the web pages is a forum selection clause. Due process might have a lot to say about the fairness of enforcing the choice of forum on unwitting consumers who were certainly never given the opportunity to negotiate the terms of their purchase contract. But *Carnival Cruise Lines* sidesteps any form of fairness analysis in favor of viewing the entire matter as a waivable contractual right. The problems of *International Shoe* are not behind us.

C.   Consent to General Jurisdiction.

The modern trend in personal jurisdiction is transactional and looks to the contacts with the forum that gave rise to the specific claim. As evident in Justice Scalia's opinion in *Burnham*, however, the transactional approach leaves unanswered the viability of the traditional forms of jurisdiction recognized in *Pennoyer*. One significant area of uncertainty concerns general—as opposed to specific— personal jurisdiction. In some sense, this form of jurisdiction is a throwback to pretransactional approaches to personal jurisdiction. General personal jurisdiction is based not on the claim that gave rise to the suit, but rather on the quality of the defendant's general relation to the forum. It is found when an entity is so closely related to a particular forum that it is considered the equivalent of the domiciliary under *Pennoyer*. The classic example is that of a corporation founded and operated within a particular state, such as General Motors, which is so connected with the State of Michigan that it can hardly claim unconstitutional prejudice from being sued in Michigan for its activities, even those not arising in Michigan. Such an entity can properly be held accountable in that forum, regardless of the location of the claimed harm.

There is much less case law development surrounding general personal jurisdiction as compared to transactionally-specific forms of jurisdiction. In *Helicopteros Nacionales de Colombia, S.A. v. Hall*,[22] the Supreme Court began restricting the reach of general jurisdiction to firms that had continuous and systematic contacts with the forum, as evidenced by company headquarters, sales operations, bank accounts, and other indicia of permanence. The test was somewhat unclear, since *Helicopteros* states the test in the negative in striking down the exercise of general jurisdiction over a company that only entered the forum state for some purchases and other single-shot events. The criteria are restrictive and are similar to the test that Justice O'Connor proposed to shore up minimum contacts in her opinion in *Asahi*. In general, a jurisdiction's being either the presence of a corporation's headquarters or its place of incorporation is a sufficient basis for an exercise of general personal jurisdiction. Beyond that, the test is quite restrictive.

---

22.   466 U.S. 408 (1984).

Subsequently, in *Goodyear Dunlop Tires v. Brown*[23] the Court confirmed the essential features of *Helicopteros* with a similarly restrictive set of requirements for the assertion of non-transaction based jurisdiction: "A court may assert jurisdiction over ... corporations to hear any and all claims against them when their affiliations with the State are so continuous and systematic as to render them essentially at home in the forum State."[24] Such restrictive requirements could be met where a corporation has its principal place of business or is incorporated, as opposed to a forum in which it has merely sold goods or engaged in transactions unrelated to the subject matter of the suit. Under the facts of *Goodyear,* this meant that a Turkish subsidiary of Goodyear that sold tires manufactured there to a bus company in France, and whose tires were alleged to have caused a fatal accident in France, could not be sued in South Carolina, no matter how much business the American parent of Goodyear does there.[25]

While limited, the general jurisdiction approach remains as an outlier from the expansion of transactional approaches for most of personal jurisdiction law. So long as the application of general jurisdiction is limited to the state of incorporation or the principal business headquarters, little is at stake. Even if claims of general jurisdiction were analyzed under the *Asahi* analysis, there would clearly be minimum contacts between the forum and the defendant, and there would be little in the fair play and substantial justice balance that would place jurisdiction in the home forum beyond due process limitations.

Unfortunately, the risk of formalist applications of general jurisdiction is not so easily discounted. In recent years, many states have responded to the uncertainties of jurisdictional law by demanding that corporations consent to general jurisdiction in order to do business there.[26] Compelled consent would recreate within the arena of general jurisdiction *Pennoyer's* formalistic categories of consent and domiciliary status. Moreover, Justice Scalia's traditionalist approach in *Burnham* and the contractual approach of *Carnival Cruise Lines* suggest that compelled consent to jurisdiction may be immune from any due process scrutiny. This area of the law remains open and reveals yet another stumbling block in the attempt to craft a modern law of personal jurisdiction.

23. 131 S.Ct. 2846 (2011).

24. *Id.* at 2851 (internal quotations omitted).

25. *See id.*

26. *See* Lee S. Taylor, *Registration Statutes, Personal Jurisdiction, and The Problem of Predictability,* 103 Colum. L. Rev. 1163 (2003).

D. Revisiting the Basics?

Whatever stability in the law of personal jurisdiction may have emerged from two decades of case law under *Asahi* came swiftly tumbling down with the Court's first major foray into this area in nearly a quarter century. In *J. McIntyre Machinery v. Nicastro,*[27] the Court confronted what should have been a more straightforward case to settle the law than either *World–Wide Volkswagen* or *Asahi.* At issue in *McIntyre* was the delivery to New Jersey of an intact industrial machine that was allegedly defective, not a subpart buried in a much larger product as in *Asahi,* or a product taken half-way across the country long after the final sale had been consummated, as in *World–Wide Volkswagen.* Here, by contrast, Nicastro, a New Jersey resident, lost half his hand in a workplace accident involving a sheet-metal shredding machine manufactured by J. McIntyre, a British company. This machine was sold to Nicastro's employer in New Jersey by an American company that was created to distribute McIntyre machines in the United States. That American distributor filed for bankruptcy before Nicastro was injured, leaving the British manufacturer as the only entity against whom Nicastro could bring a product liability suit for his injury.

Despite the division on the Court in *Asahi,* at least all nine Justices agreed on the outcome. The same cannot be said for either the reasoning or the resolution in *McIntyre.* Writing for four member of the Court, Justice Kennedy dismissed as ''metaphor'' *Asahi's* focus on the stream of commerce of goods, and instead repeatedly invoked the concept of sovereignty as the touchstone for personal jurisdiction. The exact meaning of sovereignty remained unclear, except by reference to the importance of the ''purposeful availment'' test as providing the right inquiry for determining when a defendant is subject to personal jurisdiction: ''As a general rule, the exercise of judicial power is not lawful unless the defendant 'purposefully avails itself of the privilege of conducting activities within the forum State, thus invoking the benefits and protections of its laws.' ''[28] Goods in the steam of commerce are not in themselves sufficient to establish such availment, even if a commercial defendant ''might have predicted that its goods will reach the forum State.''[29] Rather, the principles of sovereignty and purposeful availment require that the defendant have ''targeted the forum''[30]

---

27. 131 S.Ct. 2780 (2011).

28. *Id.* at 2785 (quoting Hanson v. Denckla, 357 U.S. 235, 253 (1958)).

29. *Id.* at 2788.

30. *Id.*

directly, though that is unlikely for a manufacturer of large industrial machines that sells one unit at a time, and who is certainly
unlikely to tailor the machine for specific application to New
Jersey's (or any state's) particular accumulation of scrap metal.
Justice Kennedy admitted the resulting anomaly: "Because the
United States is a distinct sovereign, a defendant may in principle
be subject to the jurisdiction of the courts of the United States but
not of any particular State."[31]

The necessary concurring votes came from Justices Breyer and
Alito. Joining the result but not the reasoning, Justice Breyer's
opinion for the two swing Justices posited that J. McIntyre had not
done enough to establish personal jurisdiction by selling at most
four machines into New Jersey (presumably no matter what their
size or cost), but that the test for why would have to await
subsequent development:

> I do not doubt that there have been many recent changes in
> commerce and communication, many of which are not antici-
> pated by our precedents. But this case does not present any of
> these issues. So I think it unwise to announce a rule of broad
> applicability without full consideration of the modern-day con-
> sequences.[32]

Writing for the three dissenters, Justice Ginsburg appeared to
hearken back to the broad jurisdictional view of Justice Brennan.
She argued that J. McIntyre, by engaging an American distributor
for its products, did in fact purposefully avail itself of any forum
along the trail of commerce. To allow the company to skirt jurisdiction by creating the intermediary of a (now bankrupt) American
distributor would have unacceptable consequences:

> The modern approach to jurisdiction over corporations and
> other legal entities, ushered in by *International Shoe*, gave
> prime place to reason and fairness. Is it not fair and reason-
> able, given the mode of trading of which this case is an
> example, to require the international seller to defend at the
> place its products cause injury? Do not litigational convenience
> and choice-of-law considerations point in that direction? On
> what measure of reason and fairness can it be considered
> undue to require McIntyre UK to defend in New Jersey as an
> incident of its efforts to develop a market for its industrial
> machines anywhere and everywhere in the United States? Is
> not the burden on McIntyre UK to defend in New Jersey fair,
> i.e., a reasonable cost of transacting business internationally, in

31. *Id.* at 2789.

32. *Id.* at 2791 (Breyer, J., concurring).

comparison to the burden on Nicastro to go to Nottingham, England to gain recompense for an injury he sustained using McIntyre's product at his workplace in Saddle Brook, New Jersey?[33]

Nearly a century and a half since *Pennoyer,* the fundamentals of personal jurisdiction still offer a continuing conundrum for American law. More troubling still is the fact that, as Justice Breyer noted, the Court has yet to confront the biggest unsettling factor in the law of personal jurisdiction.

VI. Looking Forward: Personal Jurisdiction in the Internet Age.

And then came the Internet. Electronic transactions translate poorly into the language of territoriality, grounded in a common law world of face-to-face transactions among the Crown's subjects. Territoriality is perhaps the least sound basis for coming to grips with an increasingly interdependent world. And yet, there must be accountability somewhere (and probably not just anywhere) in a world where the simple click of a button may inflict injury. Transacting parties in the Internet world may never meet, and they interact outside any concrete setting. Concepts of territoriality have almost no meaning in this context if one looks to the typical indicia of entry into the forum. There are no offices, no advertising directed at that forum in particular, not even a check drawn on a local bank since Internet transactions most often involve credit card payments handled not by the defendant but by a special Internet provider. Nor is there often any reason to know of the forum in which the other party is operating. However, none of this prevents the parties from becoming embroiled in dispute.

Two different categories of cases highlight the problems created by the Internet. The first is the direct analogue to *International Shoe,* the out-of-state firm that sells to an in-state buyer over the Internet. Unlike the seller in *International Shoe,* however, the cyberspace transaction occurs not because of the defendant's "presence" in the state, and perhaps not even at the initiation of the defendant. Rather, companies are routinely drawn into the forum state by the action of the buyer who clicks through various websites, finds a desired product, and then makes payment through some Internet billing firm. To speak of "purposeful availment" or even "foreseeability" in such circumstances stretches these concepts to the breaking point. At most, a seller puts up a web page

---

33. *Id.* at 2800–01 (Ginsburg, J., dissenting).

and allows prospective buyers to draw the seller into the forum. It is as if the stream of commerce comes to the seller, rather than vice versa. In such a world, everything is foreseeable, but this type of foreseeability is limitless.

By and large, courts have had reasonable success with the Internet sales cases. Following the well-regarded approach from *Zippo Manufacturing Company v. Zippo Dot Com, Inc.*,[34] courts have distinguished between passive web sites that are intended for informational purposes and interactive sites that are designed to invite commercial transactions. Thus, in *Zippo*, the court had to determine whether there was personal jurisdiction in Pennsylvania over a California corporation that used the word "Zippo" in its Internet domain name. Suit was brought by the manufacturer of Zippo lighters, claiming trademark infringement. The defendant moved to dismiss for lack of personal jurisdiction on the grounds that all of its contacts with Pennsylvania had occurred over the Internet, where Pennsylvania residents had signed up for Zippo's service using on-line agreement forms. Although there was no physical contact between the defendant and the forum, the court stated that, as the Internet expanded, so too must the jurisdiction analysis. Key to the court's decision was the knowing and repeated processing of Pennsylvania commercial transactions, even if initiated by the Pennsylvania purchasers. Knowingly servicing these transactions both constituted purposeful availment of the forum by Zippo Dot Com, Inc. and satisfied minimum contacts. As for fair play and substantial justice, the court credited the strong interest of the state in adjudicating trademark infringement suits and the Pennsylvanian plaintiff corporation's interest in choosing Pennsylvania as its forum. It found that those concerns outweighed the burden on the defendant.

It is not difficult to see *Zippo* as simply the extension of the *International Shoe* commitment to allow states to police commercial conduct within their frontiers, even if the seller can maintain a formal separation from the forum state. But the problem is much more difficult if we imagine an Internet spin on *Keeton v. Hustler*. Imagine a weblog or a chat room in which there is no direct commercial enterprise, but there is also no physical constraint on its reach. Imagine that someone is aggrieved by the publication of unflattering information or photos or even defamation through the web medium. Under the rule of personal jurisdiction announced in *Keeton*, the fact of publication in the forum was a sufficient basis for suit to go forward there. But web-based publication is not an act

34. 952 F.Supp. 1119 (W.D. Pa. 1997).

of willful entry into the forum by the defendant, nor is it on this account an attempt to reap the benefits of commercial contacts with people in the forum. Mechanically applied, the *Keeton* rule would expose any individual with a home web page to potential suit anywhere the web page is opened, a clearly absurd result. On the other hand, it is difficult to say to someone who is defamed in her home forum that she should have to chase the offending web publisher to remote corners of the country, or the world, in order to protect her interests. The best that can be said is that these further reaches of personal jurisdiction for broadcasting across the web are wildly undecided.

VII.   Conclusion.

The development of personal jurisdiction law gives the strong sense of doctrine chasing its tail. It may be, as this chapter suggests, that the Supreme Court can do little better than to find the jurisdictional equivalent of the familiar *Mathews* balance. At the same time, however, there is a cost associated with uncertainty and the prospect of secondary litigation not over the merits of a dispute, but over the reaches of a court's authority.

Before concluding, however, it is worth commenting on why the doctrines in this area are ultimately unsatisfying. The difficulty comes primarily from the attempt to translate the common law precepts of sovereignty developed in England under the Crown to a far different world. In part, the problem is a historical one: sovereignty-based principles of jurisdiction map poorly onto an expansive territory with 50 state sovereigns and a federal government sitting astride all of them. More fundamentally, however, as the cases from *International Shoe* to *Zippo* show, the problem is not that there are too many state sovereigns, but that they are really not sovereign at all. Fundamentally, and particularly in the commercial domain where so many of the contested jurisdictional issues arise, there is really only one sovereign and that is the market. It is an unrelenting sovereign that moves with great facility across state lines and, increasingly, international lines as well. Not only does it not confine its activities to one territory, but in its Internet form, it is hard to define its corporeal form. *Capias ad respondendum* may have been of some fleeting help in the days of *Pennoyer*, if even then. But it does not begin to address the problems of consumer-initiated entry into a forum for a cyberspace transaction, or the posting of offensive materials unrelated to any prospective transaction.

Chapter 6

FEDERALISM

As we have seen, the concept of personal jurisdiction is historically drawn from the idea of sovereignty. At English common law, courts were a projection of the power of the crown and derived their authority from the enforceability of their decrees through the territorial reach of the sovereign's might. Whatever the complications in projecting the narrow vision of territorial sovereignty onto a mobile population, corporate actors, and a robust national and international market, at least the idea of a state as a defined sovereign entity bore some relation to its common law antecedents.

Not so when we move to a distinct variant of jurisdiction called subject matter jurisdiction. Here we do not refer to the power of a court to adjudicate a dispute and impose its decree on a party or on a contested piece of property. That is the domain of personal jurisdiction in its *in personam*, *in rem*, or *quasi in rem* forms. With subject matter jurisdiction, our focus shifts from the power to enforce decrees concerning particular parties or property to the question of whether a particular court has the authority to pass on a particular issue of law.

The question of subject matter jurisdiction is an outgrowth of our federal system. One of the significant innovations of the American Constitution was the expansive use of checks and balances across the many institutions of government—what Madison referred to as the checking function by which "ambition must be made to counteract ambition" in efforts at aggrandizement of power.[1] Perhaps the most distinct innovation was the idea of shared power or dual sovereignty between the federal and state governments. Whereas the political thought of the day held, per Montesquieu, that power must ultimately reside in one sovereign, the Framers set upon creating a system of competing power divided between the states and the federal government.

Competing claims of sovereignty between state and federal courts emerge not with personal jurisdiction, where the two court systems generally share the reach of the authority of the state in which they sit, but with the types of cases that each court system may entertain. Even under the American system of dual sovereignty, there need not have been rivalrous sources of judicial power. The original constitutional design entertained the possibility, but

---

1. THE FEDERALIST NO. 51, at 322 (James Madison) (Jacob E. Cooke ed., 1961).

not the necessity, of a federal court system. Article III of the Constitution vests the judicial power of the federal government in one Supreme Court and "in such inferior Courts as the Congress may from time to time ordain and establish." The key actors in the original system of dual sovereignty were the state courts, who would be called upon not only to enforce the laws of their home states, but, in the absence of any system of lower federal courts, would be obligated to enforce federal law as well. This is the import of the Supremacy Clause[2] of the Constitution, which provides:

> This Constitution, and the Laws of the United States which shall be made in Pursuance thereof; and all Treaties made, or which shall be made, under the Authority of the United States, shall be the supreme Law of the Land; and the Judges in every State shall be bound thereby, any Thing in the Constitution or Laws of any State to the Contrary notwithstanding.

The attempt to administer dual sovereignty through a single court system was abandoned before it began. The first Congress passed the Judiciary Act of 1789, which established a system of federal district and appellate courts. The result was a dual court system, each part with ultimate right of appeal to the Supreme Court, and a corresponding need to decide which courts would be entrusted with which matters. The question of subject matter jurisdiction is a by-product of this division between state and federal court systems and of the increasingly overlapping subject matters of state and federal law. In short, the issues of subject matter jurisdiction are an unintended consequence of the uneasy division of juridical authority between the states and the federal government.

Even with the establishment of a distinct federal court system, however, the original constitutional design still has bearing on the relative roles of federal and state courts. The Supremacy Clause presumes that state courts will be established to hear state law claims, and that they will entertain claims arising under the Constitution, treaties, and laws of the United States as well. Because of the presumption that state courts are able to hear all manner of legal claims, they are referred to as courts of *general subject matter jurisdiction*. The concept of general subject matter jurisdiction refers to the range of cases that a state court may hear, and should not be confused with the general jurisdiction of a home state for *in personam* personal jurisdiction purposes. In addition, many states limit the subject matter jurisdiction of courts by, for example, allowing claims below a certain dollar amount to be

---

2. U.S. CONST. art. VI, § 1, cl. 2.

asserted in small claims courts. There are also some federal statutes—such as bankruptcy, copyright, and pension regulation—that confer exclusive subject matter jurisdiction in certain areas on the federal courts. Nonetheless, broadly speaking, state courts are presumed capable of hearing all manner of state and federal claims.

By contrast, federal courts are the products of the specific acts of Congress in creating them and vesting them with the power to hear specified claims. Federal courts are therefore deemed to be courts of *limited subject matter jurisdiction.* Any complaint filed in federal court must begin with the claimed statutory basis by which Congress conferred the subject matter jurisdiction of the court. Similarly, among the Rule 12(b) defenses, the first and most privileged defense for actions in federal court is the 12(b)(1) assertion that the district court is without subject matter jurisdiction—a defense that, when "suggested" by a party or in any other way presented to the court, may result in the dismissal of a case, even on appeal. It is the only one of the Rule 12(b) defenses that is never waived.

Under Article III of the Constitution, federal judicial power extends to all cases that arise under the Constitution, the laws, and the treaties of the United States. This is known as federal question subject matter jurisdiction. Also under Article III, the federal judicial power reaches controversies between citizens of different states. This is known as diversity subject matter jurisdiction. Here again it must be emphasized that Article III of the Constitution only authorizes that the judicial power reach both cases arising under federal law and cases involving diverse parties. The Constitution does not mandate that lower federal courts actually exist or that, if they are brought into being, they be vested with the full range of constitutional power. That remains the decision of the Congress.

At the time of the passage of the Judiciary Act of 1789, federal courts were considered necessary to overcome local prejudice in cases involving out-of-state defendants. Congress feared that hometown sentiment could sway state judges to favor parties to whom they were politically accountable. Thus, federal courts were initially created to hear cases arising under the Constitution's diversity jurisdiction. Until the period following the Civil War, cases arising directly under federal law were the province of the state courts, with ultimate appellate review by the U.S. Supreme Court. As we shall see, the areas of federal question jurisdiction, now codified as 28 U.S.C. § 1331, and diversity jurisdiction, in turn codified as 28 U.S.C. § 1332, remain the primary grants of authority to federal courts to adjudicate disputes.

The original structure of the court system reflected the relative importance of state authority in the early American republic, and the more limited role to be played by the federal government. That system accordingly presumed the primacy of state courts for the adjudication of all legal claims, regardless of their source in state or federal law. The concept of subject matter jurisdiction, as it initially developed, reflected the states' status as the primary regulators of conduct through tort, contract, and property laws. This is consistent with the role of the states as the prime governors of citizen behavior. Under this view, lower federal courts filled in only to protect against local prejudice against out-of-state parties.

The world we live in now is fundamentally different from the one envisioned in the first Judiciary Act. In the latter part of the twentieth century, the rise of the national market economy, coupled with the Supreme Court's expansive interpretation of Congress's Commerce Clause powers, provided Congress with both the motivation and the ability to regulate many types of economic activity that had previously been supervised at the state level. The rise of the modern regulatory state has, in turn, altered the roles played by the two court systems. Today, federal courts operate primarily to entertain claims brought under the expanding universe of federal law. State courts, by contrast, hear primarily state law claims.

I. Diversity Jurisdiction.

As mentioned above, federal courts derive their subject matter jurisdiction from statutes. Article III, § 1 of the Constitution gives Congress the power to create the lower courts, while § 2 defines the scope of the judicial power, which includes controversies "between citizens of different states." Congress may grant jurisdiction to the lower courts within the bounds of the judicial power as defined by § 2. In creating the lower federal courts through the Judiciary Act of 1789, now codified at 28 U.S.C. § 1332, the first Congress statutorily vested them with diversity jurisdiction, and diversity jurisdiction alone.

Diversity jurisdiction gives the federal courts the ability to hear cases between citizens from different states, as long as the amount in controversy requirement is satisfied. Currently, the amount in controversy requirement is $75,000, and is measured at the outset of the litigation by the amount reasonably claimed by the plaintiff in her complaint. Thus, if the plaintiff pleads an amount greater than $75,000 in her complaint, or if that amount is reasonably ascribed to the claim, the amount in controversy requirement would still be satisfied even if she eventually loses, or prevails for an amount less than $75,000.

Focusing on *ex ante* valuation has independent significance. As will be discussed more fully in Chapter 7's examination of the preclusion doctrines, it is important to give all parties finality in litigation for reasons of both fairness and efficiency. We have already seen in the personal jurisdiction context that a judgment entered in the absence of proper jurisdiction is void. The same principle applies even more strongly with regard to subject matter jurisdiction. Thus, Rule 12(b)(1) preserves the ability to dismiss an action for lack of subject matter jurisdiction, even on appeal. Were the amount in controversy to be assessed *ex post* rather than *ex ante*, then in any case in which a plaintiff lost or in which the award did not reach the jurisdictional threshold, there would be no jurisdiction, and, in turn, there would be no judgment. As a result, the plaintiff would be in the enviable position of either trying the case to a favorable outcome or having the opportunity to try the claim again in state court if the first case was deemed a nullity for having failed the jurisdictional threshold. The defendant would be correspondingly prejudiced by the unenviable options of losing outright or winning only the ability to defend again.

The second requirement for the exercise of diversity subject matter jurisdiction is, as the name implies, diversity of citizenship. Diversity jurisdiction requires "perfect diversity," interpreted by the Supreme Court in *Strawbridge v. Curtiss*[3] as necessitating that all plaintiffs must be diverse from all defendants. As a practical matter, this means simply that all parties on one side of the "v." in the caption of the case must be from a different state than all parties on the other side of the "v."[4] Citizenship for diversity purposes is determined by an individual's state of domicile, which is in turn defined as a party's "true, fixed, and permanent home and principal establishment, and to which he has the intention of returning whenever he is absent therefrom...."[5]

Diversity jurisdiction makes up a declining portion of the docket of federal courts, in part because federal judges are not generally welcoming of diversity cases, and in part because of the ratcheting up of the jurisdictional amount to its present level of

---

3. 7 U.S. (3 Cranch) 267 (1806).

4. This requirement is not constitutionally established, however, and the Court has held that the federal interpleader statute may allow diversity jurisdiction whenever at least two parties are diverse. State Farm Fire & Cas. Co. v. Tashire, 386 U.S. 523 (1967).

5. Mas v. Perry, 489 F.2d 1396, 1399 (5th Cir. 1974) (internal quotation marks omitted).

$75,000. But the definition of domicile for diversity purposes raises yet another problem with the continued need for this kind of jurisdiction. The concept of "domicile" as applied in defining jurisdiction assumes a sense of permanence that becomes increasingly questionable in a highly mobile society. Under the facts of one leading case,[6] a woman who had grown up in her parents' home in Mississippi was deemed a domiciliary there, even though in the intervening years she had married a Frenchman, gone off to school as an undergraduate, lived in Louisiana as a graduate student, and would later be seeking to move to an academic position, with no particular intent ever to return to Mississippi. Under the peculiarities of the law of domicile, her domicile was fixed in the last state to which her sense of permanence attached, even if that had to go back to her schoolgirl days in her parents' home.

There are some perverse consequences from tying diversity jurisdiction to antiquated notions of domicile. Similarly situated people facing a tort or contract claim can find themselves in federal court instead of a state court depending on whether one of the parties is deemed a domiciliary of another state. With a highly mobile population, many of whom have less than permanent attachments to the jurisdiction in which they happen to reside, there is the risk that divergent rules and responsibilities will emerge for everyday conduct depending on the happenstance of being in state or federal court. The logic behind raising the jurisdictional amount in diversity cases is that these are ultimately state law matters for which it may be presumed that state courts have greater expertise in the substantive area of law governing the claim. But assigning citizenship to a state other than the one in which a person functionally resides cuts in the opposite direction by increasing the proportion of the population that might find itself in federal court for relatively routine tort or even contract matters. Why should the Mississippi-raised graduate student living in Louisiana have the ability to bring her auto accident claim in a different court than the graduate student sitting next to her in class who grew up in Louisiana?

At the time the definitions of diversity developed, the population generally did stay in one place for a long time. As a result, little rested on the precision or imprecision of the definition of domicile, so long as some protection could be given to citizens of one state who faced prejudice in another state's courts. But the definition of who needs protection has not kept abreast of society's changes. Today, citizenship is much more likely established by

6. *Id.*

where an individual lives, or is registered to vote, or has been issued a driver's license, or has a checking account, than where she last lived with her parents. Increased mobility and the homogenization of the national economy combined with the rise of the national regulatory state have undermined the narrow assumptions of regionalism that undergird the inherited definitions of domicile. The tensions between modern life and the policies that underlie diversity jurisdiction raise serious concerns for the overall legal system, including judicial economy, a distaste for forum-shopping, and the reservation of the federal courts for issues of federal law.

II. Federal Question Jurisdiction.

Just as the importance of diversity cases in the dockets of federal courts diminished, the attention paid to federal question cases correspondingly rose. This required increased attention to the prerequisites for federal question jurisdiction to be properly exercised. In large part, the transformative events in federal question subject matter jurisdiction occurred far outside the world of decisional law. Most centrally, the Civil War altered the traditional relationship between state and federal powers. The Civil War amendments to the Constitution increased federal oversight of the relation between the states and their citizens and created a need for additional sources of federal jurisdiction.

While the power to extend the reach of federal judicial authority existed from the time of the original Constitution, Congress did not act on that power until after the Civil War. Under Article III, § 2 of the Constitution, "the Judicial Power shall extend to all Cases, in Law and Equity, arising under this Constitution, the Laws of the United States, and Treaties made or which shall be made, under their Authority...." Only in 1875 did Congress pass the Second Judiciary Act, now codified at 28 U.S.C. § 1331, which states that: "The district courts shall have original jurisdiction of all civil actions arising under the Constitution, laws, or treaties of the United States."

Prior to 1875, the judicial power of the United States was exercised by state judges, who were obligated by the Supremacy Clause of the Constitution to execute faithfully the laws of the United States. After 1875, however, federal and state judiciary powers were bifurcated, with federal power redirected toward federal questions and state power toward state questions. This split has become more pronounced over time. Since the 1920s, there has been no amount in controversy requirement for federal question jurisdiction, while the requirement for diversity jurisdiction has risen to $75,000. As a result of both increased jurisdictional requirements and temperament, federal courts have become overall less welcoming to state law cases brought under diversity jurisdiction.

Even with the passage of 28 U.S.C. § 1331, however, it was unclear what it would mean for cases to "arise under" federal law. The classic exposition was found in *Louisville & Nashville Railroad v. Mottley,*[7] which defined the "arising under" requirement to pertain to the plaintiff's complaint, and not to the defendant's answer. In *Mottley,* the plaintiffs had sued over personal injuries suffered in a railway accident and had settled their claim in exchange for—what else?—lifetime railroad passes. Their settlement proceeds proved short-lived because Congress, acting on its concern over fraudulent stock issuances by railroad companies, had passed legislation voiding all off-the-books contractual obligations by railroads, sweeping in the Mottleys' free passes.

The Mottleys, not surprisingly, sought to enforce their contractual rights to free lifetime passes. The problem was that even though they were suing as plaintiffs in a contract claim governed by state law, the ultimate issue in the case would be the authority of Congress retroactively to void existing contractual expectations. The Mottleys brought suit in federal court, anticipating that the Railroad would plead the new federal law as an affirmative defense to its breach of contract, and assuming that federal question jurisdiction would cover the litigation of the constitutionality of the new statute. The Supreme Court, however, held that the case did not present a federal question, because, looking just within the four corners of the complaint, no federal question was presented. On its face, the complaint charged only a breach of contract, a state law claim which, failing the requirements of diversity jurisdiction, did not fall within the contours of federal court jurisdiction. Accordingly, the case was dismissed for lack of federal subject matter jurisdiction. The Mottleys were then left to replead the suit in state court, only to have the Railroad assert the federal law as a defense to voluntary breach. The case went all the way to the Supreme Court (again), where the Court held that the federal statute was constitutional, the very issue the Mottleys sought to test in the first place.

Implicit in *Mottley* is a recognition that, with the expansion of federal regulatory power, there would have to be a realignment of the responsibility of federal and state courts. *Mottley* imposed no restriction on the power of the federal government to assume

7.   211 U.S. 149 (1908).

authority under the Commerce Clause of the Constitution to regulate greater portions of the Nation's life. Indeed, the ultimate holding on the second appeal gave the federal government broad powers to intercede in matters traditionally handled as a question of state contract law. The *Mottley* rule did, however, limit the ability of federal courts to assume increased federal power through an accretion of their common law ability to create new legal duties. This limitation on the powers of the federal courts to reach beyond congressional proclamations of a federal interest would later emerge as the core of the *Erie* doctrine[8]—as will be discussed in Section VII, below. But even at a time of expansive intervention by federal courts, the period characterized by the substantive due process doctrine of *Lochner v. New York*,[9] the *Mottley* rule required express invocation in the complaint of a distinct federal interest before federal courts could entertain a claim. As would later emerge full blown in *Erie,* the Court was drawing a distinction between the seemingly inevitable expansion of federal legislative power in the post-Civil War era, and the more circumscribed role of federal judicial power.

III.   The Boundaries of State Law in the Modern Era.

The jurisdictional grants under 28 U.S.C. §§ 1331 and 1332 neatly draw a divide between the world of federal law and traditional areas of state law, primarily common law. But with the increased reach of federal regulatory law, and with states willing to pass their own versions of antitrust or civil rights laws, this clean separation between federal and state law does not hold up. *Mottley* establishes only that whatever serves as the federal jurisdictional basis for suit in a federal question case must be apparent on the face of the complaint. It does not, however, define the federal interest itself.

In the leading case of *Merrell Dow Pharmaceuticals, Inc. v. Thompson*,[10] the Supreme Court confronted the definition of a "federal question" in deciding whether the mention of a federal statute on the face of a complaint was a sufficient basis for federal jurisdiction. The case involved Scottish and Canadian plaintiffs who claimed to have suffered birth defects resulting from their mothers' ingestion of the drug Bendectin during pregnancy. These foreign plaintiffs had brought state tort law claims in Ohio state court

---

8.   *See* Erie Railroad Co. v. Tompkins, 304 U.S. 64 (1938).

9.   198 U.S. 45 (1905).

10.   478 U.S. 804 (1986).

against Merrell Dow, the manufacturer of the drug. The plaintiffs wanted to bring suit in the United States to obtain some of the benefits of American tort law relative to that of their home countries. Oddly, in order to stay in American courts, they had to avoid presenting a federal claim. The Ohio federal courts had already ruled that suit should not go forward in the U.S. because the home court systems of the plaintiffs were a more suitable forum for their claims. This is the prudential doctrine known as *forum non conveniens,* which provides a discretionary basis for the dismissal of even jurisdictionally-proper claims that are, in the court's view, best litigated elsewhere. As a result, if there were any basis for removal of the Ohio state court cases to federal court, the cases would have been dismissed because of the federal court's prior determination of *forum non conveniens.* Nonetheless, plaintiffs did not want to avoid all questions of federal law, even though that might prompt removal to federal court. Plaintiffs sought to establish the manufacturer's liability premised in part on the failure to label adequately under a federal statute, the Food, Drug, and Cosmetic Act (FDCA).[11] According to the complaint, the misbranding of Bendectin in violation of the Act created a rebuttable presumption of negligence and was a proximate cause of the harms suffered. Thus, the plaintiffs sought to bootstrap the federal standard for labeling onto the state common law tort of negligence, the result of which would be to make Merrell Dow liable under state law for the breach of federal regulatory obligations—an example of the complicated hybrid quality of state and federal substantive law.

Merrell Dow provided the Supreme Court with an opportunity to revisit and clarify the three ways in which a federal question may be presented for subject matter jurisdiction purposes. First, and most simply, are "[t]he 'vast majority' of cases ... covered by Justice Holmes's statement that a 'suit arises under the law that creates the cause of action.' "[12] Under what is known as the "Holmes test," federal question subject matter jurisdiction exists where federal law specifically creates the cause of action. Thus, a plaintiff suing under a federal civil rights statute, or in antitrust or securities law, is claiming recovery directly under the statute that controls the case. In *Merrell Dow,* however, the underlying federal statute, the FDCA, simply required labeling and did not provide any private right for an aggrieved individual to claim damages from the failure to comply with the federal labeling requirement. Since

11.   12 U.S.C. § 301.

12.   478 U.S. at 808 (*quoting* Franchise Tax Board v. Construction Laborers Vacation Trust, 463 U.S. 1, 8–9 (1983) (*quoting* American Well Works Co. v. Layne & Bowler Co., 241 U.S. 257, 260 (1916) (Holmes, J.))).

the plaintiffs claimed recovery under state tort law and not the FDCA, their suit could not fall under the "Holmes test," even though the tort claims did incorporate the federal law as evidence of Merrell Dow's failure to meet the required standard of care.

Even if a federal statute does not directly create a "private right of action," meaning it does not provide an express basis for an aggrieved party to sue for recovery under its provisions, the Court recognized an alternative approach. As a result of a drafting error or an unanticipated anomaly, a statute may be thought to have an implied private right of action based on federal law that would constitute a federal question for purposes of jurisdiction. This situation arises most often when Congress passes a regulatory statute but does not expressly create a private right of action under it. For example, Title VII of the Civil Rights Act of 1964, which prohibits employment discrimination, creates an express private right of action allowing individual plaintiffs to recover damages upon proving that the statute has been violated. A corresponding section of the same Act, Title VI, which covers housing as opposed to employment discrimination, does not address the ability of individual plaintiffs to bring suit under its provisions. However, the statutes are designed in similar fashion to achieve similar aims and without a private right of action, Title VI would fail in its purposes. Courts therefore interpret Title VI to create what is termed "an implied private right of action" in order to further the statutory objective. As the Court explained in *Merrell Dow*, there is a "settled framework for evaluating whether a[n implied] federal cause of action lies."[13] This framework evaluates the following four factors: 1) whether plaintiffs are part of a class for whose special benefit the statute was passed; 2) whether there is evidence of a legislative intent to create or not create a private right of action; 3) whether a federal cause of action would further the underlying purpose of the legislation; and 4) whether the subject of the statute is one not traditionally relegated to state law. Although the Court elucidated this test in *Merrell Dow*, the issue was not directly presented for resolution and the Court did not find it necessary to decide in that case whether the FDCA should be read to imply a private right to sue based on mislabeling.

The most difficult area of federal question subject matter jurisdiction was the third approach, what is termed the "federal ingredient" test. This is the aspect of potential federal jurisdiction presented in *Merrell Dow*. The question here is whether the state law claim ultimately turned so indispensably on interpretation of

---

13.   *Id.* at 810.

federal law as to render it, for all intents and purposes, a federal claim. This presents a complicated question of allocation of responsibility between state and federal courts. We should start from the premise that the central thrust of contemporary subject matter jurisdiction law is that state courts should be the primary forum for resolving state law claims and federal courts the primary forum for addressing questions of federal law. In part, this reflects the initial divides of federalism.[14] But in large part this division of labor corresponds to the efficient use of the comparative expertise of each court system. State courts are more expert at questions of state law, particularly state common law. Federal courts not only have greater expertise in addressing questions of federal law, but the resolution of these issues by federal courts promotes an important interest in having uniform bodies of federal law. Much of the justification for subjecting important areas of our economic and social life to federal oversight is the need for uniform regulation of matters such as copyright or bankruptcy. It would be anomalous to enable federal oversight on this basis and then leave the interpretation and implementation to state courts acting more or less autonomously. Bringing federal law questions to federal court allows oversight by the circuit courts of appeals and allows much greater coordination through the developing law of each circuit that controls subsequent cases. The alternative would be proceeding in more spasmodic fashion through the state courts, with the only centralizing and unifying force being the remote possibility of U.S. Supreme Court review of state court final decisions.

As with all areas of law, the borders are hard to police. The question under the "federal ingredient" test is whether an interpretation of federal law is so integral to the resolution of a dispute that the state court would be required to interpret federal law in some dispositive fashion. Ultimately the definition of the federal ingredient forces courts to define the relative authority of state and federal courts in regard to the importance of the competing state and federal interests. Too broad a definition of the "federal ingredient" would risk federalizing traditional areas of common law, as so much of daily market transactions with goods and services that might give rise to a contract or tort claim are in turn covered by some aspect of federal regulatory law. On the other hand, too narrow a definition risks balkanizing federal regulations by leaving their interpretation to uncoordinated state courts.

---

14. For a fuller exposition of this point, see Barry Friedman, *Under the Law of Federal Jurisdiction: Allocating Cases Between Federal and State Courts,* 104 Colum. L. Rev. 1211 (2004).

The Court in *Merrell Dow* split five to four on the definition of the federal ingredient. The narrow majority held that the incorporation of the FDCA as evidence of negligence did not present a sufficient federal ingredient to justify federal question jurisdiction, even if a state court would have to rule on the application 'of the FDCA to the labeling of Bendectin. The majority narrowed the test for the "federal ingredient" to require some evidence that the statutory scheme would be advanced by allowing lawsuits by private parties. In effect this all but collapsed the "federal ingredient" test into little more than a restatement of the test for an implied right of action. For causes of action arising under state law, the Court ultimately reasoned, the primacy of the state interest should direct litigants to state courts.

Merrell Dow proved not to be the last word on the federal ingredient test. Most recently, in *Grable & Sons Metal Products, Inc. v. Darue Engineering & Manufacturing,*[15] the Court confronted a state claim to settle the rights to a piece of property that Grable had forfeited to the IRS for failing to pay taxes and that the IRS had resold to Darue, an odd replay of the property dispute in *Pennoyer*. Such a claim—termed an action to "quiet title"—is about as prototypical a state court action as one could envision. The difficulty in the case lay in the fact that Grable claimed that his property had been improperly seized because the IRS had not provided him with the proper form of notice required by the relevant federal tax statute. Thus, the state court claim could not be adjudicated without an examination of the underlying federal issue, the same problem the Court had confronted in *Merrell Dow*.

When Darue sought to remove the action to federal court, the limitations imposed by *Merrell Dow* became apparent. Despite the strong interest in national uniformity in the application of federal tax law, the underlying tax statute did not provide an express private right of action, and could not be read to imply one. Darue therefore sought removal on the ground that the ruling would invariably turn on the correct application of federal tax law, something that required both expertise and predictability of treatment that could only be achieved in federal court.

The clear federal interest in uniform application of the tax laws proved overwhelming, and the Supreme Court unanimously upheld the removal. In order to do so, however, the Court had to reject any reading of *Merrell Dow* that would have required either an express or an implied federal cause of action as a necessary condition for

---

15.   545 U.S. 308 (2005). For further discussion of the relation between *Grable* and the scope of federal power, see Samuel Issacharoff and Catherine M. Sharkey, *Backdoor Federalization*, 53 UCLA L. REV. 1353, 1413–14 (2006).

exercising federal question jurisdiction. This created a precarious balance, for without *Merrell Dow's* limitation, the broad scope of federal regulation threatened to bring vast swaths of state law under federal court oversight. Seeking to limit the impact of its decision, the Court stressed that not just any federal ingredient would suffice. In particular, the Court refused to adopt a "general rule" permitting federal jurisdiction in "garden variety" tort suits alleging a violation of some federal statute that did not serve as the basis for recovery.[16] Instead, as a subsequent case explained, *Grable* attempted to craft a rule that would apply to a "special and small category" of cases involving "a nearly 'pure issue of law ... that could be settled once and for all and therefore would govern numerous tax sale cases.' "[17] Whether this formulation will hold over time remains to be seen. What seems clear is that, even after *Grable*, the Court is still trying to protect state courts as the presumptively proper forum for the vast majority of causes of action arising under state law.

IV.   The Boundaries of Federal Law.

While most cases addressing the limits of federal subject matter jurisdiction arise when a federal court must determine whether it may adjudicate a state law claim, there are cases that ask whether a state court may hear a claim that may be subject to exclusive *federal* court review. The federal Copyright Act, for example, directs that federal district courts shall have *exclusive*, original jurisdiction "of any civil actions arising under any Act of Congress relating to ... copyrights."[18] Because the Act's grant of jurisdiction is exclusive, it serves to prohibit state courts from hearing claims that pertain to copyright.

Were a case to be brought exclusively as a matter of the protectability of a copyright interest, there would be little difficulty in enforcing the Copyright Act's grant of jurisdiction exclusively to federal courts. But there are also cases that are brought under state law, such as with a breach of contract claim, in which the presiding court may be called upon to examine copyright issues in conjunction with the contract or, potentially, as a defense to the state law claim. These cases thus pose the same policy tensions seen in *Merrell Dow* and *Grable*. On the one hand, an expansive definition

---

16.   *Id.* at 319 (distinguishing *Merrell Dow*).

17.   Empire HealthChoice Assurance, Inc. v. McVeigh, 547 U.S. 677, 699–700 (2006) (quoting Richard H. Fallon, Jr., Daniel J. Meltzer & Daniel L. Shapiro, Hart and Wechsler's The Federal Courts and the Federal System 65 (Supp. 2005)).

18.   28 U.S.C. § 1338(a).

of "relating to copyright" could conceivably sweep into exclusive federal court jurisdiction any state law contract or fraud claim that addressed matters potentially implicating intellectual property. On the other hand, a restrictive interpretation of "relating to copyright" threatens to undermine the policy determination of Congress that the importance of copyright demands coherent federal stewardship of the Nation's intellectual property.

Typically, the division between the two approaches turns on the question whether the federal copyright interest must be present on the face of the complaint or whether courts should inquire as to the anticipated defenses and evidence to discern whether copyright emerges as the "essence of the dispute." The dispute between these two approaches echoes the one in *Mottley*. The crux of the issue is whether, in light of the significant federal interest in copyright, federal question subject matter jurisdiction may only be found if asserted on the face of the complaint. By and large, courts have tried to mediate this tension, in much the same way that *Merrell Dow* sought to protect the integrity of state common law even in an era of regulation, by weighing the competing federal and state interests. The classic articulation of the delightfully named "thoughtful synthesis" approach is found in Judge Friendly's opinion in *T.B. Harms Co. v. Eliscu*.[19] Judge Friendly held that an action "arises under" the Copyright Act "only if the complaint is for a remedy expressly granted by the Act, e.g., a suit for infringement" or if the complaint "asserts a claim requiring construction of the Act,"[20] but then directed courts to balance the competing claims of federal and state law as reflected in the "essence of the dispute." By placing the focus of the jurisdictional inquiry on the contents of the complaint, Judge Friendly in effect imports the *Mottley* test to determine whether there is federal subject matter jurisdiction at all, but then applies a broader test to decide whether the Copyright Act vested federal courts with exclusive federal subject matter jurisdiction over the dispute. There are two facets to the Friendly rule, one implicating federal versus state policy concerns and the other turning on the successful administration of the courts.

In the first instance, Judge Friendly reiterates the fundamental concern that an expansive view of federal subject matter jurisdiction based on the mere presence of a domain of federally regulated conduct would sweep too far. Just as the presence of a federal labeling regulation could not transform a state tort law claim into a predominately federal action in *Merrell Dow*, so too the mere

19.   339 F.2d 823 (2d Cir. 1964).
20.   *Id.* at 828.

presence of an intellectual property issue should not immediately transform state law claims into exclusively federal ones. One could well imagine, for example, two parties disputing their relative shares of a business that in turn owns copyrighted works. Even though the intellectual property may be covered by copyright, the disagreement about the relative shares of ownership is a simple common law dispute, no different than if the individuals disagreed over their relative shares in a business that owned a tract of land. Thus, according to Judge Friendly, the mere fact that works may be subject to copyright "has not been thought to infuse with any national interest a dispute as to ownership or contractual enforcement turning on the facts or on ordinary principles of contract law."[21]

Perhaps more significant is the perceived need for bright-line rules concerning subject matter jurisdiction. While the application of federal procedural law has moved largely in the direction of standards rather than rules, as has been chronicled throughout this book, subject matter jurisdiction is a trap for the unwary. The constitutional concern that judgments entered in the absence of appropriate jurisdiction are a nullity is reflected in the Rules of Civil Procedure. Not only does lack of subject matter jurisdiction lead off the defenses as Rule 12(b)(1), but alone among the defenses identified in Rule 12, it is lack of subject matter jurisdiction that under Rule 12(h)(3) may be raised at any time in the litigation, including on appeal, and that may be addressed *sua sponte* by the court. The entire litigation system faces the prospect of tremendous dead-weight losses if cases are litigated extensively only to discover late in the day that all was for naught, or if parties strategically gamed the system by litigating cases in hope of a favorable outcome then challenged jurisdiction once the bloom was off the rose. Moreover, the purposes of Rule 12 would be frustrated if the interpretation of the federal interest underlying subject matter jurisdiction could not be determined at the threshold stages of litigation, but only after considerable immersion into the merits of the case. The function of Rule 12 as the legal gatekeeper to the system (as discussed in Chapter 2) would effectively be compromised if the conditions necessary for testing the legal sufficiency of claims could only be established through facts underlying the merits of the dispute.

In a subsequent Second Circuit opinion, the concern over effective administration led Judge Leval to reject the "essence of the dispute" approach for its compromise of both predictability for

---

21. *Id.* at 826.

the parties and administrability for the courts. Because the "essence of the dispute" might be "based more on the defense than on the demands asserted in the complaint, the plaintiff's attorney can have no way of telling whether the action should be filed with the exclusive jurisdiction of the federal court or in state court."[22] In like fashion, a court reviewing a motion to dismiss for lack of subject matter jurisdiction would have no means to determine whether the ultimate essence of the case would turn on copyright claims not yet in evidence, or on contract or property claims independent of any federal interest.

The example of copyright, in the more acute context of exclusive federal court subject matter jurisdiction, lends some insight into the stability of the *Mottley* rule over nearly a century. Much like the *Erie* Doctrine, to which we shall turn shortly, the *Mottley* rule seeks to preserve a respectable boundary between the proper provinces of federal and state rulemaking. It errs on the side of making rather formal, noncontextual bright-line decisions at very early stages of litigation. Here again there are fundamental policy implications for what would first appear as a highly technical rule. The assignment of jurisdictional authority to federal or state courts is a matter of administration rather than a first-order question of justice. Without an overriding equitable consideration at stake, the systemic concern for efficiency emerges front and center. That systemic concern requires a clear and dispositive resolution of jurisdiction so that the investment of resources in litigation will not be futile. While the *Mottley* opinion does not elucidate this line of reasoning, we may speculate that the efficiency gain from a bright-line rule for jurisdictional gatekeeping has contributed to the stability of *Mottley*. Many courts, the Supreme Court included, and many commentators have acknowledged that our procedural system could clearly survive a relaxation of the "four-corners" rule for determining subject matter jurisdiction. Nonetheless, the efficiency gains from having clear rules at the threshold stages of litigation have a command all their own—a command that has allowed the *Mottley* rule, despite its apparent formalism, to survive.

V. Removal and Forum Allocation.

While the *Mottley* rule anticipates a division of responsibility between state and federal courts, it is not self-executing. The presentation of a case to the proper tribunal is determined by the parties, and they in turn have bountiful strategic reasons for trying to manipulate the forum. For the plaintiff, who is in the enviable

---

22. Bassett v. Mashantucket Pequot Tribe, 204 F.3d 343, 353 (2d Cir. 2000).

position of initiating the litigation process, the initial decision is simply whether to file in state or federal court. The defendant is then in position to challenge a decision to file in federal court under a Rule 12(b)(1) motion to dismiss, or to seek to remove a case from state court to federal court under 28 U.S.C. § 1446, the federal removal statute.

Many of the leading jurisdictional cases are really battles over state versus federal courts. For example, in *Merrell Dow,* the plaintiffs had initially brought the action in the defendant's home forum, the state of Ohio, where the company was headquartered. Under the provisions of removal law, Merrell Dow could not seek to remove the case to federal court for diversity reasons because there is no diversity removal from state courts in the defendant's home state. This makes sense because the purpose of diversity-based removal is to cure hometown prejudice, and a defendant could not claim to be prejudiced by local sentiment in its home state. Thus, the defendant had to argue that a federal question existed in order to obtain removal. Any federal question would suffice to remove the case and, in light of prior court rulings, result in dismissal for *forum non conveniens.* Similarly, in the personal jurisdiction case *World–Wide Volkswagen v. Woodson,*[23] discussed in Chapter 5, the ability to sue the New York dealership in Oklahoma state court was a critical issue. The local state courts were believed to be a welcoming forum for the injured plaintiffs and the pleadings were designed to make sure that the case stayed where the plaintiffs originally filed it. Although the plaintiffs had no realistic prospect of recovering from the New York defendants, their presence in the case would have been dispositive on the choice of forum. Diversity jurisdiction, and removal based on diversity, requires complete or "perfect" diversity between all plaintiffs and all defendants. Under the facts of *World Wide Volkswagen,* the plaintiffs were still considered domiciliaries of New York, their last permanent home at the time of the accident, and the inclusion of the dealership would have defeated diversity and prevented removal. The entire fight over personal jurisdiction in that case was in fact a battle over the conditions necessary for removal of the case to federal court.

To a large extent, the *Mottley* rule gives a first-mover advantage to the plaintiff. Looking only to the complaint to determine the presence of a federal question favors plaintiffs over defendants by giving the former greater latitude in selecting a forum. The plaintiff can choose to raise only state law claims to stay in state court, raise federal claims to gain the federal forum, or sue an in-state defen-

---

23.　444 U.S. 286 (1980).

dant in order to defeat diversity. The choice between federal and state court is purely a matter of strategy not principle. One side or the other may look upon evidentiary rules more favorably in one court system. There may be advantages to the smaller area from which a jury pool is typically chosen in state court as opposed to federal court. Or the fact that state judges are oftentimes elected and potentially subject to political pressures may favor one side or the other. While these considerations are significant to the litigants, the court system as a whole has no stake in systematically favoring one side or another. Rather, the systemic interest must lie in predictability and reinforcing the general trend toward federal law cases in federal courts and state law cases in state courts.

The most contested area of law on removal is, perhaps paradoxically, the use of joinder to bring in-state nominal defendants into a case in order to prevent removal on diversity grounds. Courts have traditionally been stringent in reviewing claims of "fraudulent joinder," presumably in recognition of the principle that the plaintiff is the master of the complaint. Increasingly, however, federal courts have begun to reconsider their reluctance to allow removals whenever an in-state defendant is named. There remains considerable uncertainty in this area, though a relaxation of the fraudulent joinder rule would result in more state law cases being brought into the federal courts.

VI. Supplemental Jurisdiction.

We now turn from deciding whether cases raise federal *or* state claims, to the issue of what to do with cases that raise both federal *and* state claims. Clearly, if the claims are transactionally related, it would be a tremendous waste of judicial and litigant resources to have the federal and state components litigated separately. For example, although the merger of two businesses might trigger both state and federal laws, there would be little sense in having an antitrust challenge to the merger proceed in both state and federal court. However, any rule that allowed subject matter jurisdiction over both types of claims would necessarily have the effect of joining the claims in either state or federal court, thereby implicating the delicate division of labor between the two court systems. Further, because federal courts are courts of limited subject matter jurisdiction, allowing them to adjudicate claims that do not have some independent basis for federal jurisdiction raises further problems.

The need to create some capacity to resolve overlapping claims led initially to the separate concepts of ancillary and pendent jurisdiction. Ancillary jurisdiction arose when parties in a diversity action would need to include a claim against a nondiverse party, without whom complete adjudication would be impossible. A clear example is impleader, in which a defendant in a tort suit might need to add a claim against her insurer, even when there is not diversity of citizenship. Courts would invoke the judicially-created doctrine of ancillary jurisdiction to hear this related claim. In the case of pendent jurisdiction, a party might sue under a federal statute and subsequently add a state claim. For example, if a party brought a federal antitrust claim against its competitor and then added a state unfair competition claim, the federal court could exercise pendent jurisdiction to hear both claims. These "add-on" jurisdictional powers served important policies of efficiency and equity.

Creating "add-on" powers was problematic for two reasons. First, it appeared that the courts were prescribing their own jurisdictional powers, raising constitutional questions about the source of their authority to do so. Second, while efficiency might dictate that some additional jurisdiction was necessary, there were different federalism implications in creating liberal jurisdictional rules for cases that presented state law claims (as with the diversity claims in an ancillary action) and those that were based primarily on federal law (as with the federal claims to which pendent jurisdiction might attach).

The key decision comes from *United Mine Workers of America v. Gibbs*,[24] a case that raised both federal and state claims emerging from a labor dispute. The plaintiff, Gibbs, had been hired as a mine superintendent, but ran afoul of the mineworkers' union and began to lose trucking contracts and mining leases as a result of what he claimed to be a concerted union effort to harm him. Gibbs brought both federal and state claims against the union, claiming that the interference with his business opportunities constituted a prohibited "secondary boycott" under federal labor law and tortious interference with contract under state law.

Clearly the state and federal claims covered identical conduct. Since there was no diversity of citizenship, however, Gibbs could only raise the state law claim in federal court if the court's federal question jurisdiction provided a basis for sweeping in related state claims. As we saw with *Merrell Dow* and *Grable*, however the line is drawn here, there is a risk of either denying the federal forum to federal claims or encouraging federal intrusion into matters of state law. In deciding that the court had jurisdiction to hear the state

---

24.   383 U.S. 715 (1966).

claim, the Supreme Court devised a five-part test that erred on the side of assuring litigants with substantial federal claims access to federal court without having to sacrifice their transactionally related state law claims. This test basically asked whether: 1) the claims were sufficiently transactionally related so as to present "one constitutional case"; 2) the federal claim was substantial enough to merit adjudication; 3) there was a common nucleus of operative fact between the claims; 4) state issues did not predominate; and 5) the court, at its discretion, agreed to hear both claims. While perhaps imprecise, the core of the *Gibbs* test emphasizes judicial economy and strikes a liberal balance in favor of keeping federal law in federal court, even at the risk of federalizing state law in certain instances.

In cases arising under diversity jurisdiction, however, the policy justification for the *Gibbs* rule does not hold. The underlying claims in diversity by definition do not involve the use of federal courts as the prime arbiter of federal law. In *Owen Equipment & Erection Co. v. Kroger*,[25] for example, the Court confronted a wrongful death suit in which the plaintiff's estate sued a diverse defendant, who in turn implead Owen, a third party not diverse from the original plaintiff. The plaintiff then sought to add a claim against Owen despite the lack of diversity between Owen and Kroger. Had the Court directly applied the *Gibbs* test, it would likely have found there to be jurisdiction. The claims were undoubtedly transactionally related and efficiency would command that they be tried together. The Court declined to do so, however, finding that the plaintiff could not manufacture diversity jurisdiction by waiting for the defendant to implead a nondiverse party.

While puzzling from the standpoint of efficiency, the outcome in *Kroger* confirms the general division of labor between state and federal courts. Where the litigation is organized around a federal question, as in *Gibbs,* the federal courts will craft a welcoming jurisdictional principle allowing a plaintiff both to use the federal forum for the resolution of federal claims *and* achieve efficiency by trying related state claims together in the federal forum. Where the plaintiff chooses the federal forum as a preferred forum for a state law claim based on diversity of citizenship, however, federal courts will offer no expansive jurisdictional rules to allow for the efficient prosecution of related state claims. If the plaintiff wants to realize the efficiencies of unitary litigation, the plaintiff may file all the related claims against all the related parties in state court. There is no systemic reason for federal courts to be particularly solicitous of

25. 437 U.S. 365 (1978).

what are ultimately matters of state law. Thus, in *Kroger* there is no special reason for the plaintiff to go forward in federal court because all the claims arise under state law. Although efficiency would be served by allowing Kroger to bring both claims in federal court, as in *Gibbs*, there is a countervailing policy interest in avoiding the federalization of state law.

Congress subsequently took care of the uncertain constitutional pedigree of judicially-created jurisdictional rules by supplanting the common law doctrines of ancillary and pendant jurisdiction with a supplemental jurisdiction statute, 28 U.S.C. § 1367. Although not free from some uncertainty in statutory design, the statute basically sought to codify the distinct approaches in *Gibbs* and *Kroger*. The statute begins in § 1367(a) by adopting the *Gibbs* definition to allow federal courts that have jurisdiction over a claim to exercise jurisdiction over all other transactionally related claims that are part of the same constitutional case. While broad, this jurisdictional grant is immediately limited by § 1367(b), which excludes from the broad definition of supplemental jurisdiction cases in which the court's original jurisdiction is based on diversity rather than the presence of a federal question. When the case is brought in federal court on the basis of diversity, the district courts are not granted supplemental jurisdiction to adjudicate claims by the original plaintiff against parties brought into the suit under Federal Rules of Civil Procedure 14, 19, 20, and 24. As in *Kroger,* a plaintiff seeking the unitary resolution of a diversity case with some nondiverse potential defendants is advised to keep the matter in state court.

VII. The Erie Doctrine.

Before the emergence of modern federal question jurisdiction and the rise of the modern regulatory state, federal courts directed their attention only to diversity cases. Of necessity, this required that they adjudicate matters of state law that would have been presented to state courts but for the citizenship of the parties. In this capacity, the only role of the federal courts was to interpret state law. But this left open the question as to what exactly was state law. As the nation expanded into new states carved out of western territories, and prior to any systematic body of published state court decisions, identifying the exact source of state law, particularly decisional law, was no small undertaking. Beyond the practical difficulties of identifying state law was a deeper concern about the role of the common law, particularly in the newly formed states of the nineteenth century. The common law in the original states drew heavily from its British antecedents. But as the country grew and a new national identity was being forged, should not the new nation stake out its own sources of law, even common law?

So thought Justice Joseph Story, the most dominant early nineteenth century member of the Court after the first Chief Justice, John Marshall. Story was a remarkable figure who not only served as a Justice of the Court, but simultaneously taught at Harvard Law School and published an astonishing set of commentaries on the law. Story believed that legal institutions would play a critical role in forging a new national identity. In his view, national unification depended on the ability of federal judges to develop a new federal common law that would address the distinct needs of the ascendant republic. In seeking to unburden the new American state from its British and colonial inheritances, Story in *Swift v. Tyson* held that, while federal judges sitting in diversity were obligated to honor state law, "state law" would be defined to mean only state statutes, not state common law.[26] Thus, in the absence of express state statutes, federal judges were charged with articulating a "federal common law." For Story, such a federal common law, particularly in matters of commercial exchange, would help cement the integrated national market that was at the heart of the founding of the Republic.

Justice Story's efforts at using the common law in aid of nation-building ran into the problem of a dual court system and the risk of divergent bodies of law seeming to control the same daily activities. Federal courts became more enamored of their new common law powers, with Justice Swayne subsequently proclaiming for the Supreme Court, "We shall never immolate truth, justice, and the law, because a State tribunal has erected the altar and decreed the sacrifice."[27] Although wonderfully colorful, Justice Swayne's formulation ignored the problem that state courts remained faithful to the "altar" of state decisional law and that the precise requirements of "truth" and "justice" were a tad hard to predict ahead of time. As a result of the widespread use of federal common law in diversity cases, the same case could well be decided differently depending upon the accident of citizenship of the parties. Rather than serve as a unifying agent for the nation, *Swift v. Tyson* threatened arbitrariness, subjecting parties to two different standards of law in their everyday affairs.

26.   41 U.S. (16 Pet.) 1 (1842); see also William A. Fletcher, *The General Common Law and Section 34 of the Judiciary Act of 1789: The Example of Marine Insurance*, 97 Harv. L. Rev. 1513, 1520 (1984) (describing the rise, in the early nineteenth century, of "the notion of a uniquely American common law").

27.   Gelpcke v. Dubuque, 68 U.S. (1 Wall.) 175, 206–07 (1863).

The *Black & White Taxicab* case epitomized this problem.[28] Brown & Yellow Taxicab, a Kentucky corporation, had secured an exclusive contract to provide taxi services at a Kentucky railroad station, thereby preventing its competitor, Black & White Taxicab, another Kentucky corporation, from competing in that market. However, Kentucky courts had refused to enforce exclusive dealing contracts as contrary to public policy. Federal courts, operating under *Swift,* were not obligated to honor Kentucky state decisional law, and had in fact found exclusive dealing arrangements lawful and enforceable. Brown & Yellow therefore reincorporated in Tennessee, and then, armed with diversity of citizenship, successfully brought an action against Black & White in federal court. By manipulating its citizenship to take advantage of federal as opposed to state courts, Brown & Yellow was able to enjoin its rival from interfering with its exclusivity contract, a legal maneuver that was ultimately upheld by the Supreme Court. This sort of manipulation of citizenship to control the legal rules governing the same exact contractual relationship at a Kentucky train station exposed the ultimate vulnerability of *Swift.*

Unpredictability was not the only source of disenchantment with *Swift.* The general common law powers of federal courts had been one of the lynchpins of federal efforts to derail labor activism during the Progressive Era, with the most notorious form of intervention being the use of injunctions to halt strikes. Federal courts also earned the enmity of reformers by using the Constitution to strike down progressive legislation in decisions like *Lochner v. New York.*[29] The hostility to expansive federal court power only intensified when the Court struck down the National Industrial Recovery Act and other early pieces of the New Deal. By 1938, however, the Court's resistance to social legislation was beginning to buckle, President Roosevelt's appointees were taking hold, and the Supreme Court was prepared to rein in the far reaches of the federal common law.

The confrontation with *Swift's* legacy came in *Erie Railroad Co. v. Tompkins,*[30] a seemingly quite ordinary state law tort suit. The plaintiff was injured by a protruding door on a passing train. The injury occurred while Tompkins was walking on a "commonly used beaten footpath" on railroad property alongside train tracks near his Pennsylvania home. Under Pennsylvania law, Tompkins would have been deemed a trespasser to whom no legal duty was

28.   Black & White Taxicab & Transfer Co. v. Brown & Yellow Taxicab & Transfer Co., 276 U.S. 518 (1928).

29.   198 U.S. 45 (1905).

30.   304 U.S. 64 (1938).

owed. Had the case gone forward in state court, therefore, Tompkins would have lost. But armed with diversity jurisdiction, Tompkins brought suit in federal court in New York against the Erie Railroad, a New York corporation. The critical issue is not the fact that the suit was in New York, but that it was in federal court. Once the federal district court found that Pennsylvania had no statute on point, the legacy of *Swift* meant that the federal court was free to find its own common law. Reaching for broad principles of equity, the federal court imposed a tort duty upon the defendant under the federal common law, treating Tompkins in effect as an invitee because of the open and frequent use of the footpath, rather than as a trespasser, as he would have been under Pennsylvania common law.

In an opinion by Justice Brandeis, the Supreme Court reversed. At a technical level, the opinion concerned the interpretation of one of the oldest federal statutes, the Rules of Decision Act (RDA), which required federal courts exercising diversity jurisdiction to obey the decisional law of the state in which they sat. The RDA was critical to the entire enterprise of federal common law since it was Justice Story's construction of the rule of decision as including only state statutes that had freed federal courts, after *Swift v. Tyson,* to disregard state common law. Based on an amalgam of arguments, some resting on the original intent of the statute and some on broader conceptions of federalism, Justice Brandeis ultimately found that the "Rule of Decision" must include state court rulings and not just legislative pronouncements. In other words, federal courts must apply the same substantive law as if the case had been litigated in state court. By making federal courts act as much as possible as if they were state courts in the same jurisdiction, the Court read the RDA as designed to thwart forum shopping and avoid the inequitable administration of the law, what subsequently became known as the "twin aims" of *Erie.* By eliminating the ability of parties in diversity cases to pick strategically between a given state's laws and the federally developed common law, *Erie* indicated that while diversity of citizenship may control the forum in which the dispute is adjudicated, it should not control the outcome.

The *Erie* rule turns on a distinction between the statutory commands on federal courts under the RDA and the Rules Enabling Act (REA).[31] Under the RDA, federal courts are obligated to follow state substantive law in diversity cases. At the same time, however, the REA authorizes federal courts to develop their own

---

31. *See* John Hart Ely, *The Irrepressible Myth of Erie,* 87 Harv. L. Rev. 693, 718–38 (1974).

procedural system, which we now have as the Federal Rules of Civil Procedure, and to utilize those rules in both diversity and federal question cases.

As a practical matter, *Erie* set store by the ability of courts to draw the line between matters of substance and procedure. But that line was unlikely to be drawn effectively in the political climate surrounding *Erie*. The ascendant New Dealers believed that so long as federal courts were dominant, there could be no progress in American society. On this view, *Erie* should be understood not as a case about the limits of federal power, but as the resolution of the boundaries of federal *judicial* power.[32] Indeed, the same Court that decided *Erie* also upheld New Deal legislation that shifted the locus of economic and social regulatory power to the federal legislative and executive branches. Thus, the liabilities of a railroad carrier— the issue before the Court in *Erie*—would soon be preemptively defined by federal law governing all railroads. In effect, the question in *Erie* was that of the scope of federal court intervention, rather than a federalism decision about the broad sweep of Congress's power under the Commerce Clause.

In the hands of the New Deal generation, *Erie* became an instrument to scale back the federal judiciary even further. No case embodied that more clearly than *Guaranty Trust Co. v. York*,[33] and no Justice of the Court more fully articulated that view than its author, Felix Frankfurter. The issue in *York* was whether a federal court could entertain a diversity claim even though the state statute of limitations had run. While the issue could have been addressed under *Erie* as a matter of procedure versus substance, the Court went further. According to Justice Frankfurter, the obligation of federal courts sitting in diversity was to replicate all aspects of how the claim would be treated in state court; the use of federal practices was barred if they could prove to be "outcome determinative." The Court stated that *Erie* "did not merely overrule a venerable case [*Swift v. Tyson*]. It overruled a particular way of looking at law which dominated the judicial process long after its inadequacies has been laid bare." Thus, "if a plea of the statute of limitations would bar recovery in a State court a federal court ought not to afford recovery." The case therefore stands for the rule that if a state procedural rule is outcome determinative, federal courts must follow state law.

---

32. Thomas W. Merrill, *The Common Law Powers of Federal Courts,* 52 U. Chi. L. Rev. 1, 13–19 (1985).

33. 326 U.S. 99 (1945).

The problem is that under the *York* test for outcome determinativeness, *any* difference between state and federal practice could be outcome determinative when examined in retrospect. Under the right circumstances, even a trivial difference, such as not paying the right filing fee or using the wrong color paper on the cover of a brief, might result in a case never getting docketed, thereby altering the "outcome." The result was an extraordinarily constricted view of federal court procedural power, as is well reflected in *Ragan v. Merchants Transfer & Warehouse Co.*,[34] decided shortly after *York*. In *Ragan*, the Court considered a personal injury suit brought in a federal district court in Kansas under diversity of citizenship. In order to be timely under state law, both the filing of the complaint and service of process had to occur within the statute of limitations, while under the Federal Rules, a party had 120 days after timely filing the complaint to perfect service. Because the plaintiff had filed the complaint within the Kansas two-year statute of limitations, but did not serve the defendant until after that period had run, the action was either timely under the Federal Rules or time-barred under state law, depending on which law applied. The Court held that the state rule should be followed, because the plaintiff should not be able to maintain a case in federal court that would have been dismissed in state court.

This strict interpretation of the outcome determinative test seems to require absolute fidelity to state practices, an approach that reaches even beyond the commands of *Erie* itself. It not only undoes the broad common law powers federal courts had given themselves in the period running from *Swift* through the *Lochner* era, but also effectively compromises the REA, in which Congress granted the federal courts the power to organize their own procedures through the Federal Rules.

As the Supreme Court moved into the era associated with *Brown v. Board of Education*[35] and other cases assertively staking out a more central social role for the Court, the *Erie* rule and its manifest distrust of federal courts became increasingly anomalous. The first significant retreat from the outcome determinative rule came in *Byrd v. Blue Ridge Rural Electric Cooperative, Inc.*,[36] which sought to introduce a test balancing the state's interest in applying its own procedures and the federal courts' efficiency interest in procedural uniformity. Unfortunately, this balancing test lacked clarity as applied and opened the door to being second-guessed as

34. 337 U.S. 530 (1949).
35. 347 U.S. 483 (1954).
36. 356 U.S. 525 (1958).

the facts of a case emerged. As we previously examined in the discussion of the *Mottley* rule for pleading a federal claim, there are times when the litigants need clarity on shaping their case. A balancing test on the controlling law introduces too much uncertainty on what elements of a claim need to be plead, on what discovery is relevant, and so forth. *Byrd* tried to move away from the formalism of *York* but substituted imprecision in the standards for determining controlling law.

The critical repudiation of the *York* doctrine came in *Hanna v. Plumer.*[37] Here, the Court confronted a conflict between state law requiring in-hand service of process and the more liberal procedures for service available under Federal Rule 4. Under state law, only service made directly on the defendant could properly initiate suit, but the plaintiff in *Hanna* had served the executor of a tortfeasor's estate by leaving copies of the summons and complaints with the executor's wife at his residence. Under the Federal Rules, the case was properly engaged; under state law, the case would have been dismissed for failure to properly execute service. In "outcome determinative" terms, the contrast was clear.

Writing for the majority, Chief Justice Warren forcefully asserted the federal prerogative under the Rules Enabling Act. Wherever there was a federal rule directly on point, the Court found that lower courts should not be concerned about the "relatively unguided *Erie* choice." Rather, a federal court should apply the federal rule, so long as it was within the constitutional powers of Congress and the courts under the REA. Since the Federal Rules are developed through the combined efforts of the Supreme Court, acting through the rules drafting process, and Congress, sitting in oversight, a finding that the Federal Rules should cede to state law would require a determination that the Court, the Rules Advisory Committee, and Congress had all acted beyond their constitutional authority. In other words, the Rules always trump.

Although clear in its application, Chief Justice Warren's opinion did not elucidate a theoretical framework for deciding what happens when state and federal practices conflict, but there is no federal rule directly on point, as with statutes of limitations, filing fees, color of briefs, and a host of other practices both significant and trivial. The key for such situations proved to be Justice Harlan's concurrence, which tried to limit the categorical approach of the majority and set out only the parameters of when the federal interest should trump. While Justice Harlan did not carry the day on what happens when a federal rule is on point (the federal rule

---

37.   380 U.S. 460 (1965).

always gets applied in federal court), his opinion proved indispensable in bringing coherence to the application of *Erie*.

For Justice Harlan, the key to the *Erie* problem is the difficulty of ordinary citizens controlling their lives in the face of legal uncertainty. Going back to the *Black & White Taxicab* case, for example, both cab companies had an overriding interest in clear legal rules governing exclusive dealing contracts so as to be able to make such critical business decisions as whether to invest in new cabs. Having dual sovereigns with competing commands on such first-order questions of rights in the society threatened just the sort of uncertainty that led Montesquieu and other political thinkers of centuries gone by to conclude that any ordered society must ultimately have one sovereign power.

Justice Harlan's key insight was that most procedural rules, even if outcome determinative after the fact in litigation, do not affect how citizens conduct their everyday lives. If the cover of a brief must be red or blue, if a filing fee is $50 or $75, parties will adjust accordingly in the litigation process. But no one orders his or her business affairs differently depending on the color of a brief cover or small variations in a filing fee. By contrast, parties *do* order their business affairs quite differently depending on whether or not exclusive dealing contracts are enforceable. For Harlan, the elusive line between procedure and substance, the potentially conflicting commands of the Rules Enabling Act and the Rules of Decision Act, was made visible by the contrast between those sorts of decisions that would affect the conduct of life's daily affairs, and those that simply involve the mechanical steps that must be taken once in the judicial arena. Justice Harlan's *ex ante* approach enables the Court to meet *Erie*'s twin aims: avoiding forum shopping and the inequitable administration of the law. The perceived harm driving *Erie* is that the legal results of primary conduct (such as whether damages are available for contract breach) will depend on whether the parties are in state or federal court. Thus identical conduct may lead to arbitrary differences in outcomes depending on which rules are employed. Chief Justice Warren's opinion in *Hanna* intuits this problem by commanding the use of the Federal Rules whenever a Rule is on point. Justice Harlan's concurrence furthers this aim by forcing courts, in circumstances in which there is not a rule directly on point, to ask whether prior to the litigation, in the *ex ante* state of affairs, the choice of rule would influence primary conduct. Thus the *Hanna* doctrine resolves the policy concerns of *Erie* while providing an easily administrable rule for the lower courts. The effect of both the Warren and Harlan opinions is to preserve the ability of the states to regulate the types of primary conduct—property, contract, tort—that have long been the province of state law, regardless of whether that law derives from statutes or common law decisions.

While *Hanna*, and particularly Justice Harlan's concurrence, may have provided the best organizing principles for *Erie* cases, it was not the last word. More recently, the Court in *Gasperini v. Center for Humanities, Inc.*[38] introduced a hybrid concern for state court practices of sufficient magnitude as to be "outcome affective." *Gasperini* involved the appellate standards for setting aside an award of damages. Had the case been adjudicated in the state courts of New York, the site of the litigation, the jury award could have been overturned if it "deviates materially from what would be reasonable compensation." Under Federal Rule 59, however, a district court's authority to set aside a jury award was limited to truly extreme cases. Under either of the *Hanna* approaches, the federal standard would have controlled, either because there was a Federal Rule on point or because the question of what standard controls motions to set aside a jury award is unlikely to have any bearing on primary conduct.

In an opinion by Justice Ginsburg, the Court appeared to straddle all lines of *Erie* jurisprudence. The "outcome affective" test employed by the Court to order the district court to revisit the jury award appears to revive the "outcome determinative" test developed by Justice Frankfurter and then jettisoned unceremoniously. The Court's attentiveness to the weighing of the federal and state interests hearkens back to *Byrd*. Meanwhile, the concern that runaway jury awards might dampen commercial contracts could possibly be read as consistent with Justice Harlan's attention to primary conduct in *Hanna*. As with developments in personal jurisdiction law after *Asahi Metal Industry v. Superior Court of California*,[39] the main effect of *Gasperini* was to create a fair amount of confusion in an area needing clarification.

In its most recent opinion on the balance between state and federal law, the Court seemed disinclined to follow *Gasperini* or to limit the clear application of federal procedure in federal court. In *Shady Grove Orthopedic Associates v. Allstate Insurance*,[40] the Court, per Justice Scalia, confronted a New York law that allowed certain consumer claims, but not class action aggregation of those claims. Justice Scalia turned back to *Hanna* to restore an overwhelming presumption that federal procedure would carry the day

38.   518 U.S. 415 (1996).

39.   480 U.S. 102 (1987).

40.   130 S.Ct. 1431 (2010).

in federal court, regardless of how the state courts would have handled the same issue: "We do not wade into *Erie's* murky waters unless the federal rule is inapplicable or invalid."[41] For so long as *Shady Grove* remains the settled law, the Court will have in effect returned to the firm rule handed down by Chief Justice Warren in *Hanna*. Whatever the cost of inflexibility that Justice Harlan pointed out in his concurrence in *Hanna*, there is the great gain of procedural clarity in federal court litigation.

VIII. Conclusion.

The federalist experiment in dual sovereignty is still a work in progress. The jurisdictional battles accompanying subject matter jurisdiction, whether in the narrowly drawn *Mottley* rule or in the more expansive domain of *Erie,* ultimately return to an allocation of power between the state and federal systems. In turn, these jurisdictional battles get played out in the courts on matters ranging from the procedural to the substantive. Perhaps more than any other area of procedure, the risk of caprice from uncertain sources of legal authority, as exemplified in the *Black & White Taxicab* case, makes this an area in great need of clear guideposts. *Mottley* provides an example of a fairly firm rule that works fairly well. Where the law is less developed, as with the supplemental jurisdiction statute or with the tension between *Gasperini* and *Shady Grove,* the lack of clarity returns us to the insights of early political theorists who well understood the stability afforded by unalloyed sovereign authority.

41. *Id.* at 1437.

Chapter 7
REPOSE

Legal procedure is part of a complicated interaction between what has been termed private ordering and public intervention. As we have seen throughout this book, modern society brings people together in a variety of settings and injects an active state presence into all manner of everyday activities. Inevitably, there are disputes, and the purpose of a procedural system is to secure the just and efficient resolution of those disputes. Yet, as we have also seen, disputes do settle all around us, based on social norms or simply on an understanding of what is right and what is wrong, what is contestable and what is not, without the necessity of the full resources of the system. Still, the very fact that the full system exists does much to induce this state of affairs. Every settlement occurs against the backdrop, sometimes but certainly not always explicitly invoked, of what might occur were the matter to be taken to court, with all its associated costs and other demands, including the time and disruption associated with legal proceedings. In this sense, disputants outside the legal system are said to be bargaining "in the shadow of the law."[1]

But the shadow of the law is not always enough to induce private ordering of disputes, and so they arrive in court. When this happens, three public interests arise beyond the scope of the narrow claims of each party to satisfy his or her assertion of rights. The first is to provide a public resolution of the issues, such that future, similarly situated disputants may be better able to anticipate what are the likely outcomes of their own actions should they proceed to litigation. The second is to provide finality so that the disputants themselves may get on with their affairs. The third is to do this while utilizing scarce judicial resources in the most efficient manner possible.

The first public interest is addressed through the elaborate artifact of reported decisional law. For those who brave the wilds of litigation through to an adjudicated conclusion, the law provides for written judgments that not only inform the litigants of how and why their dispute was resolved as it was, but also inform others as to what would likely occur were they to press their disputes to an adjudicated resolution. In the last chapter, we shall return to the

---

1. The term comes from the classic article, Robert H. Mnookin & Lewis Kornhauser, *Bargaining in the Shadow of the Law: The Case of Divorce*, 88 YALE L.J. 950 (1979).

troubling question of why anyone would be so foolhardy as to actually seek a full and costly adjudication of a claim. But, for now, it suffices that decisional law not only informs the litigants of the reasons for a particular outcome, but also provides a public good to the world of prospective litigants by informing private negotiations, thus actually facilitating settlement.

As can be deduced from the title of this chapter, it is the second public interest that provides an overarching theme for the material to come: the enduring aim of achieving finality through dispute resolution. Not only do courts provide a forum for argument and an impartial and well-reasoned adjudication of a dispute, courts attempt to provide closure; the object is to put a quiet end to altercations that would otherwise continue indefinitely, so that life may proceed without being consumed by festering grudges and feuds which might reignite, even escalating into violence, at the slightest future provocation. At a colloquial level, courts can be thought to offer us an escape from a society of Hatfields and McCoys: rival private bands whose conflicts are both enduring and violent. The benefit, therefore, of a court system to society and to the litigants that enter it must be measured not just by the ability of parties to have meaningful access to it, and not simply by the just quality of adjudication that it offers, but by the finality that can be achieved through litigation therein.

Finality may be realized in many ways. The procedural rules are structured so as to give increasing closure to each level of adjudication in any particular piece of litigation.[2] There are rules that channel litigation so as to force conclusive disposition of as much of the dispute between the litigants as possible. There are formal doctrines of preclusion—claim preclusion, issue preclusion, and the lesser variant of the law of the case—that foreclose relitigation of issues or claims that were or could have been raised in the first proceeding. And, in more recent times, the concept of "virtual representation" has emerged to challenge the ability of parties not even involved in the original lawsuit to litigate issues that were decided there.

I. Complete Litigation.

One of the animating concepts in the law of repose is the idea of transactional completion. When suit is brought, the court looks back in time at whatever incident went awry that gave rise to the

---

2. An example here would be the limited scope of appellate review of any factual findings of a trier of fact. This facet is not explored further.

claims of the action, and requires that any and all other claims arising out of the same incident be pleaded in tandem. In the terminology of the Federal Rules, claims are grouped according to whether they arise from the same "transaction or occurrence," or even the same "series of occurrences."[3]

What emerges may be thought of as the "transactional" approach to litigation. The anticipation is not, however, that the parties will bring every claim that arises out of the same transaction, but rather that the parties will select a subset of all possible claims as their focus for actual litigation. But just as the potential ambit of litigation is now to be defined transactionally, so too must the finality achieved by litigation be defined that way. The result of omitting a claim that arises out of the same transaction or occurrence as the original is the permanent foreclosure of the unpleaded claim.

The clearest example within the Rules comes with the definition of a counterclaim under Rule 13. A counterclaim is simply a related legal claim asserted in the same legal proceeding by the defendant against the original plaintiff. There are two kinds of counterclaims anticipated by the Rules: those that are compulsory under Rule 13(a) and those that are permissive under Rule 13(b). As may be gleaned from the terminology, compulsory counterclaims must be pleaded in the same action or risk being forever lost, while permissive counterclaims may be raised subject to the managerial concerns of Rule 42(b), which allows the court to sever claims for purposes of efficiency or fairness. The distinction between the two forms of counterclaims brings into sharp relief the "transactional" approach to litigation: a party is obligated to raise only those counterclaims that arise "out of the same transaction or occurrence that is the subject matter of the opposing party's claims." Any other counterclaims—those that do not arise from the same transaction or occurrence—are deemed permissive, and a party may bring them as it wishes, provided the court has subject matter jurisdiction.[4]

It follows that the effect of failure to raise a compulsory counterclaim is that a party loses the ability to do so in the future. Much, therefore, turns on the definition given to "the same transaction or occurrence," the operational language of the Rules. However, as anyone who has made it to this point in the book will suspect, there is little to be gained from parsing the words of the

---

3. The phrase "transaction or occurrence" is used throughout the Federal Rules, and appears in either the text or notes of FED. R. CIV. P. 7, 8, 10, 13, 14, 15, 18, 20, 21, 26, 42, 54, 56, and 59.

4. *See* Chapter 6.

Rules—they do not offer a bright-line rule for when a party must raise a counterclaim and when not. Thus, the leading exposition from the Supreme Court would explain the key operative terms of Rule 13 as follows:

> [A] "transaction" is a word of flexible meaning. It may comprehend a series of many occurrences, depending not so much on the immediateness of their connection as upon their logical relationship.[5]

Thus, a critical instruction is couched only in terms of "logical relationship." Little will be gained from trying to patch the holes in this particularly porous definition through elaborate wordsmanship.

In place of a textual approach, courts over the years have attempted to craft a functional account of what it means for claims to be transactionally related. One early approach was to define a compulsory counterclaim as one which would give rise to a *res judicata* bar—and therefore be lost—were the claim not to be raised.[6] Yet this definition suffered a tautological infirmity: the concept of *"res judicata"* refers to the preclusion of claims that were previously deemed adjudicated. As a result, the preclusive effect was both the issue to be decided and the test to determine whether preclusion would indeed attach. That is, this test says no more than that a claim is compulsory (and will be precluded if not raised), if it would be precluded if not raised. This does not clarify anything. Alternatively, courts have focused on whether the same evidence or the same issues of fact and law would be litigated in both the original claim and the potential counterclaim. This gets closer to the functional account desired by the Rules, but it is still flawed. The problem is that defendants must decide what constitutes a compulsory counterclaim at the point of answering the complaint—well before discovery and pre-trial motions have defined what the operational evidence, facts, or law will be as the case matures. Defendants are not certain to have enough information to make that decision so early in the litigation.

---

5. Moore v. New York Cotton Exch., 270 U.S. 593, 610 (1926). Although this language originally referred to Rule 13's predecessor, "this is [also] the rule generally followed by the lower courts in construing Rule 13(a)." Baker v. Gold Seal Liquors, Inc., 417 U.S. 467, 469 n.1 (1974). An early case gives some indication of the hopelessness of the textual inquiry, defining the same transaction or occurrence to incorporate "whatever may be done by one person which affects another's rights and out of which a cause of action may arise." Williams v. Robinson, 1 F.R.D. 211, 213 (D.D.C. 1940).

6. *See, e.g.,* Big Cola Corp. v. World Bottling Co., 134 F.2d 718 (6th Cir. 1943).

Ultimately, courts have done no better than to allow the flexibility of the "logical relationship" test to stand. In part, this reflects the fact that courts have difficulty putting in place a pleading regime that assumes more information than the parties can be expected to have so early in the litigation. In larger part, however, the reason for the lack of clarity is that there is relatively little case law on the scope of compulsory counterclaims. Since misestimation of what constitutes a compulsory counterclaim may result in the foreclosure of future claims, risk-averse defendants have every incentive to "plead first, evaluate later." Here the imprecision of the Rules yields a systemic inefficiency as parties are forced to plead defensively and thereby inject claims into litigation that may very well have lain dormant and never been actually asserted.

II.   Claim Preclusion.

A direct corollary to the rules requiring complete pleading of claims is the doctrine of *res judicata*, or claim preclusion. Stated most directly, the rule of *res judicata* provides that "[a] final judgment on the merits of an action precludes the parties or their privies from relitigating issues that were or could have been raised in that action."[7] That is, a party cannot bring a claim or cause of action against another if, in a previous suit, the same parties or their privies were involved, the first suit arose from the same transaction or occurrence as the new suit, and the first suit had a final judgment entered on it by the court.[8]

The basic proposition underlying *res judicata* is fairly straight-forward. Once a discrete controversy between two parties has been litigated to judgment, there is every reason to accord that judgment finality. It is wasteful to litigate each cause of action in a suit separately, and so, continuing the example above, we see that Rule 13 is really just an explication of the consequences of *res judicata* in the realm of counterclaims. Even if compulsory counterclaims were not defined, *res judicata* would dictate that certain counterclaims—those that are logically and efficiently grouped together with the original claim—must either be raised in the original action or lost. Similarly, while Rule 18 purports to "allow" the joinder of claims,

---

7. Federated Dep't Stores, Inc. v. Moitie, 452 U.S. 394, 398 (1981). Note that by "issue" the Court is referring to legal issues, or causes of action, and not to factual issues, which are the focus of issue preclusion, discussed below.

8. The more formal rendition of this concept is to speak of a final judgment comprising "merger" and "bar" orders. Under this older account, a judgment serves to merge all claims and defenses into the judgment itself, such that they may no longer be asserted, and then to bar formally their reassertion.

the doctrine of *res judicata* in fact requires that they either be raised or foregone. The efficiency interests of the judicial system in realizing some benefit from the litigation are clearly advanced by grouping claims together in this way. So too are the equitable interests of the parties in securing the benefits of resolution. Thus, Rule 18 provides the procedural vehicle to achieve the complete resolution of disputes required by the preclusion doctrine.

The primary contested issues in *res judicata* concern the rigidity and the scope of the ensuing preclusion. With regard to the rigidity of the preclusion, consider a hypothetical in which Jones sues Smith, claiming that Smith is improperly creating widgets for which Jones allegedly holds exclusive patent rights. Assume that the case proceeds to trial and Jones loses. The doctrine of claim preclusion would, as a general matter, prohibit Jones from again suing Smith over the patent to the widgets. But consider what would happen if the reason Jones lost his first claim was that his patent had not yet been approved. Now imagine that Jones sues a year later over the continued use of his patent, but that in the interim his patent has been granted. In that case, due to the intervening change in facts, Jones's new claim would not be barred. Or imagine that Jones lost his first case because of a special law foreclosing the ability to enforce patent rights in widget production. Imagine that in the intervening period, the legal regime had changed, such that these rights were now enforceable. Here an intervening change in law would defeat the prospective prohibition on raising a new claim for infringement of patent rights. Thus courts recognize an exception to the customary prospective operation of *res judicata* "where between the time of the first judgment and the second there has been an intervening decision or a change in the law creating an altered situation."[9] A similar principle governs intervening changes in material fact. It is important to bear in mind that changes in material fact or applicable law do not give occasion to revisit the initial judgment; they are simply the basis for curtailing the *prospective* effects of the earlier judgment.

In each case of subsequent change, we must be careful to distinguish the validity of the original judgment from its prospective preclusive effect. The change in the law governing the patent eligibility of widgets or the subsequent grant of the patent to the plaintiff do not call into question either the correctness or the enforceability of the original judgment. Neither a subsequent change in law or fact results in an ability to reopen the original case and seek the original remedy from the original litigation.

9. State Farm Mut. Auto. Ins. Co. v. Duel, 324 U.S. 154, 162 (1945).

Rather, what is at issue is the prospective effect. The doctrine of claim preclusion concerns what may be contested after the first suit is over. Even when an exception to claim preclusion is triggered, the original judgment stands as before, though the legal relationship between the parties may be subject to subsequent modification.

Of greater difficulty is the question how far the doctrine of claim preclusion should extend. In formal terms, this is sometimes referred to as the "bar order," signifying the enforceability of a prohibition on subsequent litigation. Despite the modern emphasis on transactional completion, it is important to realize that this was not always the touchstone for *res judicata* and that there are genuine policy concerns over the imprecision in the expansion of the preclusive reach of judgments. *Rush v. City of Maple Heights*, an early case from Ohio and a favorite of many casebooks, presents the dilemma that courts face in confronting the scope of preclusion.[10] The facts are illustrative of the multiple claims that can arise within a simple tort action. Rush was riding as a passenger on a motorcycle driven by her husband when the motorcycle crossed a bumpy stretch of road full of potholes. The motorcycle crashed, and Rush was thrown off and injured. Traditionally, under the common law, a plaintiff like Rush could bring separate actions for property damage and for personal injuries, on the theory that the two kinds of damages would be proven through different kinds of evidence and that each claim would constitute an independent pleading, hence a separate action. This is precisely what Rush tried to do: she initially brought a negligence action against the city for property damage to the motorcycle in which she prevailed and recovered $100. With this judgment in hand, Rush filed a personal injury claim and tried to leverage the earlier judgment, arguing that the city should be barred from contesting liability and hence the only issue was the scope of damages. The trial court agreed, and ordered the jury to assume liability, with the jury in turn awarding $12,000 in damages.

Rush exposed a conflict between liberal pleading rules, whose aim was to accommodate efficiently all aspects of a dispute within a single lawsuit, and the remaining formal strictures of preclusion law. Each system had its trade-offs. The older rule offered certainty that preclusion could run no further than a single pleading, even at the risk of inviting strategic trial sequencing, as in *Rush*. By contrast, a rule that allowed preclusion to follow the capacity to bring all actions together gained efficiency, but risked imprecision

---

10.   167 Ohio St. 221, 147 N.E.2d 599 (1958).

in just how far preclusion would reach. On appeal in *Rush,* the Ohio Supreme Court opted for the modern emphasis on transactional efficiency. The Court pointed to the absurdities created by the older rule by quoting Lord Coleridge: "it seems to me a subtlety not warranted by law to hold that a man cannot bring two actions, if he is injured in his arm and in his leg, but can bring two, if besides his arm and leg being injured, his trousers which contain his leg, and his coatsleeve which contains his arm, have been torn."[11] The Court further noted that the two-action rule had produced much "vexatious litigation," and could no longer be reconciled with an era of liberalized pleading.[12]

The decision of the Ohio Supreme Court exposed a major fault line between the modern era of transactional efficiency and the common law tradition of precision in pleading. Although the Court did not elaborate its analysis, it was clear that it was making a policy choice between two distinct approaches. The clearest basis for its choice is the efficiency gain, both in terms of litigant resources and the ability to claim a court's attention with multiple iterations of the same underlying dispute. But there was also an equitable concern over the ability of a litigant, as in *Rush,* to lead with a low value claim—perhaps lulling the defendant into not investing in the case—then making additional claims once liability had been established as a matter of law.

In recent decades, courts have generally fastened on the concept of related transactions or occurrences, the same terminology followed in the Rules, to define the bounds of preclusion. While this concept intuitively applies to simple scenarios like the motorbike accident in *Rush*, it is difficult to give it a clear definition that can be precisely applied to more difficult cases. Thus, the Restatement (Second) of Judgments can offer only that the test for *res judicata* is:

> to be determined pragmatically, giving weight to such considerations as whether the facts are related in time, space, origin, or motivation, whether they form a convenient trial unit, and whether their treatment as a unit conforms to the parties' expectations or business understanding or usage.[13]

Such open-ended ruminations on the intersection of time and space are a welcome introduction to each episode of *Star Trek,* but are rarely of much help in settling legal disputes. When pressed to

---

11. *Id.* at 606 (quoting Brunsden v. Humphrey, (1884) 14 Q.B. 141 (U.K.) (Coleridge, L., dissenting)).

12. *Id.* at 606–07.

13. RESTATEMENT (SECOND) OF JUDGMENTS § 24 (1982).

make the test more concrete, courts have added a functional account of what could have been efficiently tried together. As one court expressed it, this becomes "a fact-based inquiry into whether the cases are based on the same factual predicate or came from the same nucleus of operative fact. If they did, they are the 'same' for the purposes of *res judicata* ... [as] 'one nucleus of operative fact.' "[14] This then returns to the same transaction approach used in the Federal Rules whereby the question for *res judicata* purposes is, "whether the same transaction or connected series of transactions is at issue, whether the same evidence is needed to support both claims, and whether the facts essential to the second were present in the first."[15]

The lack of precision should not distract from the intuitive appeal of the doctrine of claim preclusion. As the Supreme Court has recently reaffirmed, preclusion protects "against 'the expense and vexation attending multiple lawsuits, conserv[es] judicial resources, and foste[rs] reliance on judicial action by minimizing the possibility of inconsistent decisions.' "[16] From the perspective of the parties who invoke the formal decisionmaking processes, there is and should be an expectation of finality to adjudication. Parties who have actually invoked the litigation process through substantive trial or summary judgment are in a fundamentally different posture than those facing uncertainty at the early pleading stage. Here, despite the imprecision, the expectation is that formal adjudication should serve as an instrument of repose by providing as much finality as possible.

III. Issue Preclusion.

The development of issue preclusion, also called collateral estoppel, is more complicated than that of claim preclusion. In the latter, the concerns of efficiency and equity point toward a need for finality to the dispute between the litigants. Using the concept of the same "transaction or occurrence" indicates not just the concern with careful deployment of scarce judicial resources, but also the need to permit parties to rely upon the resolution of the dispute so as to order their affairs. Issue preclusion is not quite so neatly wrapped up. Instead of providing finality as between parties, the concern with issue preclusion is more directed at the efficient use of

14. Trustmark Ins. Co. v. ESLU, Inc., 299 F.3d 1265, 1270 (11th Cir. 2002).

15. Woods v. Dunlop Tire Corp., 972 F.2d 36, 38 (2d Cir. 1992) (internal quotations omitted).

16. Taylor v. Sturgell, 553 U.S. 880, 892 (2008) (quoting Montana v. United States, 440 U.S. 147, 153–54 (1979)).

factual determinations by courts. The idea is primarily that, once invoked, a court determination of fact is deemed conclusive, absent the normal processes of appellate review.

We must be careful to distinguish not just the functions of claim preclusion and issue preclusion—one applying to whole claims and one applying to factual determinations within a single claim—but also the different rationales underlying the two. As we have seen, claim preclusion is intended primarily to provide finality between the actual litigants to the dispute. Putting aside for the moment the question of *who* may be bound by the first proceeding (a topic that will be taken up in section V), the focus of claim preclusion law is essentially the question of *what* a party might be bound to. The classic formulations for *res judicata* all turn on the notion that a final disposition of the case—whether by full adjudication, or a sufficiently broad encounter with the merits of a case, or even the entry of negotiated final decree—binds the litigants to all matters that were or could have been raised in that proceeding.

Issue preclusion operates quite differently. Although finality is implicated, the primary purpose of issue preclusion is the completeness of resolution through actual adjudication, which is an issue of efficiency. It is possible to think of issue preclusion in terms of maximizing the benefit of the tremendous investment of societal resources represented by a trial. The object then becomes to limit waste of those resources. The history of issue preclusion has been one of a steady expansion in the scope of potential preclusion, and this expansion from its relatively narrow historical origins fully conforms to an efficiency explanation. The unmistakable thread in the decisional law expanding issue preclusion is the not quite stated yet exasperated admonition of, "but has this not already been decided against you?" And the corollary is inescapably, "have *we* the judiciary not already been called upon to decide this?" As David Shapiro aptly summarizes the distinction:

> The function of issue preclusion ... is not to prevent litigation of an issue because it *might* have been litigated before [as with claim preclusion], but rather to prevent *relitigation* of an issue because it *was* litigated before.[17]

In its early form, issue preclusion effectively did not preclude very much. Its primary function was to serve as an accessory to claim preclusion by providing an expansive form of closure for the litigants—and for the litigants exclusively—that assured that any factual issues litigated between them would never again emerge.

---

17. David L. Shapiro, Civil Procedure: Preclusion in Civil Actions 48 (2001) (emphasis in original).

Returning to our earlier hypothetical, imagine that Jones had sued Smith at Time 1 (T_1) for ownership rights in a patent for widgets, and that Jones had then lost based on a jury determination that he did not own those rights. Suppose that Smith had subsequently opened a second production facility making a variant of the same widgets and that Jones had sued again at Time 2 (T_2) claiming, as before, that Smith was in violation of Jones's patented widgets. Claim preclusion would not apply here. Since the second production facility was not in existence at T_1, it was not previously the subject of litigation, nor could it have been. Yet it would be preposterous for a judicial system to engage repeatedly Jones's inflated sense of his prowess at patents. Nor could a sound legal system tolerate the capacity for mischief if Jones could repeatedly force Smith to bear the costs of defending her right to manufacture widgets or perhaps have to pay off Jones to be spared litigation costs. On these facts, Jones could be precluded from arguing that he owned the patent for widgets produced by Smith, because of the earlier determination that he did not in fact hold the patent. Diagrammatically:

Classic Issue Preclusion

Original Patent Suit (T_1) Jones v. Smith	Second Patent Suit (T_2) Jones v. Smith
Decided: J does not own the patent.	J may not argue that he owns the patent.

Both parties could, as with claim preclusion, argue that there had been some intervening change in law or fact that should allow for relief from the preclusive effects of the prior judgment. Absent such extraordinary interceding events, however, both parties were subject to the preclusive effects of a mutually dispositive factual finding.

The key to this early form of issue preclusion was the concept of *mutuality of obligation*. That is, a prior factual ruling could be applied to a future suit if, and only if, the determination of fact could be deemed binding on both parties to the dispute. If the second suit involved anyone other than the original parties, any factual dispute from the original suit could be relitigated because there was no mutually enforceable obligation between the parties arising from a prior decision.

As should be evident, so long as the doctrine of mutuality of obligation held, issue preclusion would be of limited utility. It furthered the objective of repose between the parties, but did relatively little to maximize the other overriding goal of preclusion law: efficiency. The potential for a broader payoff from adjudicatory fact-finding was being wasted.

A simple example shows the shortfalls of the mutuality requirement. Imagine that Jones filed the suit at T_2 not against Smith, but against another widget manufacturer. Now, all of a sudden, Jones would be free to claim anew that he was indeed the holder of the patent rights, notwithstanding the finding in *Jones v. Smith*. In the new litigation, Jones could not be bound because of the mutuality doctrine. There could be no mutuality because Jones's new adversary could not be bound by the outcome of the first proceeding. Any attempt to bind Jones's new adversary to the first proceeding would run afoul of the "principle of general application in Anglo–American jurisprudence that one is not bound by a judgment in personam in a litigation in which he is not designated as a party or to which he has not been made a party by service of process."[18] As a result, Jones would be free to pursue the same claim against as many new adversaries as he desired, a decidedly inefficient outcome, and one that could give rise to wildly inconsistent rulings.

Results of Classic "Mutuality of Obligation" Requirement

Original Patent Suit (T_1) Jones v. Smith	Second Patent Suit (T_2) Jones v. A, B, C
Decided: J does not own the patent.	J *may* argue that he owns the patent, even though he can't if he sues Smith.

In *Blonder–Tongue Laboratories, Inc. v. University of Illinois Foundation*,[19] the Supreme Court set about repairing just this anomaly. Confronted with back-to-back claims of patent infringement, the Court found that a plaintiff who had raised a claim and had it decided against him on the merits could be bound to the result in subsequent cases, even against parties who did not participate in the initial proceeding. There was no longer a need for perfect mutuality of obligation so long as the plaintiff had had a full and fair opportunity to assert the claim, and so long as the factual determination was necessary to the outcome of the case. The plaintiff against whom issue preclusion was asserted could hardly claim unfairness in its application, even if there were no corre-

18. Hansberry v. Lee, 311 U.S. 32, 40 (1940).

19. 402 U.S. 313 (1971).

sponding possibility for a mutual preclusion against his new adversary. After all, the plaintiff had chosen the forum of the original litigation and had chosen which claims to pursue to judgment. There was, therefore, no reason not to hold him to the consequences of his choices. By permitting issue preclusion against a losing plaintiff, courts could avoid allowing the waste of judicial resources on deciding the same issue, and avoid risking inconsistent judgments in the two trials. This proved a decisive step in garnering efficient returns on the investment of judicial resources in finding facts, and quickly was adopted not only as federal law, but also essentially as the law of all states. The effect was to sound the death knell of the mutuality of obligation doctrine.

Jones v. Smith under *Blonder–Tongue*

Original Patent Suit (T$_1$) Jones v. Smith	Second Patent Suit (T$_2$) Jones v. A, B, C
Decided: J does not own the patent.	**J now *may not* argue that he owns the patent, the same as if he sues Smith.**

But *Blonder–Tongue* was unlikely to be the final resting point for courts seeking to harness efficiency gains from cases that had actually been pushed through the litigation process all the way to trial. The case law quickly moved beyond *Blonder–Tongue*'s neat little surgical incursion into the inherited common law mutuality of obligation doctrine. The breakthrough came in *Parklane Hosiery Co. v. Shore*,[20] a case that for the first time allowed preclusion against a losing *defendant*. Before this, when a defendant lost on a particular issue, she was still allowed to defend that issue in the next suit. Thus, the polluter of a river whose claim that it had only dumped clean water had been rejected in one toxic tort case could argue the same thing in the next one. The premise was that, unlike the losing plaintiff, the losing defendant had not chosen the forum or the time to engage the merits. Absent that consent to put the matter at issue, the defendant was still allowed the choice to relitigate facts found against her. After *Parklane Hosiery*, that option was closed.

In *Parklane Hosiery*, the government prevailed against a defendant in a criminal antitrust case. The question then became whether the defendant could be bound to the litigated factual findings of the adverse judgment in a subsequent private civil case arising out

20. 439 U.S. 322 (1979).

of the same course of conduct. Although the narrow logic of *Blonder–Tongue* would not apply, the Court allowed issue preclusion to attach. Perhaps surprisingly, it did this despite the fact that the defendant had had no choice about the forum or the desirability of litigating these particular issues in the original suit—the factors that had been decisive in overturning the mutuality requirement in *Blonder–Tongue*. But in the end, efficiency demanded the result.

At the same time, in contrast to the Court's unhesitating endorsement of the expansion of issue preclusion in *Blonder–Tongue,* its holding in *Parklane Hosiery* was considerably more guarded. The Court's key concern was for the strategic "wait-and-see" plaintiff. This is a party who wishes to prosecute a case on the merits, but who awaits a ruling in another case involving an issue necessary to his own case. If the first plaintiff to go to trial prevails, the strategic sideliner gains the advantage of claiming issue preclusion against the litigated defenses of the mutual defendant. If the first case loses, then wisdom about trial approaches may be gained cheaply and with no risk of any prejudice to the second case. From the vantage point of a defendant in a mass harm case, the risks are overwhelming. If the plaintiffs were to try their cases *seriatim*, in each successive case the defendant stands either to win the one case at bar, or to risk a preclusive ruling that would spell defeat in all subsequent cases. Simply put, the defendant is at strategic risk in each case of either winning one case or losing a thousand.[21]

Parklane Hosiery

Original Mass Harms Suit (T_1) A v. B	Subsequent Mass Harms Suits C, D, E v. B
Held: B guilty of harming A.	B's hands may be tied by the factual findings of A v. B, B may not be able to defend by rearguing facts already decided.

By changing the risks faced by the parties, the Court introduced a new dimension of strategic use of preclusion. The effects are by no means easy to map. For example, a defendant facing many cases may suddenly feel pressure to invest in full-bore litigation even in a case that does not merit such attention. A defendant might even spend more than is at stake in any particular case in order to both avoid the risks of preclusion and to send a message to any individual litigant that any case would be a war of massive

---

21. For a fuller exposition of the strategic consequences of issue preclusion, *see* ROBERT G. BONE, CIVIL PROCEDURE: THE ECONOMICS OF CIVIL PROCEDURE 246–53 (2003).

escalation. To give but one example, for many years it was thought that this was the litigation strategy of tobacco defendants, for whom any loss was perceived as an invitation to disaster. The general perception was that a case against tobacco would end up costing more to prosecute than could likely be obtained by judgment. But strategic considerations abound. On the other side of the courtroom, coordinated plaintiffs might decide among themselves to present the most sympathetic case first, in the hopes that the emotional impact of the case will lead to judgment in their favor, after which the defendant will be helpless against the rush of those waiting in the wings.

The Supreme Court qualified its holding in *Parklane Hosiery* by not granting automatic issue preclusion from an earlier adverse judgment. Instead, the expansion of preclusion was to be determined under the specific facts of the case by a judge presiding over the second litigation. The Supreme Court specifically expressed skepticism about the appropriateness of preclusion in the case of a party who had had a full opportunity to participate in the first proceeding, but who chose strategically to sit on the sidelines. This introduced a strong equitable qualifier on the potential strategic misuse of expansive preclusion law. But the Court's qualifier may have been too little, too late. Once the Court stripped aside the last of the bars to the prospective application of adverse rulings in earlier litigation, the efficiency mandates were irresistible. Despite initial caution in the acceptance of *Parklane Hosiery*, the broader interpretation of issue preclusion was off and running and has by now been accepted in the overwhelming majority of American jurisdictions.

By way of concluding this section, a note on terminology: while *Blonder–Tongue* significantly advanced the scope of preclusion law, it also introduced an unfortunate nomenclature into this area of law, one that persists to this day. *Blonder–Tongue* introduced a distinction between permissible *defensive* collateral estoppel and impermissible *offensive* collateral estoppel. The former was the attempt by a defendant in the second case to use preclusion as a defensive shield to protect against the losing plaintiff in the first case pressing the same claim anew, as in *Blonder–Tongue*. Under *Blonder–Tongue,* such preclusion was appropriate because the plaintiff had had his day in court, in the forum of choice. The latter conception, the *offensive* use of collateral estoppel as a sword, rather than a shield, was an improper attempt by a victorious plaintiff in one case to preclude a subsequent defendant from mounting an independent defense in a subsequent case. Here preclusion would be used to foreclose a defendant who never had a day in court from mounting a defense, an impermissible outcome. This distinction was faithful to the holding of *Blonder–Tongue* and this notion of impermissible offensive collateral estoppel came to be the terminology of choice in the courts and among lawyers generally.

With *Parklane Hosiery* the terms remained, but their meanings changed. Although lawyers and courts clung to the "offensive" versus "defensive" collateral estoppel language, the terms began to take on distinct and incompatible definitions. After *Parklane Hosiery*, the terms stood for the proper use of preclusion as a defensive shield against a party who was a participant in a prior judicial resolution of contested facts, as opposed to the impermissible use of preclusion offensively by a party in an earlier proceeding seeking to bind a party who has not yet had his day in court. There is no evident gain in continuing to use terminology that corresponded to the line drawn by *Blonder Tongue* once the logic of that case has been superseded. The important thing to understand is that both tactics that were termed "offensive" by the two courts remain impermissible uses of issue preclusion. A plaintiff may not estop a defendant from defending herself simply because the plaintiff won an issue in prior litigation with someone else. Similarly, a victorious defendant cannot shield himself from future litigation from parties who might be able to do a superior job than the original plaintiff.

Far simpler than trying to jigger the definitions of what is offensive and defensive is the straightforward intuition that preclusion is not permitted against a party who has never had her day in court. Most questions of issue preclusion may be resolved by asking whether the party against whom preclusion is sought has had a chance to press his claim or defense in some prior proceeding. If the answer is no, absent some direct privity between that party and a losing party in a prior case, then preclusion will not be permitted.

No Preclusion Allowed

A v. B(T$_1$)	A v. C(T$_2$)
A wins an issue.	C can argue the same issue, because she wasn't in court the first time.

A v. B(T$_1$)	C v. B(T$_2$)
B wins an issue.	B is not shielded; C may argue the issue. Perhaps C can do a better job than A.

The modern focus is therefore best conceptualized by focusing on what issue was decided against whom, as expressed by the concept of issue preclusion, rather than on collateral estoppel, either offensive or defensive. Thus, under the contemporary rule, followed in most American jurisdictions, a party may be held to an adverse finding in a proceeding in which he participated, but may not seek to bind a previously unrepresented party to the outcome of the earlier case. The Court's commitment to the day-in-court ideal would demand no less.

IV. The Law of the Case.

Looking back across the preclusion spectrum reveals the controlling role played by the systemic interest in finality and efficiency. The development of preclusion law follows a general efficiency-driven trail toward greater resolution of disputes each time the adjudicatory process is invoked by litigants. The distinction between the broader form of claim preclusion and the more stringent requirements of issue preclusion may be thought of as turning on the complementary equitable concern of the actual litigants to finality. Once thought of in these terms, the preclusion doctrines fall at the far reaches of a *continuum* that begins with the concept of precedent or *stare decisis*. Decisional law is also an application of the need to realize efficiency gains from the resolution of disputes by informing prospective disputants of their likely fates in the courts. Midway along this *continuum* is the most yielding of the preclusion doctrines: the law of the case.

The law of the case refers to the principle that an issue, or question of law, decided at one stage of a case is not to be relitigated and redecided at a subsequent stage of the case should it arise again.[22] While the rules of preclusion prevent relitigation of the same claim and the same factual issue, they are concerned specifically with relitigation in *successive suits*; law of the case is instead concerned with relitigation of the same issue in successive *stages* of a single suit or trial proceeding.[23] Law of the case determinations, therefore, seek to regulate affairs *within* a proceeding and do not apply between separate cases. Unlike *res judicata*,

22. *See generally* Allan D. Vestal, *Law of the Case: Single Suit Preclusion*, 1967 UTAH L. REV. 1.

23. Rezzonico v. H & R Block, Inc., 182 F.3d 144, 148 (2d Cir. 1999) ("[L]aw of the case is similar to . . . *res judicata* in that it limits relitigation of an issue once it has been decided. However, law of the case is concerned with the extent to which law applied in a decision at one stage of litigation becomes the governing principle in later stages of the same litigation. *Res judicata* does not speak to direct attacks in the same case, but rather has application in subsequent actions.").

law of the case does not deem conclusive all questions that were present in the case and that may have been decided, but were not; actual decision of a question is necessary to establish law of the case, and unlike issue preclusion, law of the case applies to factual determinations whether or not they turn out to be necessary to the judgment. The law of the case doctrine, therefore, "merely express- es the practice of courts generally to refuse to reopen what has been decided, not a limit to their power."[24] It becomes more significant in highly complex litigation that spans many districts and long periods of time, and involves numerous parties and attorneys, where it would quickly become extremely wasteful to redecide every determination made in every stage of the litigation.

What limits law of the case is that it is purely an efficiency- driven device, and does not implicate the equitable aim of allowing parties repose. As one court expressed it, the law of the case "ensures judicial efficiency and prevents endless litigation. Its elementary logic is backed by elementary fairness—a litigant given one good bite at the apple should not have a second."[25] As a result, in practice, law of the case doctrine is much more flexible and far less binding than the other preclusion doctrines.

V.   Further Reaches.

Perhaps in some era long past it was possible to resolve fully a particular case by providing closure to the immediate litigants and the immediate litigants only. Unfortunately, the dictates of mass society oftentime frustrate closure absent resolution of claims or potential claims of third parties. As explained above, *res judicata* limits only the original parties or those in "privity"[26] to them, and issue preclusion does not bind those who have not had their day in court; therefore, formal legal doctrine would foreclose the expansive use of preclusion doctrines against anyone outside these bounds. That concept has yielded, however, to a recognition that under the federal *res judicata*, "a person may be bound by a judgment even though not a party if one of the parties to the suit is so closely

---

24. Messinger v. Anderson, 225 U.S. 436, 444 (1912).

25. Perkin–Elmer Corp. v. Computervision Corp., 732 F.2d 888, 890 (Fed. Cir. 1984).

26. Under a standard formulation, privity "is merely a word used to say that the relationship between the one who is a party on the record and another is close enough to include that other within the *res judicata*." Bruszewski v. United States, 181 F.2d 419, 423 (3d Cir. 1950). Thus, for example, a parent and a subsidiary corporation may be found in sufficient privity for a judgment against one to have preclusive effect against the other.

aligned with his interests as to be his virtual representative."[27]

For decades, lower courts have tried to expand the application of *res judicata* by pressing on the definition of what it means for a party not in the lawsuit to be so closely aligned with another as to allow preclusion to extend beyond the named parties to a litigation. However, the idea of binding virtual representation runs into conflict with "our 'deep-rooted historic tradition that everyone should have his own day in court.' "[28] The conflict is best exemplified in a 1989 Supreme Court case, *Martin v. Wilks*,[29] concerning a consent decree between the City of Birmingham and a group of black firefighters claiming race discrimination in the granting of promotional opportunities. As part of the settlement, the City of Birmingham agreed to overhaul its traditional seniority-based promotional system in order to overcome the history of racial exclusion. The decree was promptly challenged by the incumbent white firefighters, whose union contract enshrined seniority-based promotions. The question posed was whether court approval of the consent decree could bind the white firefighters. Since the white firefighters had not participated in the earlier action in their own capacity, the case turned on whether the City of Birmingham could serve as their stand-in representative in the first action. Arguably, there were many reasons to doubt the adequacy of the virtual representation by the City, particularly since by altering seniority-based opportunities the City settled claims for damages for which it directly would have been responsible.[30] At the same time, it was unlikely that there could be any resolution to the race-based denial of promotional opportunities without some adverse impact on the incumbent white firefighters. Thus, it was questionable that the interests of the City and the white firefighters were truly "so closely aligned."

Thus framed, *Martin v. Wilks* offered a direct conflict between the resolution of apparently bipolar litigation and the third-party effects of the traditional litigation model. The Supreme Court resolved the matter in favor of limiting the preclusive effects of judgments or decrees on parties who had not had their day in court. The risk of collusion at the expense of the unrepresented is too great when parties to the dispute have not only their own gains and

27. Meza v. General Battery Corp., 908 F.2d 1262, 1272 (5th Cir. 1990).

28. Martin v. Wilks, 490 U.S. 755, 762 (1989) (quoting 18 Wright & Miller, Federal Practice and Procedure § 4449, at 417 (1981)).

29. 490 U.S. 755 (1989).

30. This aspect of the case is discussed at length in Samuel Issacharoff, *When Substance Mandates Procedure:* Martin v. Wilks *and the Rights of Vested Incumbents in Civil Rights Consent Decrees*, 77 Cornell L. Rev. 189 (1992).

losses to weigh, but also the high temptation to foist the costs of their resolution on those who have never had an independent opportunity to protect their interests. Thus the Court, in reaffirming the traditional limitations of the preclusion doctrines, placed the burden of binding third parties squarely on the litigants:

> Joinder as a party, rather than knowledge of a lawsuit and an opportunity to intervene, is the method by which potential parties are subjected to the jurisdiction of the court and bound by a judgment or decree. The parties to a lawsuit presumably know better than anyone else the nature and scope of relief sought in the action, and at whose expense such relief might be granted. It makes sense, therefore, to place on them the burden of bringing in additional parties where such a step is indicated, rather than placing on potential additional parties a duty to intervene when they acquire knowledge of the lawsuit.[31]

A similar result obtained in litigation arising from two successive challenges to the imposition of an occupation tax in Jefferson County, Alabama. The tax was challenged first by the City of Birmingham—evidently a favorite litigant of the preclusion bar—and three individual taxpayers, and subsequently by a class of employees subject to the tax. The Alabama Supreme Court found the second suit to be barred because of a "substantial identity of parties." The Supreme Court reversed, holding, in the spirit of *Martin v. Wilks,* that preclusion without participation was to be soundly disfavored:

> [I]n Anglo–American jurisprudence ... one is not bound by a judgment *in personam* in a litigation in which he is not designated as a party or to which he has not been made a party by service of process.... As a consequence, a judgment or decree among parties to a lawsuit resolves issues as among them, but it does not conclude the rights of strangers to those proceedings.[32]

Despite these holdings, the pressure to expand the preclusive effect of judgments continues to be felt. This is particularly the case where the claims at issue are in some sense "public," meaning that there is nothing particularly distinctive about the individual claimant who comes before the courts. *Taylor v. Sturgell,* the most recent Supreme Court case on point, well demonstrates the conflict.[33] Taylor was an antique aircraft enthusiast who filed a claim

---

31. 490 U.S. at 765 (footnote omitted).

32. Richards v. Jefferson County, 517 U.S. 793, 798 (1996) (internal quotations omitted).

33. 553 U.S. 880 (2008).

arguing that the Freedom of Information Act (FOIA) should provide him access to Federal Aviation Administration (FAA) records relating to a WWII–era plane that caught his fancy. Prior to Taylor's suit, his friend Herrick—a member of the same vintage airplane club—had brought an unsuccessful suit against the FAA to obtain the same records, represented by the same lawyer. In all respects, therefore, the suits were identical, and the particular identity of the claimant made no difference to the controlling legal issue whether FOIA granted access to the FAA records.

The Supreme Court rejected the preclusion claim, recognizing that binding Taylor to the outcome of Herrick's litigation would, *de facto,* transform the first filed suit into a class action, with none of the structural protections of Rule 23. Nonparty preclusion—the troubling doctrine of virtual representation—could be justified only where there were clear procedural protections, as in class actions, or where there was a specific legal relationship between the party to the judgment and the party to be bound (such as a subrogation agreement in insurance or the privity between the preceding and succeeding owners of property).

Taylor drew the line at those legal relationships that either preexisted the litigation or were created under a court's supervision. Most significantly, the Court refused to allow a *post hoc* preclusion doctrine to be created through a broad reading of "adequate representation," finding that Herrick was not necessarily an adequate representative for Taylor just because Herrick had a strong incentive to litigate and Taylor and Herrick shared the same lawyer. The Court stressed that representation is adequate to justify preclusion only when, at a minimum, "the interests of the nonparty and her representative are aligned" and "either the party understood herself to be acting in a representative capacity or the original court took care to protect the interests of the nonparty."[34]

Still troubling was the inescapable fact that, barring collusion or a failure to prosecute in the first case, Taylor should have lost just as Herrick had already lost. A system that allows two identically situated litigants to obtain different outcomes by successively litigating an identical claim has more in common with the croupier at a roulette wheel than a court of justice. This is the most compelling argument advanced by the FAA as a reason to apply nonparty preclusion more liberally in "public law" cases where a duty is owed to the public generally. The Court acknowledged that such duties create the risk of "vexatious litigation" because "the number of plaintiffs with standing is potentially limitless." Howev-

---

34.　*Id.* at 900.

er, it concluded that *stare decisis*, along with "the human tendency not to waste money," rendered this risk more theoretical than real.[35] As with all claims by the Supreme Court to empirical expertise in how matters will play out, there is reason for caution in accepting that this will indeed be the case across the full range of public law disputes.

A variant of the *Taylor* preclusion problem was presented in *Smith v. Bayer Corp.*,[36] a complicated case involving the effect of the denial of class certification on subsequent efforts to certify a similar class in other courts. *Smith* had to resolve the difficult issue of cross-jurisdictional preclusion, a matter beyond the scope of this book. For our purposes, the relevant issue was whether a non-named member of a claimed class action could in any way have her rights adjudicated by a court deciding that the matter should not be a class action. Following in the spirit of *Taylor,* the Court in *Smith* held that "[t]he definition of the term 'party' can on no account be stretched so far as to cover a person . . . whom the plaintiff in a lawsuit was denied leave to represent."[37] From that, Justice Kagan concluded: "Neither a proposed class action nor a rejected class action may bind nonparties. What does have this effect is a class action approved under Rule 23."[38] As with *Taylor,* the Court found that the hoped for conclusion of litigation would have to come through the less formal instructive features of litigation:

> [O]ur legal system generally relies on principles of *stare decisis* and comity among courts to mitigate the sometimes substantial costs of similar litigation brought by different plaintiffs. We have not thought that the right approach (except in the discrete categories of cases we have recognized) lies in binding nonparties to a judgment.[39]

In sum, although the pressure to relax the general prohibition on third-party preclusion continues to mount, the Supreme Court has consistently cabined such preclusion to a limited set of exceptional circumstances. The clear direction of the law is toward an increasingly expansive view of conclusive resolution of claims presented and issues litigated as against parties. Thus far the expansion of the preclusion doctrines has been held in check by the preservation of the day-in-court opportunity for those not parties to the litigation.

35. *Id.* at 903–4 (internal quotations omitted).
36. 131 S.Ct. 2368 (2011).
37. *Id.* at 2379.
38. *Id.* at 2380.
39. *Id.* at 2381.

VI. Relief From Judgment.

As the problems of public law litigation and class actions reveal, the inherited preclusion doctrines map poorly onto the more expansive forms of modern litigation. The traditional doctrines of both claim and issue preclusion, including the mutuality of obligation requirement of collateral estoppel, drew from a conception of litigation that was tightly bound to two (and only two) parties disputing a single claim over a retrospective event. All the preclusion doctrines were aimed simply at allowing the resolution of that dispute to be binding and affording the parties their due sense of repose.

The expansive form of modern litigation changes the application of preclusion law. For the most part, we have seen how this results in broader uses of preclusion than the common law would have allowed. At the same time, the capacity of concluded litigation to have prospective effects on broader parties and a broader set of issues also compels a corresponding expansion of the ability to revisit the prospective preclusive effects of a judgment. While repose remains the object of dispute resolution, courts must also be attentive not only to the resolution of a dispute at the time it was litigated, but also to the propriety of its continuing to bind parties prospectively.

In recent years, the Supreme Court has had to revisit the question of not only *who* may be precluded by a judgment, as was discussed in the last section, but also *how long* a judgment may remain preclusive, as will be discussed in this section. Again, questioning how long a judgment may remain preclusive is not to revisit the correctness of the judgment at the time it was entered. Once the normal processes of appellate review have concluded, judgments must be final and parties must be allowed to get on with their lives. Instead, asking how long a judgment may remain preclusive is to ask what changes in circumstance can justify relieving parties from the prospective effects of a prior judgment.

The Supreme Court's recent decision in *Horne v. Flores*[40] provides the context for isolating the prospective effects of a judgment. At issue in *Horne* was the proper application of Rule 60(b)(5), which allows a party in concluded litigation to be relieved from the ongoing effects of a final judgment when "applying [the judgment] prospectively is no longer equitable." The case took the form of what is known as "structural injunction" litigation—that is, public

---

40. 129 S.Ct. 2579 (2009).

interest cases aimed at changing the operation of large institutions, generally governmental practices. In this case, a federal district court had issued an injunction ordering the state of Arizona to increase its funding for programs designed to assist non-native English speakers in overcoming their language barriers, as mandated by federal law. At the time of the litigation of the dispute, the district court found the level of funding for these programs in Arizona to be deficient enough to constitute a violation of governing federal law. Almost a decade after this injunction had been issued by the district court, Arizona sought to be relieved of its obligations under the court injunction, arguing that conditions had fundamentally changed in the intervening period—once again, not challenging the initial decree, but its continued operation. As the Court explained:

> Rule 60(b)(5) may not be used to challenge the legal conclusions on which a prior judgment or order rests, but the Rule provides a means by which a party can ask a court to modify or vacate a judgment or order if a significant change either in factual conditions or in law renders continued enforcement detrimental to the public interest.[41]

The Court also noted that, "Rule 60(b)(5) serves a particularly important function in what we have termed institutional reform litigation," because injunctions produced by such litigation "often remain in force for many years."[42] For this reason, courts "must take a flexible approach to Rule 60(b)(5) motions,"[43] especially in institutional reform cases, in which the prospective effects of prior litigations are particularly salient.

41. *Id.* at 2593 (internal quotations omitted).

42. *Id.*

43. *Id.* at 2594 (internal quotations omitted).

Chapter 8

MANAGEMENT

I. The Managerial Turn in Judging.

The world of procedure draws a divide between "inquisitorial" and "adjudicative" courts. The "inquisitorial" model prevails in the civil law processes of Europe and in countries whose legal system draws from Roman law. In this model, judges are expected to shoulder active responsibility for investigation and development of the case. Underlying this approach is the assumption that judges must be given the ability to focus the litigation process from the early investigative stages to the actual examination of witnesses at trial. In contrast, the "adjudicative" model of Anglo–American common law systems assumes a triadic division of responsibility between two adversaries and a judge weighing what is put before her. The adjudicative model sees the judge as a passive recipient of information and arguments provided by the various parties, who themselves bear primary responsibility for case investigation and development. The assumption here is that the parties have the incentive and the authority to control litigation, including expenditures, in pursuit of their private objectives, and that the court's job is to facilitate this.

There are other significant differences between the two systems. To take just one important example, no civil law countries use juries for non-criminal cases. Because of this, cases may be presented to the court in rolling fashion, allowing information to be acquired or discovered as it proves necessary. In some civil law countries, such as Italy, the acquisition and introduction of new information may even continue into the appeal. In American procedure, however, this type of rolling discovery is not possible. The focus of litigation, should there be no pre-trial disposition or settlement, is on a fixed trial of all the evidence. The evidentiary resolution is meant to take place either before a jury or, per Rule 52, in a dispositive ruling by the court. All trial findings of fact, whether by a jury or by a court, are entitled to substantial deference on appeal and may not be set aside unless "clearly erroneous," to use the language of Rule 52.

Despite the extensive literature detailing the differences between inquisitorial and adjudicative litigation models, the growing wisdom is that there is actually a great deal of convergence between the two. Notwithstanding the finality of trial in the American system, there have been great revisions in the presumed judicial passivity in the face of litigation, which have turned American judges into centrally active participants in the process. Correspondingly, the effects of globalization and increased cross-border transactions have led civil law systems to become more accustomed and more receptive to elements of adversarial control in the litigation process.

As we have seen, the 1938 Rules took the first steps in the direction of more direct engagement of courts in the dispute resolution process. The key development came with Rule 26 and the rest of the discovery provisions, which provided that information would be gathered under the aegis of the courts. The introduction of the discovery rules began the process of easing the presumed passive role of the court as dispassionate arbiter of whatever the parties might present. But while the new discovery rules allowed judges a slightly more active role in the process of framing the factual predicates of the dispute, it still left them in a relatively passive role overall: they would not act absent a party request for some form of intervention through the filing of a motion. Thus, as originally formulated, Rule 26 still did not allow judges actively to shape or to limit the discovery process absent extraordinary events and the request for judicial relief.

This began to change officially in 1983, with the adoption of a systematic series of reforms to the Federal Rules intended to encourage what Judith Resnik has termed "managerial judging."[1] First and foremost, the 1983 reforms sought to give courts a greater role in the shaping of the dispute. This approach, while still different from the ongoing supervisory power of inquisitorial civil law courts, unmistakably moved American courts in that direction. We have seen some evidence of this already in the earlier discussions of the summary judgment trilogy from 1986 and the subsequent ramping up of the scope of judicial review of the factual plausibility of a claim at the motion to dismiss stage, both of which heralded a greater judicial role in screening the factual bases of a case for trial. These case developments were, in fact, influenced by the same ideas that spurred the 1983 reforms. Underlying all these developments was the growing recognition that a declining percentage—barely one percent at present—of cases actually go to trial and that meaningful management of litigation requires judicial participation in *all* phases of the litigation process, including the power to create incentives toward settlement.

1. Judith Resnik, *Managerial Judges*, 96 HARV. L. REV. 374 (1982).

A clear example of the new direction paved by the 1983 reforms was the wholesale revision of Rule 16, the title of which was changed from "Pre–Trial Procedure, Formulating Issues" to "Pre-trial Conferences; Scheduling; Management." Prior to 1983, the limited managerial role of the court involved only the actual trial of a case: Rule 16 allowed for conferences on the eve of trial in order to, as the Rule's title made clear, clarify what the major issues at trial would be. This allowed the court to maintain control over the efficient use of *judicial* resources in a trial. But with only a small number of cases actually going to trial, extensive judicial power to craft the trial presentation gave the courts little power to regulate the conduct of the major part of litigation.[2] The limited reservoir of judicial managerial authority stopped short of permitting or promoting court supervision of *litigant* resources. As a result, there was a "widespread feeling that amendment [was] necessary to encourage pretrial management that meets the needs of modern litigation."[3] The 1983 amendments, therefore, granted courts the formal power to manage the litigation process, even when it occurred outside the courtroom. Indeed, with the 1983 amendments came the first overt recognition that "case management" was an integral function of the trial court.

Although the 1983 amendments expanded the managerial authority of the court, that authority continues to differ to a great degree from the civil, inquisitorial model in one important respect: there is no *requirement* that courts undertake this role. For example, Rule 16(b) mandates a "scheduling order" in each case, which "encourages the court to become involved in case management early in the litigation,"[4] but does not *require* a pretrial conference. The practical result of this is that the parties must report to the court at an early stage how the case is to be litigated, and the judge in turn *may* become more involved as the case demands. Similarly, the 1983 amendments to Rule 26 governing discovery increase the potential managerial oversight of the courts. In order to eliminate "burdensome" discovery, Rule 26(b)(2), as amended, authorizes, but does not require, a supervising court to act on its own initiative. Again, the reforms, while vesting courts with increased managerial authority, stopped well short of compelling judges to assume administrative oversight over litigants, as would be required in an inquisitorial system.

2. ARTHUR R. MILLER, THE AUGUST 1983 AMENDMENTS TO THE FEDERAL RULES OF CIVIL PROCEDURE 21 (Federal Judicial Center 1984).

3. H.R. DOC. No. 98–54, at 46 (1983).

4. *Id.*

Another major change of the 1983 amendments is the redirection of the court's attention from the trial of a case to its resolution, whether at trial or before. Thus, amended Rule 16(c) outlines what may be discussed at a pretrial conference, and directs courts to inquire as to "the possibility of settlement or the use of extrajudicial procedures to resolve the dispute."[5] As amended, this Rule provides an important array of managerial tools aimed at winnowing a case and perhaps prodding settlement. Judges now possess these powers from the outset of litigation. Should these tools prove insufficient, litigants must still establish their reasons for trial. Courts are empowered to demand a pretrial order from parties that lists (and must justify) every disputed issue of fact meriting trial, a stipulation as to nondisputed facts, a clear statement of the disputed issues of law, and a statement of agreed-upon legal standards. The Rule then compels the parties to come before the court prior to trial with a person having settlement authority over the claim. In effect, Rule 16 encourages active judicial intervention to resolve the case, with trial seen as an unlikely and perhaps unfortunate result.

The changes to the Federal Rules outlined so far represent a concerted effort to provide incentives for parties to settle their disputes before trial becomes necessary. But judicial involvement in promoting settlement should not be seen as a matter of all carrots and no sticks. The 1983 amendments not only changed the way courts approach pretrial litigation, but also inaugurated an era in which judges increasingly use coercive mechanisms, including mechanisms aimed at attorneys, to move litigants out of the courtroom. Among the tools made more readily available to courts since 1983, three stand out for specific attention: the use of sanctions to limit strategic or abusive behavior; the redirection of litigants away from courts and into alternative systems of dispute resolution; and the utilization of court-directed awards of attorneys' fees to limit claims.

II. Sanctions.

The original 1938 design of the Rules envisioned a world of litigation that was largely self-regulated until such time as a court was called upon to make dispositive rulings. The required pleadings were minimal and the court would not engage the litigants prior to trial, absent a specific request for judicial action filed in the form of a motion. Under this scheme, a court exercised power through its

---

5. In the 2007 stylistic revisions to the Rules, this language from Rule 16(c) was rewritten to direct courts to consider ways of "settling the case and using special procedures to assist in resolving the dispute. . . ."

rulings on matters presented for resolution. Not surprisingly, the turn toward a managerial court required not only procedures for earlier intervention into legal disputes, but increased power to compel desired litigant behavior. The world of presumed litigant autonomy was coming to a close and one clear indication of this was the emergence of sanctions as a disciplinary tool. Thus, the 1983 amendment to Rule 16 pretrial practices included a new section 16(f), which provided for extensive sanctions upon failure to comply. As the congressional report accompanying the amendment to Rule 16 made clear, "[E]xplicit reference to sanctions enforces the rule's intention to encourage forceful judicial management."[6]

In tandem with new Rule 16 were the amendments to the discovery rules, primarily Rule 26. Discovery was initially created to be self-regulating. Parties would acquire what information was necessary for the resolution of their dispute and no more. Although predating the extensive integration of economic analysis into law, the original discovery rules anticipated an efficient equilibrium in which no party would have an incentive to overlitigate. Any unjustified or strategically-motivated attempt to escalate discovery would be met by a corresponding reply, escalating into the litigation equivalent of mutually assured destruction.[7] The risk of escalation alone, however, proved an insufficient deterrent to excessive discovery. Discovery gives rise to what economists term a "moral hazard," which is defined as a situation in which parties are not forced to internalize directly the costs of their conduct. The easiest and most common example of this concept is parties with insurance who, once insured, may not take ordinary levels of care since, if the insurance is sufficient, they may be indifferent to the consequences of their conduct. Likewise, in discovery, other than the danger of retaliation, it typically costs very little to ask for documents or propound interrogatories, and it may be quite costly for the other side to answer these requests. Therefore, parties may take a "what the heck" approach to asking for whatever suits their fancy, knowing that they do not bear the brunt of the costs of producing the information.[8] As a result, the self-regulating, efficient use of discovery anticipated by the Rules may not have been realized in real life.

---

6. H.R. Doc. No. 98–54, at 53 (1983).

7. *See* John K. Satear, *The Barrister and the Bomb: The Dynamics of Cooperation, Nuclear Deterrence, and Discovery Abuse,* 69 B.U. L. Rev. 569 (1989).

8. For a discussion of the impact on settlement of the apparently "free" good of asking for information, see Samuel Issacharoff & George Loewenstein, *Unintended Consequences of Mandatory Disclosure,* 73 Tex. L. Rev. 753 (1995).

As previously discussed in Chapter 3, it is no longer the case that, as the Rules originally stated, "the frequency of use of [discovery] methods is not limited." Instead Rule 26(b)(2), as amended in 1991, imposes presumptive limitations with an eye towards eliminating "burdensome" discovery. Again, the court is allowed to act on its own initiative, which allowance was "intended to encourage judges to be more aggressive in identifying and discouraging discovery overuse,"[9] and "contemplates greater judicial involvement in the discovery process and thus acknowledges the reality that it cannot always operate on a self-regulating basis."[10] Whether instigated by a motion or *sua sponte,* a judicial finding that discovery was sought inappropriately *requires* the court to impose sanctions on parties, attorneys, or both. The unusual mandatory character of this Rule is designed to overcome what the drafters of the amendments considered to be the "asserted reluctance to impose sanctions on those who abuse the discovery rules."[11]

The most significant managerial innovation of 1983, however, addressed not the conduct of attorneys or parties during litigation, but their reasons for coming into court in the first place. The vehicle was the 1983 alteration to Rule 11, a previously little-considered provision that had required only that the original pleadings in a case be signed. Under revised Rule 11(b), the signature of an attorney on any pleading or document filed with the court took on a new meaning: the signature became a certification that the submitting party and attorney had made a "reasonable inquiry" into any factual assertions or legal arguments within the document—an objective inquiry designed to require litigants to carefully consider a document before signing it—and that the document in question had not been put forward for any improper purpose, including delay or harassment. Before the 1983 amendments, failure to comply with Rule 11 resulted in the court simply striking the offending pleading or document. But the new penalties were much more severe: the court, "upon motion or upon its own initiative," "shall" impose "an appropriate sanction" on anyone violating the above provision (knowingly or otherwise). Again, of special note is the mandatory nature of the sanction, the ability of the court to act on its own, and the strict approach to liability. Although the court was also allowed to punish the client if that was appropriate, the practical result of these changes was to shift the repercussions from the client, who had previously suffered all of the ill effects of Rule

---

9. H.R. Doc. No. 98–54, at 57 (1983).

10. *Id.* at 58.

11. *Id.* at 60.

11, to the attorney. Although courts in theory had always had the power to intervene on their own initiative, the *sua sponte* provision was added "to overcome the traditional reluctance of courts to intervene unless requested by one of the parties."[12] According to the Advisory Committee, such initiative was in fact "part of the court's responsibility for securing the [judicial] system's effective operation."[13]

Revised Rule 11 transformed federal practice. The courtly custom that lawyers did not challenge the professional integrity of other lawyers quickly succumbed to the routine filing of motions for sanctions against the losing party. The effects of "hindsight bias" or "Monday morning quarterbacking" made it appear that the losing party had been pursuing a losing strategy all along and that the failure to confess error must have been the product of contumacious conduct. In turn, sanctions practice set off a new cycle of collateral litigation. Motions for sanctions begat cross-motions for sanctions for the filing of frivolous Rule 11 sanctions motions, and so forth. In short order, sanctions practice became a commonplace part of federal litigation, indeed a veritable "avalanche" of collateral litigation was precipitated, with the threat of sanctions motions an everyday event.[14]

Two issues came to dominate the application of new Rule 11. The first concerned the purpose of sanctions. The "American rule" of litigation makes each party responsible for its own attorneys' fees. Unlike the "British" or "continental" rule that allows the winning party to recover the costs and fees associated with the case, American practice does not permit fee-shifting as part of the judgment, unless specifically authorized by statute. As a result of Rule 11, the American rule came under pressure as judges began to award fees to the prevailing party as a sanction for improper litigation.

12. *Id.* at 38.

13. *Id.*

14. As described by one commentator, "The 1983 Advisory Committee's invitation to use Rule 11 to attack pleadings and motions triggered an avalanche of 'satellite litigation.' Beginning in 1984, the volume of cases decided under the rule increased dramatically. By the end of 1987, the number of reported Rule 11 cases had plateaued. Even though the number of reported cases leveled off, motions under the amended rule continued to be made routinely, especially by defense counsel, as many attorneys were unable to pass up the opportunity to force their adversaries to justify the factual and legal bases underlying motions and pleadings. Indeed, one study found that in a one-year period, almost one-third of the respondents to the survey reported being involved in a case in which Rule 11 motions or orders to show cause were made. The same study showed that almost 55% of the respondents had experienced either formal or informal threats of Rule 11 sanctions." Georgene Vairo, *Rule 11 and the Profession*, 67 Fordham L. Rev. 589, 598 (1998) (footnotes omitted).

More significantly, Rule 11 began to encroach upon the enforceability of certain substantive rights. Unlike discovery sanctions or penalties for failing to comply with the settlement exploration procedures under Rule 16, the sanctions authorized under amended Rule 11 went to the decision to litigate itself. In most instances, the sanctionable event became the decision to invoke the judicial forum, to enter court. Plaintiffs suffered disproportionately under this regime since a failed lawsuit both took the initiative of commanding the time and costs of litigation and invited an after-the-fact finding that the claim was meritless all along. Lawyers were most at risk in cases in which they had to rely on their client's account of facts before filing suit, which had a predictable adverse impact on plaintiffs' counsel in cases where liability turned on matters, such as the state of mind of the defendant in any action for intentional wrongdoing, in which critical evidence could only be examined once the discovery process got underway. This was a particular problem in cases that typically turned on documentary evidence that could not be examined prior to formal discovery—as in employment discrimination cases, for example. The prevalence of Rule 11 sanctions after a failed claim, and the rise of fee-shifting as the preferred sanction, led many lawyers to abandon fields such as civil rights and environmental cases on the plaintiff's side. Since these were the fields where Congress had created a statutory right for prevailing plaintiffs to recover fees from a losing defendant in order to induce lawyers to represent indigent clients, the impact of revised Rule 11 was to undercut the willingness of lawyers to take on cases which Congress had sought to promote, a conflict between procedural law and the substantive policy considerations of the underlying legislation. The impact of amended Rule 11 created a firestorm of controversy.

In 1991, Rule 11 was altered to dampen the rush to sanctions at the end of a losing case. First, under new Rule 11(c)(2), the amount of sanctions was limited to that necessary to deter improper conduct, rather than to provide compensation to the prevailing party. Second, and most significantly, the procedures for seeking sanctions were altered. No motion for sanctions could be submitted to the court unless first presented to the opposing party with specific identification of the offending pleading and the reasons for its being sanctionable. Moreover, a request for sanctions could be made to the court under new Rule 11(c)(1)(A) only after the party charged with sanctionable conduct had had 21 days to consider withdrawing or amending the offending pleading. Although courts retained the power to sanction improper conduct *sua sponte,* the 21–day safe harbor effectively ended the practice of sanctions motions following successful motions to dismiss or for summary judgment. Though coming to define a major part of federal practice in the initial period after 1983, the 1991 amendments returned Rule 11 to the relative backwaters of the managerial arsenal.

III.   Alternative Dispute Resolution.

One of the most significant developments in the litigation landscape over the past 20 years or so has been the rise of alternative dispute resolution (ADR) mechanisms as an alternative to the formal processes of court-focused litigation. Numerous factors prompted the rise of these alternative mechanisms, but none loom so large as the perceived potential for unchecked cost escalation in formal litigation. A court battle can be prohibitively expensive. In addition, repeat litigants, such as commercial entities that anticipate routine disputes arising from the implementation of contracts with many parties, often sought a mechanism that would provide them with *an* answer to disputed issues at lower cost, even if it proved not to be *the* answer that might have emerged from full investigation of the facts in formal litigation. Further, the presumption of public availability of pleadings and accompanying documentation created difficulties for litigants who feared disclosure of business secrets or other matters of confidence through the normal operations of the public litigation system. Key to private dispute resolution mechanisms is that they are just that: private.

ADR procedures are typically more informal than litigation under the Federal Rules. There is generally no discovery permitted and the results are kept confidential to the parties. Moreover, the procedures can be tailored to the needs of the litigants, and range from mediation to more formalized arbitration. In mediation, a neutral party attempts to facilitate settlement by serving as an intermediary between the parties, seeking common ground for resolution of the dispute. A mediator will generally communicate offers and counteroffers in an attempt to narrow the range of dispute, hopefully eliminating the rancor or strategic posturing that may serve as a barrier to settlement. Arbitration consists of an actual presentation of claims and defenses to a neutral decisionmaker or, in some cases, a panel of decisionmakers. Often arbitrators are drawn from the ranks of retired judges. They render a decision that is binding upon the parties and, under the terms of the Federal Arbitration Act,[15] is entitled to overwhelming deference by courts.

---

15.   9 U.S.C. § 4.

The rise of ADR mechanisms is not without controversy. As with any area in which relatively well-heeled private parties can bypass public institutions, there is an accompanying loss of prestige and public support for the corresponding public ventures (e.g., private support of private schools diminishes support of the more privileged classes for public ones). Moreover, to the extent that areas of law shift to the less visible private sphere, as with commercial disputes, the development of the public law may be compromised. And there are those who question both the efficacy and the equity of private dispute resolution. Advocates of ADR often cite high success rates in settlement, with figures reaching 95 percent and sometimes better. Critics respond that the formal litigation system reaches comparable figures for pretrial resolution of disputes, an argument that calls for difficult empirical assessments of the relative cost and frequency of dispute resolution under the two systems. Finally, there are those who contend that informal processes tend to reproduce power imbalances between the parties. For example, feminists contend that women tend to fare poorly in mediated divorces where conditions of dependence or intimidation may reassert themselves.[16] Similar concerns have been voiced with regard to consumer and employment arbitration requirements that are, for all practical purposes, imposed by the offeror, usually the party with the upper hand economically.

Whatever the criticisms, ADR is an important and growing feature of the dispute resolution landscape. Indeed, there are several ways in which ADR is increasingly influential within the court system itself. First, courts have interpreted the mandate of Rule 16(c) to include seeking out ADR mechanisms to take advantage of "special procedures to assist in resolving the dispute." One interesting example of this is the use of the "summary jury trial" as pioneered in the federal courts of Ohio.[17] Instead of holding a full-blown trial, a six-person jury is "empanelled" to hear opening and closing arguments, and a summation of the evidence by the attorney for each side. The jury deliberates, typically within view of the parties, comes to a conclusion and suggests an award. Unlike a trial, however, the jury is not a legally constituted body and has no power to enter a judgment. The point of the exercise is to offer a streamlined reality check for litigants overly enamored of their particular side of a dispute—a point that will be explored more fully

16. *See* Trina Grillo, *The Mediation Alternative: Process Dangers for Women*, 100 YALE L.J. 1545, 1548 (1991); *see also* LINDA BABCOCK & SARA LASCHEVER, WOMEN DON'T ASK: NEGOTIATION AND THE GENDER DIVIDE (2003) (describing propensity of women not to demand as much compensation as men do).

17. *See* Thomas D. Lambros, *The Summary Jury Trial—An Alternative Method of Resolving Disputes*, 69 JUDICATURE 286 (1986).

in Chapter 9. While only some jurisdictions have experimented with the summary jury trial, virtually all jurisdictions offer some form of court-annexed mediation services. These allow for confidential efforts to explore settlement without the direct participation of the court. Some jurisdictions, such as Floridas state courts, now require mandatory mediation prior to the commencement of discovery and other litigation procedures.

Second, courts have broadly construed the scope of the Federal Arbitration Act to grant increasing finality to private dispute resolution. In a series of decisions over the past 20 or so years, the Supreme Court has imparted great finality to arbitral decisions and limited the scope of judicial review. In effect, these decisions have made arbitration the dispositive forum for the resolution of large areas of claims between contractually related parties. The foundation for the expansive view of arbitration is found in a series of cases known as the *Steelworkers' Trilogy*. There the Court held that arbitration under a union collective bargaining agreement provided the sole forum for resolving employment disputes, that the question of the scope of the arbitration agreement was itself a matter for arbitration, and that federal courts had almost no authority to reexamine the merits determinations of arbitrations.[18] More recently, the Court found that contractual agreements to arbitrate all disputes in the employment context meant all disputes, even those that might otherwise be directly actionable in federal court under the employment discrimination laws.[19]

An important issue is the potential tension between arbitration agreements and class actions. Increasingly, arbitration agreements are "shrink-wrapped" into all sorts of products, from computer software to consumer goods purchased from catalogues or over the Internet. In much the same fashion as the forum selection clause at issue in *Carnival Cruise Lines, Inc. v. Shute*,[20] discussed in Chapter 5, these provisions require arbitration of all disputes arising from the transaction. The difficulty in many consumer transactions is that the amount at issue from an unacceptable consumer product is not worth the cost or trouble to arbitrate on a one-by-one basis, just as it is not worth litigating in court contested small claims. Where there is no arbitration agreement in place, similarly situated plain-

---

18. *See* United Steelworkers v. American Mfg. Co., 363 U.S. 564 (1960); United Steelworkers v. Warrior & Gulf Navigation Co., 363 U.S. 574 (1960) (presuming an arbitration clause to cover a situation unless it was *impossible* to do so); United Steelworkers v. Enterprise Wheel & Car Corp., 363 U.S. 593 (1960).

19. *See* Gilmer v. Interstate/Johnson Lane Corp., 500 U.S. 20 (1991); Circuit City Stores, Inc. v. Adams, 532 U.S. 105 (2001).

20. 499 U.S. 585 (1991).

tiffs could overcome this collective action problem through the mechanism of the class action. The question in a growing number of cases is whether the presence of an agreement to arbitrate all claims stands as a barrier to any form of class certification. There is scant experience with classwide arbitrations, and even where possible, the ability to bind absent class members to a decree requires a court order, which makes even more complicated the relation between arbitration and judicial proceedings. Further, the Supreme Court ruled that whether class treatment is permitted within arbitration is a matter determined by the underlying contract provision, and as such must be interpreted by arbitrators.[21] Seemingly, the result of this may be that potential defendants need only insert a mandatory arbitration provision in a contract and couple it with a "no-class-arbitration" clause in order to avoid class actions altogether, either in court or in arbitration.[22] The prevalence of such clauses prompted a judicial backlash. California state courts began to challenge the enforceability of mandatory arbitration clauses and have refused to compel individual arbitration in the context of consumer class claims, holding, to the contrary, that courts may compel classwide arbitration.[23] Other courts have also acted to curtail the compelled individual arbitration clauses in the case of small value claims, such as credit card overcharges or cell phone billing disputes.[24]

Most recently, the Supreme Court limited the ability of states to refuse to enforce arbitration agreements from out-of-state contracts, even if deemed violative of state public policy. In a technical preemption challenge to a California state refusal to enforce a mandatory non-class arbitration clause, the Court in *AT&T Mobility v. Concepcion*[25] held that, "the [Federal Arbitration Act] prohibits states from conditioning the enforceability of certain arbitration agreements on the availability of classwide arbitration procedures."[26]

21. Green Tree Financial Corp. v. Bazzle, 539 U.S. 444 (2003).

22. *See* Myriam Gilles, *Opting Out of Liability: The Forthcoming, Near–Total Demise of the Modern Class Action*, 104 MICH. L. REV. 373 (2005).

23. Keating v. Superior Court, 31 Cal.3d 584, 645 P.2d 1192 (1982); Discover Bank v. Superior Court, 36 Cal.4th 148, 113 P.3d 1100 (2005).

24. *See, e.g.*, Kristian v. Comcast Corp., 446 F.3d 25 (1st Cir. 2006); Lowden v. T–Mobile USA, Inc., 512 F.3d 1213 (9th Cir. 2008); Dale v. Comcast Corp., 498 F.3d 1216 (11th Cir. 2007); Luna v. Household Finance Corp. III, 236 F.Supp.2d 1166 (W.D. Wash. 2002); Lozada v. Dale Baker Oldsmobile, Inc., 91 F.Supp.2d 1087 (W.D. Mich. 2000); State ex rel. Dunlap v. Berger, 211 W.Va. 549 (2002); Powertel, Inc. v. Bexley, 743 So.2d 570 (Fla. Dist. Ct. App. 1999).

25. 131 S.Ct. 1740 (2011).

26. *Id.* at 1744.

In sum, it is now clear that the most obvious consequence of the cost of legal procedure is that many disputes cannot be processed because they do not justify the likely costs. There is also the strong public regulatory interest in viewing the court system as a scarce public resource that must be rationed in some rational fashion. The result has been increased attention to all manner of ADR systems. Some of these operate as an adjunct to the court system, as with court-mandated mediation and innovative procedural shortcuts, such as the summary jury trial. Other results include the greater judicial willingness to enforce contractual commitments to arbitration and the increased willingness to impart finality to arbitral decisions. In all of these approaches there is a self-conscious trade-off between the quality of the adjudication (as reflected in the presence of attorneys, the availability of discovery, the use of the rules of evidence, and the presence of an appeals process) and the cost. Proponents of ADR herald the cost saving and the potential greater conciliation available outside the litigation setting. Critics bemoan the loss of public values coming from public dispute resolution and question the claim that ADR resolves disputes more effectively. Under either view, it is clear that the pressure to move outside the litigation system is the direct result of that system's commitment to party-controlled adjudication based on fully revealed information. That commitment may not be sustainable. When unconstrained, the litigation system may impose an unchecked and unrealizable cost obligation on parties who may just need some resolution of a dispute, even if it is not the perfect resolution.

IV. Judicial Control of Fees.

Consistent with the overriding commitment to party autonomy, the American rule of attorneys' fees makes each party liable for his or her own litigation expenses. The sole (and minor) exception to this rule is provided by 28 U.S.C. § 1920, which permits administrative taxing of "costs" against the losing party in litigation. Because such costs are defined narrowly to include only filing fees, reproduction costs of court pleadings, and other technical costs associated with notice and filing requirements, the taxing of costs has little impact upon litigation strategy.

Nonetheless, there is one provision of the Rules that tries to use the taxable cost structure to create disincentives against quixotic litigation endeavors. Under the terms of Rule 68, a plaintiff who is offered a settlement and turns it down will not be considered a prevailing party for purposes of assignment of costs if he or she goes to trial and does not obtain a judgment exceeding the prior offer. Under such circumstances, the plaintiff would be able to recover costs up to the time of the initial settlement offer, but not after. From that moment forward, the *defendant* would be considered to have prevailed and would be entitled to recover costs from the plaintiff. On its face, Rule 68 is designed to create pressures to settle, a subject that has fascinated academic commentators.[27] In practice, however, Rule 68 has almost no significance. The reason is quite simple: taxable costs are too small a component of litigation expenses to have much bearing on settlement incentives.

Even the exceptions have exceptions, and there is one unique setting in which Rule 68 has actual significance. There are cases in which the American rule that parties bear their own expenses does not hold. In a number of substantive areas of law, Congress has determined that there would be insufficient enforcement of publicly important laws if litigants had to carry their own freight. For example, consider the significant costs associated with prosecuting a school desegregation suit on behalf of a class of schoolchildren— or a voting rights case, or a prison conditions case. Under 42 U.S.C. § 1988, a prevailing plaintiff in these cases is allowed to recover not only costs but also attorneys' fees from a losing defendant. The object of this exception to the general rule against fee-shifting is to induce publicly beneficial lawsuits in circumstances where the financial returns from litigation are insufficient, or simply not available.

In *Marek v. Chesny*,[28] the Court confronted the interplay between Rule 68 and fee-shifting under 42 U.S.C. § 1988. The question was whether an offer of judgment, meaning an offer to settle, would serve to cap fee-shifting in addition to cost-shifting if the offer were not superseded by the judgment at trial. The technical issue was whether the term "costs" in Rule 68—up to now understood as only the administrative costs of the case—would be read to also include *fees*—the money paid by the party to its lawyers—even though the two terms are carefully segregated in both the Rules and governing statutes. The Court concluded that allowing the recovery of fees for work that produced no additional benefit made no sense and held that the Rule 68 offer of judgment capped not only costs, but recoverable fees as well. But the problem with that solution in this case, involving a shooting death by a police officer, is that it produces an incentive for the plaintiffs' *lawyer* to want to accept a low settlement (or risk not getting paid), while the plain-

---

27. *See* Geoffrey P. Miller, *An Economic Analysis of Rule 68*, 15 J. LEGAL STUD. 93 (1986).

28. 473 U.S. 1 (1985).

tiffs, the decedent's family, had little reason to accept that same offer. On the contrary, given that the only consequence to the plaintiffs if they received a lower judgment later would be the failure to recover the minor technical costs available under Rule 68, they had hardly a thing to lose by continuing. Since the family was not liable for fees, this produced a split between the incentives of the plaintiffs' lawyer and the plaintiffs themselves.

Beyond the technical issues of the applicability of Rule 68, *Marek* starkly raises questions about the dual role of lawyers as faithful agents of clients on the one hand, and as officers of the court on the other. This is an issue we briefly confronted in Chapter 3 in discussing *Hickman v. Taylor*,[29] in which the Court created the work-product privilege precisely to keep the incentives between client and attorney aligned. As Justice Jackson noted in *Hickman*, by playing the role of zealous advocates for their clients, lawyers allow individuals, even culpable ones, to navigate the shoals of the legal system.[30] The ability to secure faithful representation by a trained advocate is one of the hallmarks of a mature legal system and has come to be viewed as a central component of due process. At the same time, lawyers owe a duty of honor to the legal system that necessarily imposes limitations on advocacy. Much as lawyers may seek to advance the interests of their clients, they may not destroy documents, suborn perjury, or facilitate unlawful conduct. As with all the polar positions in law, considerable controversy attends the gray areas between advocacy and duty to the legal system overall.

Much like a lawyer's responsibility to the legal system, the question of payment—the lawyer's responsibility to herself—complicates the attorney-client relationship. For economists, this insight is likely second nature: attorney-client relations are a subset of principal-agent problems, and there is always a risk of self-serving behavior on the part of an agent. Whether the agent is a real estate salesperson, a doctor, a mechanic, or a lawyer, there is always a problem. We turn to agents to handle our affairs precisely because of our inability to handle them ourselves. Yet self-interest on the part of our agents is always present, and the very reason we turn to them compromises our ability to monitor them successfully. We rely on the mechanic because we do not really know what is wrong with our car; yet our ignorance makes us unable to know whether the mechanic is doing a good job, taking too long, overbilling us, and so forth. Reliance on the fact that a mechanic seemed

29.   329 U.S. 495 (1947).

30.   *Id.* at 515 (Jackson, J., concurring).

an honest chap, or that the doctor had good bedside manner, is a poor substitute for the ability to assess meaningfully how our agents are discharging their duty.

The law has resisted this easy understanding of the economics of principal-agent relations. Much of the law governing the conduct of lawyers mandates exclusive attentiveness to the interests of clients and disregard of the lawyer's financial interests. There is little that addresses directly the problem of conflicting economic motives in the relation between lawyers and clients. Instead we rely on notions of professionalism and fiduciary obligations, backed up by threats of discipline or malpractice, to compel attorney fidelity to the interests of clients.

Marek poses a paradox because it is an area where, as a result of fee-shifting, one party may, in effect, seek to play the other party's lawyer against the interest of the client. As we have seen, under the facts of the case, the offer to settle would serve as an incentive for the lawyer to seek to end the litigation, while the client had relatively little to lose by not accepting the low offer. For the Court, this was not a problem. As Chief Justice Burger expressly acknowledged, "[a]pplication of Rule 68 will serve as a disincentive *for the plaintiff's attorney* to continue litigation after the defendant makes a settlement offer."[31] This is the first time the Court has acknowledged the propriety of using incentives to push a wedge between the interests of attorneys and their clients, in order to induce those clients to choose settlement as a result of the compromised position of the attorney. The Court looked to the inherent principal-agent tensions in attorney-client relations to provide an independent set of incentives for lawyers to settle claims, even where their clients might not stand to benefit. *Marek* seeks systemic benefits from compromising the fragile alliance between lawyer and client.

The willingness to allow one side to maneuver the other's vulnerability with regard to client interests to promote settlement was posed even more acutely in *Evans v. Jeff D.*[32] There a lawyer representing a class of institutionalized, mentally ill minors found himself in the unenviable position of being offered a generous settlement by the defendant, the state of Idaho, only on condition that he waive his claim for attorneys' fees under § 1988. Focusing on the legal system's interest in settling cases efficiently, the Court rejected arguments that offers of settlement without fees might compromise the willingness of lawyers to take civil rights cases in

---

31. *Id.* at 10 (emphasis added).

32. 475 U.S. 717 (1986).

the future—something that presumably ran counter to Congress's intention in passing § 1988. The Court reasoned that defendants are unlikely to settle without knowing the full cost of the total settlement, including attorneys' fees, and that bundling the considerations was not only inescapable but appropriate. Taken together, *Marek* and *Evans v. Jeff D.* signal the willingness to use fee-shifting and judicial control of fee awards as instruments to promote settlement, even at the cost of some disruption to the attorney-client bond.

V. Limits on the Managerial Model.

The U.S. is not the only common law country facing the difficult issue of cost burdens from litigation. In Great Britain, the problem of cost escalation had gotten so extreme by the early 1990's that whole ranges of everyday disputes, such as a disagreement with a contractor, became prohibitively expensive to litigate, which effectively prevented recourse to the courts to all but the very wealthy or those subsidized by state-provided legal services. In part, the problems in Britain were the result of the system of loser-pays fee-shifting. Assume, for example, a case in which each party has a 50–50 chance of winning. In effect, each incremental dollar spent on litigation has an anticipated cost of only 50 cents, since the other side stands a 50 percent chance of having ultimately to pick up the cost. In addition, each incremental expenditure by the other side not only has a 50 percent chance of being picked up by the adverse party, but also increases the risk that the entire cost of litigation will be passed on to the adverse party if the incremental expenditure proves helpful in determining the outcome of the litigation. As a result, the best understanding of litigation dynamics under a loser-pays system is that parties are less likely to litigate, but once in litigation, are more likely to accelerate expenditures.[33]

Unlike the American response to date, however, the British response has been far more managerial, while at the same time seeking to facilitate recourse to the courts, rather than forcing litigants out of the court system. In 1994, the Lord Chancellor appointed Lord Woolf to head an investigation charged with improving access to justice and reducing the costs of litigation. The Woolf Report concluded that in order to achieve the objective of "appropriate and proportionate means of resolving disputes,"

---

33. This is the best understanding in the academic literature to date. *See* Avery W. Katz & Chris William Sanchirico, *Fee Shifting in Litigation: Survey and Assessment* (Univ. of Pennsylvania Inst. for Law and Econ. Research Paper No. 10–30), *available at* http://papers.ssrn.com/sol3/papers.cfm?abstract_id=1714089.

"there is no alternative to a fundamental shift in the responsibility for the management of civil litigation in this country from litigants and their legal advisers to the courts."[34] Perhaps the most striking feature of the Woolf Report was its willingness aggressively to ration litigation resources to prevent parties from being overwhelmed by costs. Most noteworthy is the creation of a "fast track" for parties of limited means:

> The fast track is intended to provide improved access to justice for litigants with modest cases by providing a strictly limited procedure designed to take cases to trial within a short but reasonable timescale at a fixed cost that litigants can afford. It is intended to be a procedure without frills. It will ensure equality of treatment between litigants even if they are of unequal means. It will provide little scope for a wealthy party to indulge in aggressive tactics designed to wear down his opponent. It will be designed so that the litigant's maximum liability for costs, even if he is unsuccessful, can be anticipated with certainty. . . .

The fast track was designed to improve access to justice for those who at present cannot afford to litigate.[35]

The Woolf Report represented a strong administrative initiative to provide for a rationed and rational system of judicial resolution of disputes. Unlike expanded ADR processes that serve as alternatives to courts, or the managerial initiatives that induce litigants to seek private resolution, this British reform approach was strikingly court-focused. Even in Britain, however, the problem of litigation cost continues to plague the system, despite the inroads into a more managerial approach to court access.[36]

Such rationed justice proposals are not unknown in the U.S. Many state court systems provide for local small claims courts in which disputes are resolved quickly, without discovery, and often without counsel. But these courts typically have very limited jurisdiction, allowing them to hear cases involving at most a few thousand dollars. More ambitious were the efforts of Judge Robert Parker in the Eastern District of Texas, who used a tracking system much like that implemented in Britain. Under the local rules of court, prior to the commencement of any expenditures,

---

34. LORD HARRY WOOLF, ACCESS TO JUSTICE: INTERIM REPORT TO THE LORD CHANCELLOR ON THE CIVIL JUSTICE SYSTEM IN ENGLAND AND WALES 26 (1995).

35. *Id.* at 41.

36. LORD RUPERT JACKSON, REVIEW OF CIVIL LITIGATION COSTS: FINAL REPORT (2009), *available at* http://www.judiciary.gov.uk/NR/rdonlyres/8EB9F3F3–9C4A–4139–8A93–56F09672EB6A/0/jacksonfinalreport140110.pdf.

litigants were assigned to one of six tracks by a judge who was charged with managerial oversight of the case. Based upon the issues in the case and the amount in controversy, the parties were assigned to one of the following tracks:[37]

Track One	No discovery.
Track Two	Disclosure only.
Track Three	Disclosure plus 15 interrogatories, 15 requests for admission, depositions of the parties, and deposition on written questions of custodians of business records for third parties.
Track Four	Disclosure plus 15 interrogatories, 15 requests for admissions, depositions of the parties, depositions on written questions of custodians of business records for third parties, and three other depositions per side (i.e., per party or per group of parties with a common interest).
Track Five	A discovery plan tailored by the judicial officer to fit the special management needs of the case.
Track Six	Specialized treatment and program as determined by the judicial officers.

Despite some court-focused efforts to manage litigation in the U.S., such as the tracked litigation system in the Eastern District of Texas, the main thrust of the managerial revolution has been to increase the authority of courts to move litigants out of the litigation system, rather than actively oversee their efforts. The end product is not a mandatory level of judicial supervision of the litigation process. Instead, the upshot is an uncomfortable hybrid in which the managerial powers of the courts are increased, the disfavoring of trial as compared to settlement is formally acknowledged, and the demands of parties for judicial assistance is treated increasingly as another claim for limited societal resources. Managerialism thus far has not served to systematize and rationalize how parties may adjudicate a dispute. Rather, it has primarily empowered courts to induce settlement, sometimes coercively, or to force litigants out of the court system altogether.

37. Order Amending Civil Justice Expense and Delay Reduction Plan, No. 93–13 (E.D. Tex. Sept. 2, 1993).

Chapter 9

WHY LITIGATE?

The astute reader will have noticed how little attention is given in this book to the processes of trial and appeal. It is, of course, true that most disputes are resolved prior to formal adjudication or even litigation. Our lives are surrounded by disputes such as those between siblings as to who gets the larger portion of dessert, or among spouses as to whose turn it is to take out the garbage. Fortunately, these everyday squabbles rarely enter the legal system. And it is further true that even among the great bulk of cases that do enter the judicial system, the vast majority are resolved well short of trial. We might add as well that the great work of our system of civil procedure is to facilitate the resolution of disputes, even after they have entered the formal processes of litigation. Yet a book on civil procedure must acknowledge those few cases in which litigants do engage the formal dispute resolution processes of the court system and which are pursued to final resolution through trial.

Moreover, there is something particularly salient about legal resolution of litigated outcomes in the instruction of future lawyers. Each year, first-year law students are introduced to the study of law through the case method. The minds of future lawyers are sharpened by considering the misfortune of the fellow with chest hair on his palm;[1] the people chasing each others' foxes through the forest;[2] the dimwitted brothers seeking to farm the Oklahoma hardscrabble;[3] or the individuals who, unable to make monthly installment payments on their home appliances, appeal all the way to the U.S. Supreme Court for relief.[4] While the claims of injustice are real, there is scant attention paid to the puzzling issue of why these individuals and organizations would give of their time and money to litigate cases to judgment and opinion, and thereby provide such a rich source of teaching material. What's more, these valiant contributors to the education of law students seek no compensation for their efforts, demand no copyright in the product created, and claim no protection against the snickers and guffaws

1. Hawkins v. McGee, 84 N.H. 114, 146 A. 641 (1929).

2. Pierson v. Post, 3 Cai. R. 175 (1805).

3. Peevyhouse v. Garland Coal & Mining Co., 382 P.2d 109 (Okla. 1962).

4. Mitchell v. W.T. Grant, 416 U.S. 600 (1974); Fuentes v. Shevin, 407 U.S. 67 (1972).

that inevitably accompany the repeated recitation of their misfortunes.

What makes the behavior of these litigants all the more peculiar is the fact that they are clear losers as soon as they enter the litigation process. Litigation ensures that the disputants collectively are worse off than they were before. Whatever the stakes in a dispute between two parties, there is only one way in which they can preserve their joint welfare. Any division of the stake between them, whether it be one side taking all, or half-and-half, or anything in between, leaves the parties jointly in the same position as when they began their dispute: however they slice it, they will still have the entire pie to share. It is only by bringing lawyers into the mix and by subjecting themselves to the inevitable costs of litigation that the parties consign themselves to being worse off. Once lawyers and courts and filing fees and witnesses and depositions and all the rest are brought into the picture, the pie starts getting smaller and smaller. Because this is perfectly obvious, and perfectly obvious to all rational disputants right from the get go, the penchant of our casebook warriors to litigate requires some explanation.

The explanation cannot be found simply in the short-sightedness of the disputants. Even if it were not perfectly clear at the very beginning that a trip through the litigation minefield is costly, that lesson is soon brought home to litigants. Regardless of the contractual terms with their attorneys, and even if represented on a contingency basis, clients soon realize that they are signing away a significant amount of resources to their newly acquired legal representatives. In fact, most parties quickly learn this lesson, and a remarkably stable 95 percent or more of cases manage to get resolved well short of trial. And even though—as described in Chapter 3—the number of tried cases has been falling of late in the U.S., some small percentage of cases do nonetheless make it to court, and some even persist in going on to appeal. What accounts for these volunteer heroes of subsequent legal instruction?

The point of departure for considering this issue could be the prevailing understanding of two or so generations ago. At a time when the question of why cases were fought to conclusion was not considered pressing, the common metaphor for explaining disputes that went to trial was that they were as rare and random as lightning strikes. But this earthy metaphor cannot survive our changed understanding of the physics of lightning. We now understand that swinging a golf club in an exposed field during a thunderstorm can affect one's chances of making the evening news. So, too, our legal intuitions have advanced a bit. In concluding this book, it is worth turning our attention to the emerging understanding of why cases are actually litigated. To do so, I start by presenting a streamlined explanation of the first major improvement in our understanding, the law and economics model of why cases are litigated. I then consider the limitations that this model faces in accounting for the actual choices of human beings.

I. The Law and Economics Model.

Law and economics draws from the pioneering work of Nobel laureate Gary Becker of the University of Chicago and is important as the first coherent view of why cases reach and travel through the process of litigation. It provides insight into what is likely the central paradox of litigation: the fact that taken together, the parties to a lawsuit are losers from the moment they enter the process of adjudication. Becker's insight was that the neoclassical economic model of "marginal trade-offs" could be applied with success (if not always the same degree of it) to less clearly economic decisions made in the domains of criminality, love, marriage, and law.[5] An unexpectedly broad range of behaviors could be explained by the discounted utility that individuals could expect to achieve from among a set of alternatives. Why do some individuals engage in criminal activity while others do not? An answer might be found in the likely trade-offs between the risk of getting caught and the opportunities foregone if one or another person might have to spend time incarcerated.[6] Why do people marry? Love may be part of the answer, but so are the search costs of seeking alternative partners and the opportunity cost of a foregone present relationship.[7]

Hopefully, these caricatured renditions of complex human motivations will be found wanting. But nonetheless, they do capture a part of the motivation behind why those with less to lose or whose youth allows an unrealistically low estimation of the prospect of getting caught are those most likely to engage in unlawful conduct. Similarly, that human relationships are fraught with complex emo-

---

5. *See* GARY S. BECKER, THE ECONOMIC APPROACH TO HUMAN BEHAVIOR (1976) (applying an economic model to "Law and Politics" (Part 3), "Marriage, Fertility, and the Family" (Part 6), and other "Social Interactions" (Part 7)).

6. *See id.* at 47 ("[T]here is a function relating the number of offenses by any person to his probability of conviction, to his punishment if convicted, and to other variables, such as the income available to him in legal and other illegal activities. . . .").

7. *See id.* at 212 ("The gain from marriage has to be balanced against the costs, including legal fees and the cost of searching for a mate, to determine whether marriage is worthwhile.").

tions does not render irrelevant to the success of a relationship the age of the individuals and the diminishing prospects of finding "Mr. or Ms. Right" waiting at the next bus stop. That the law and economics approach is not so ecumenical as to capture the full range of factors affecting human decisionmaking should not diminish the tremendous intellectual energy unleashed by this inquiry into human motivation. The use of marginal utility to assess human conduct was as bold a conceptual breakthrough as the advent of probabilistic reasoning a century earlier.[8]

As applied to litigation, the critical economic insight comes from asking a simple question about the incentives that would lead people to actually seek a trial resolution in a case. If, rather than assuming that the prospect of litigating through to trial and appeal is random, we instead inquire as to the conditions under which rational parties might find themselves in an escalating conflict over rights and wrongs, then the world of litigated dispute resolution begins to look remarkably different.[9] The key insight begins with a very simple model that assumes each party enters the litigation process with an expected value attached to the claim of the plaintiff. At its simplest, the model appears as follows:

$$EV^\pi \; = \; P \times A \; \text{minus} \; C^\pi$$

In this simple model, EV^π represents the expected value of the case to the plaintiff. As set forth in this account, the plaintiff's expectations are a function of her probability of success (P), the likely award to be obtained (A), and the costs associated with prosecuting the claim (C^π). This calculation can then also be expressed as the defendant's expected loss from a plaintiff's claim. Here the scaled-down version of the model for the defendant appears as follows:

$$EV_D \; = \; P \times A \; \text{plus} \; C_D$$

8. For a compelling account of the role of statistical probabilities in reshaping intellectual thought after the Civil War, see Louis Menand, The Metaphysical Club 177–200 (2001).

9. *See* George L. Priest & Benjamin Klein, *The Selection of Disputes for Litigation*, 13 J. Legal Stud. 1, 4 (1984) ("According to our model, the determinants of settlement and litigation are solely economic, including the expected costs to parties of favorable or adverse decisions, the information that parties possess about the likelihood of success at trial, and the direct costs of litigation and settlement.").

The defendant's calculation is the mirror image of the plaintiff's, with one critical difference: the costs are added to the defendant's likely loss, whereas they are subtracted from the plaintiff's likely recovery.[10] Thus, these streamlined equations reflect the fact that the costs associated with litigation are a joint loss to the parties and subtract from their joint welfare.

By combining these two equations, it is possible to isolate what is termed a "settlement zone," in which two parties with convergent expectations of the likely award and the probability of the plaintiff prevailing are able to negotiate a mutually advantageous end to the litigation.[11] This may be represented as follows:

SETTLEMENT ZONE CREATED BY C^{π} plus C_D,

WHEN PARTIES AGREE ON VALUES OF P AND A

If parties can agree on the likely value of P (the probability of the plaintiff winning) and A (the amount that will be awarded if she wins), what they are really arguing about is how to divide up the costs of litigation, C^{π} and C_D. Consider then a concrete application:

> If each party would pay $25,000 to litigate a $200,000 claim that the plaintiff has a 50 percent chance of winning, the gross expected value of the claim, not considering the costs of litigation, would be $100,000. Once those costs are taken into account, though, the plaintiff stands to gain only $75,000 if she wins, and the defendant stands to lose $125,000 if he loses. Any settlement of more than $75,000 and less than $125,000, if made before those costs of litigation are sacrificed, makes each party better off.

10. *See* RICHARD A. POSNER, ECONOMIC ANALYSIS OF LAW 597 (7th ed., 2007) ("[S]ettlement negotiations will fail, and litigation ensue, only if the minimum price that the plaintiff is willing to accept in compromise of his claim is greater than the maximum price the defendant is willing to pay in satisfaction of that claim."); *see also* Evans v. Jeff D., 475 U.S. 717, 734 (1986) ("Most defendants are unlikely to settle unless the cost of the predicted judgment, discounted by its probability, plus the transaction costs of further litigation, are greater than the cost of the settlement package.").

11. *See* Steven Shavell, *Suit, Settlement, and Trial: A Theoretical Analysis Under Alternative Methods for the Allocation of Legal Costs*, 11 J. LEGAL STUD. 55, 56–57 (1982) ("If the plaintiff does decide to bring suit, it is assumed that he and the defendant will reach a settlement if and only if there exists some settlement amount that both he and the defendant would prefer to going to trial.").

For this model to work, however, the parties' understanding of the estimated value of the case must converge. The parties' estimates, in turn, reflect their respective assessments of how likely the plaintiff is to prevail and how much the prospective damage award will be if she does indeed triumph.[12] If there is agreement on both the probability of the plaintiff prevailing and the likely size of the ensuing award, cases should settle almost immediately, before much of the pie is eaten away by the transaction costs associated with litigation. There may, of course, be disagreement about how to apportion the savings from the portion of the pie that would otherwise have been lost.[13] And some portion of cases may fritter away resources as the parties posture to claim a greater willingness to go to trial.[14] But life has a way of removing from the gene pool individuals whose sense of sport involves repeatedly playing chicken with oncoming cars. So, too, we would expect parties with an inflated sense of righteousness or greed or simply *amour-propre* to be pushed to the margins if they indulge themselves in costly attempts to squeeze out the last dime from mutually advantageous settlements.

How, then, can the parties' estimates of probable success and the likely award be made to converge? This turns out to be an essential function of the American rules of civil procedure. The basic law and economics insight is to claim that the source of divergence between the parties must rest on incompatible assessments of either the facts or the law governing a particular case.[15] Since the parties (and society) are best served by promoting quick settlements that conserve the joint resources of the parties, the rules of procedure should attempt to intercede to remove this source of divergence between the parties. This is one way of understanding the simple mandate of Federal Rule of Civil Proce-

12. *See* Russell Korobkin & Chris Guthrie, *Psychological Barriers to Litigation Settlement: An Experimental Approach*, 93 MICH. L. REV. 107, 112 (1994) (noting that under an economic model, "as long as both sides make an identical estimate of the likely outcome of the trial, the case should settle") (footnote omitted).

13. *See* POSNER, *supra* note 10, at 597 (noting that the "larger the settlement range, the more the parties will stand to gain from hard bargaining and the likelier (it may seem) the parties are to end up litigating because they cannot agree how to divide the available surplus").

14. *See* ROBERT COOTER & THOMAS ULEN, LAW & ECONOMICS 487–92 (1988) (describing how strategic behavior can frustrate settlement).

15. *See* Patrick J. Borchers, *Jurisdictional Pragmatism:* International Shoe's *Half–Buried Legacy*, 28 U.C. DAVIS L. REV. 561, 585 (1995) ("Unstable and unpredictable legal doctrine inhibits the convergence of the parties' estimates of the case value, thus inhibiting settlement.").

dure 1, which states that the object of the Rules is to foster the just, speedy, and inexpensive resolution of disputes.[16]

Disagreement on the governing law is addressed relatively directly. To begin with, as a society we invest heavily in the creation of the public good known as decisional law. We build courthouses, staff them with respected community leaders called judges, stock them with bright clerks, and demand that their experiential wisdom be reduced to written form. The resulting case law forms the heart of the common law enterprise and is publicly available to counsel to inform their assessments of the strength of the claims put forward on behalf of their clients.[17] In addition, as we have seen, we allow for a relatively quick reality check of the legal basis for a plaintiff's claim through the Rule 12(b)(6) motion to dismiss. In some circumstances, we may even allow for interlocutory appeals, *mandamus*, or certification of a case to a state appellate court, all for the purpose of providing an early look at the governing legal principles.

Factual disagreements are more difficult. Here the true rendition of the factual strength of a party's claim lies not in the public domain but frequently in the private knowledge of the litigants themselves.[18] A key insight of law and economics is that as long as the parties have private information about their side of the case, the prospect of settlement may be significantly compromised.[19] As was discussed in Chapter 2, the Federal Rules assume, as a general matter, that defendants are likely to have more information about liability, while plaintiffs tend to know more about the precise

16. FED. R. CIV. P. 1 ("[These rules] shall be construed and administered to secure the just, speedy, and inexpensive determination of every action."); *see* POSNER, *supra* note 10, at 601 ("How do rules of procedure affect the settlement rate? ... A full exchange of the information in the possession of the parties is likely to facilitate settlement by enabling each party to form a more accurate, and generally therefore a more convergent, estimate of the likely outcome of the case....").

17. *See* Robert G. Bone, *Case Five: Complex Litigation and Prior Rulings Issues*, 29 NEW ENG. L. REV. 703, 716 (1995) ("The larger the body of historical data about outcomes in individual cases, the more likely it is that the parties' estimates of settlement value will converge on a reasonable figure."); John P. Gould, *The Economics of Legal Conflicts*, 2 J. LEGAL STUD. 279, 296 (1973) ("The concept of legal precedent is in effect a means to provide stationarity over time to the probabilities and hence to increase the opportunities for out of court agreements.").

18. *See* Leandra Lederman, *Which Cases Go to Trial?: An Empirical Study of Predictors of Failure to Settle*, 49 CASE W. RES. L. REV. 315, 323 (1999) ("Asymmetric information models, also based on divergent expectations by the parties, allow party estimates of outcome to differ not based on party optimism but based instead on information held by only one party (asymmetric information), so that one side has a truer estimate of the likely outcome at trial.").

19. *See* Robert H. Gertner, *Asymmetric Information, Uncertainty, and Selection Bias in Litigation*, 1993 U. CHI. ROUNDTABLE 75, 81 (arguing that divergent expectations "based on differences in information rather than opinion" account for trials).

amount of damages. Thus, suppose we have a simple case in which the standard of liability turns in part on the state of mind of the defendant, such as with an intentional tort or a claim of discrimination. Here the defendant will likely have a much more informed sense of the prospects for proving liability than would the plaintiff. On the damages side of the equation, it is the plaintiff who is likely to have the better quality information as to the exact nature of the injuries suffered.[20] Because such private information is not likely to be available in the public sphere, there is a grave risk of inefficient impasses in the ability of parties to settle.

Here, too, as we have also previously seen, the rules of procedure seek to intercede. Rather than draw on a body of knowledge that is maintained in the public domain, as with published decisional law, the combined effects of notice pleading and liberal discovery serve to create a limited domain of shared information between the parties. The expanse of discovery is the single most distinctive feature of American procedure and its scope and cost not only draw attention but also typically shock foreign litigants who find themselves in American courts.[21] But under the economic model of litigation, the costs of discovery serve two important functions. First, the fact that parties face significant costs in the litigation process expands the potential settlement zone and creates a greater possibility of mutually advantageous settlement, even if the parties do not have perfectly matched assessments of the case's likely outcome were it to go to trial. More significantly, the costs of discovery are justified to the extent that they bring the parties' assessments of the case into line at some point prior to trial. Under this approach, discovery not only allows for a trial to be "on the merits" if the parties are unable to settle, but the investment in mutually shared information makes settlement much more likely.[22]

---

20. *See* Robert H. Gertner & Geoffrey P. Miller, *Settlement Escrows*, 24 J. LEGAL STUD. 87, 89 (1995) ("Consider a typical tort claim. The plaintiff may have better information about the extent of damages because the effect of the injury may be difficult for another party to observe. A defendant may have better information about liability because he knows his level of care."); Geoffrey P. Miller, *Settlement of Litigation: A Critical Retrospective, in* REFORMING THE CIVIL JUSTICE SYSTEM 13, 16 (Larry Kramer ed., 1996) (noting that in tort cases plaintiff usually has better information as to the magnitude of his damages).

21. *See* John H. Shenefield, *Thoughts on Extraterritorial Application of the United States Antitrust Laws*, 52 FORDHAM L. REV. 350, 355 (1983) ("Foreign discovery procedures are generally narrowly tailored to issues directly involved in the litigation. By contrast, more liberal American discovery procedures permit inquiry into a wide range of matters that may never receive the direct attention of a foreign court.").

22. Marshall E. Tracht, *Renegotiation and Secured Credit: Explaining the Equity of Redemption*, 52 VAND. L. REV. 599, 632–33 (1999) ("Discovery proceedings encourage settlements in a number of ways. First, by facilitating the exchange of informa-

Once the parties have discovered all the information relevant to the claims and defenses in the case, to use the language of Rule 26, and once they have read from the same decisional law and tested the application of the law through motions to dismiss and motions for summary judgment, there is no reason to believe that the parties should not settle. And, indeed, our experience confirms that parties do settle in droves, including the famous settlement on the courthouse steps.

The next step in this analysis will be to question the assumptions made by the law and economics model as to how people actually behave under conditions of stress and uncertainty.[23] But for the moment there remains a critical question for the law and economics approach: why then do any cases go to trial once the lawyers have tested the law and discovered the facts? The economic model gives two answers. First, there is the possibility of parties just getting it wrong. Simply because we provide all the tools necessary to resolve the dispute does not mean that all litigants will take the hint. In a world full of claims that Elvis still lives, it would be sheer folly to suppose that any system that engages masses of people will be free from error. Second, and perhaps more significantly, there are always new areas of law, new claims, new conceptions of rights and duties. It may be that the pretrial system has given the parties all the tools necessary mutually to assess the facts and to evaluate the decisional law as it stands. But it may still be the case that parties diverge in their estimations of likely trial outcomes because the law is unsettled in the particular domain in which their dispute arose.

Thus, there are two potential explanations for cases going to trial. The first is mistake and the second is uncertainty in the state of the law.[24] As a result, parties who invest of themselves in providing fodder for future generations of law students do so either

tion, they reduce the informational asymmetries that may block negotiations. Second, the prospect of costly and time-consuming discovery may encourage the parties to settle."); Robert B. Wilson, *Strategic and Informational Barriers to Negotiation*, in BARRIERS TO CONFLICT RESOLUTION 108, 114 (Kenneth J. Arrow et al. eds., 1995) ("Discovery procedures ... contribute to an equalized evidentiary basis for the trial, and before the trial they can narrow the informational gap and promote settlements; even the prospect of costly discovery can encourage early settlement.").

23. For a collection of the leading early studies of decisional processes under conditions of uncertainty, see JUDGMENT UNDER UNCERTAINTY: HEURISTICS AND BIASES (Daniel Kahneman et al. eds., 1982) [hereinafter JUDGMENT UNDER UNCERTAINTY].

24. *See* Richard B. Stewart, *The Discontents of Legalism: Interest Group Relations in Administrative Regulation*, 1985 WIS. L. REV. 655, 662 ("The more certain the law—the less variance in expected outcomes—the more likely the parties will predict the same outcome from litigation, and the less likely that litigation will occur because of differences in predicted outcomes.").

because they are foolish or because they have the misfortune to find themselves in an area where few others have tread in the past. As to the former, well, there is not much we can do except be bemused as we read of their disputes. As to the latter, their decision to pursue the case and create the public good of decisional law turns out not to be a selfless act but the product of seeking a just solution in an area where society could not provide enough certainty. But, in either case, the methodology of the system of civil procedure stands vindicated as trying to protect individuals from their own folly or providing as much certainty as possible in the assertion of their legal rights.

One final point should be made about this conception of the litigation process. Under either explanation for why parties might actually go to trial, there is no reason to believe that the cases that actually do get litigated should favor one or the other side. If parties simply make mistakes, or if the law is uncertain, then the likely winner at trial could as easily be the plaintiff as the defendant. In other words, the selection of cases for trial should be random as between the parties. This observation was formulated by Professors George Priest and Benjamin Klein, in what is known as the Priest–Klein hypothesis. If indeed the sources of trial are either mistake or uncertainty in the law, then Priest–Klein predicts that there would be no systematic bias to cases that do go to trial and that plaintiffs and defendants should each win about half of all litigated cases.[25] Early empirical attempts to assess this hypothesis were generally confirmatory, although some subsequent analyses introduce complexity depending on the repeat quality of the defendant, the presence of an insurer, and a host of other strategic variables.[26] Nonetheless, as a general matter, the basic insight that litigated cases tend to split between the parties has held up fairly well.[27]

25.   Priest & Klein, *supra* note 9, at 4–5.

26.   *See* Frank B. Cross, *In Praise of Irrational Plaintiffs*, 86 CORNELL L. REV. 1, 11 (2000) ("The relatively high general tort rates are quite consistent with the predictions of Priest and Klein's fifty percent hypothesis, although the low product liability plaintiff win rates are suspicious and evidence that strategic litigation may be transpiring.") (footnote omitted); Samuel R. Gross & Kent D. Syverud, *Getting to No: A Study of Settlement Negotiations and the Selection of Cases for Trial*, 90 MICH. L. REV. 319 (1991).

27.   Joel Waldfogel, *Reconciling Asymmetric Information and Divergent Expectations Theories of Litigation*, 41 J.L. & ECON. 451, 452 (1998) ("Considerable evidence supports the main prediction of the ... model, Priest and Klein's 50 percent rule, that as the fraction of cases going to trial approaches zero, the plaintiff win rate at trial approaches 50 percent.").

II. Do Litigants Behave as the Economic Model Would Predict?

A. *The World of Human Complexity.*

If proven, the Priest–Klein hypothesis may confirm that the parties who get to trial are a random distribution from among the world of litigants, meaning that the cases going to trial reflect no systematic bias in favor of plaintiffs or defendants. The hypothesis may further confirm our sense that we have designed a pretty good system in which all but the foolish and the trailblazers can resolve their disputes prior to trial. And the hypothesis may even confirm an intuition that the cases going to trial are basically the right ones. But the economic model and its confirmatory hypothesis cannot assure us that the process of selecting out cases prior to trial is an efficient one. It may be that the selection of cases for trial works pretty well, but only at a tremendous cost to all settling litigants—costs that end up being borne by the settling parties and by society as a deadweight loss. If, for example, the pretrial screening that is provided by discovery and motions practice were to be far more costly than trials themselves, it may turn out that there is not much systemic gain from sorting through disputes to find the right ones for trial.

To conclude that parties are being helped to settle in an efficient manner, we need to assume that they will integrate the shared knowledge of the facts and the law in such a way as to further their achievement of shared assessments of the case. In other words, we need to have a behavioral theory of how parties make decisions in conditions of uncertainty as they go about the process of acquiring the costly information about the relevant law and facts through the litigation system. For the law and economics model to hold fully, we must have confidence that sharing information will result in parties reassessing their positions in light of the new information. We must further assume that they will integrate the new information in a parallel manner so that their assessments of the value of settlement actually converge. In short, we need a behavioral theory showing that parties objectively reevaluate information in a cold, dispassionate fashion. For if information were not integrated in such a way as to permit a dispassionate reassessment of the position of the parties, our confidence in the efficiency gain from the tremendous costs associated with the pretrial process would be shaken.

Unfortunately, there is every reason to question this behavioral account of how litigants respond to information.[28] To begin with,

---

28. For a good summary of this critique, see Daniel A. Farber, *Toward a New Legal Realism*, 68 U. CHI. L. REV. 279 (2001).

the law and economics model failed to take robust account of the more nuanced model of strategic behavior that emerged from game theory.[29] Here the challenge lay in identifying the mechanisms through which information asymmetries between the parties could be exploited in ways that undermined the simple assumption of converging expectations. Whereas the early law and economics approach saw the litigation process as a mechanism to overcome asymmetries in information, more sophisticated game theoretic approaches would ask whether the existing asymmetries would be strategically exploited by the better-situated parties. I will not attempt to address the broad range of strategic complications here. Rather, I wish to focus on the behavioral assumptions of the law and economics model more directly. Here I turn to an increasing body of social science evidence about decisionmaking under conditions of uncertainty, to draw on the title of the pathbreaking work by Amos Tversky and Daniel Kahneman and their behavioralist collaborators.[30] The critical psychological insight in this work is that we all make decisions based on a number of heuristics that impede the smooth reassessments of information called for in the economic model and that lie at the heart of the presumed efficiency of the modern procedural devices.[31] I will examine a couple of these heuristics to suggest where the next generation of law and economics work has headed and the types of challenges that will inform the coming scholarly and policy assessment of the processes of litigation.

To be clear, the concern here is not over the benefits of liberal pleading and court-supervised discovery compared to some more formalized common law pleading regimes from days gone by. The concern is over the assumption of how parties will respond to the new regime. To go back to the work of Gary Becker, the challenge is to the underlying account of how people integrate information. For Becker, the account is one of people acting as rational central-processing units: "[T]he economic approach does not assume that decision units are necessarily conscious of their efforts to maximize or can verbalize or otherwise describe in an informative way

29. *See generally* Christine Jolls et al., *A Behavioral Approach to Law and Economics*, 50 STAN. L. REV. 1471, 1473 (1998) (discussing deficiencies in the law and economics model and offering "an approach to economic analysis of law that is informed by a more accurate conception of choice, one that reflects a better understanding of human behavior and its wellsprings").

30. JUDGMENT UNDER UNCERTAINTY, *supra* note 23.

31. *See* Samuel Issacharoff, *Can There Be a Behavioral Law and Economics?*, 51 VAND. L. REV. 1729, 1732–33 (1998). For a survey of these heuristics, see Russell B. Korobkin & Thomas S. Ulen, *Law and Behavioral Science: Removing the Rationality Assumption From Law and Economics*, 88 CAL. L. REV. 1051, 1075–1102 (2000).

reasons for the systematic patterns in their behavior. Thus it is consistent with the emphasis on the subconscious in modern psychology. . . .''[32] These decision units (a.k.a. "people") are assumed to have internalized a rational calculus deep in their subconscious. But rather than posit the truth of that, as did Becker and by extension the first generation of law and economics scholarship, this is an empirical claim that may be tested and challenged.

Looking back at Becker's claim a quarter century later, we have reason to be skeptical that it can hold up. We know, for example, that there is a litany of psychological evidence on the heuristics and biases in human reasoning.[33] We know with a fair degree of certainty that people individually, and even aggregated through market transactions, simply do not see the world through the lenses offered up by the expected-value economic calculus.[34] We can look at some of the more well-established models to see how far we have moved since Becker would have attributed his insights to the core of the human psyche.

For example, we know that contrary to what economists would tell us, people value losses more than gains and will invest more heavily in seeking to avoid a loss than realize a gain, even of equal value.[35] In other words, people value what they have over what they may aspire to have. This is known as the endowment effect[36] and is a robust effect, even if the goods are of equal value. We also see the real world applications of this effect. Thus, people will refuse to sell a possession for a fixed amount of money even if they would not buy another for the same amount of money.[37] Also, people tend to hold losing stocks too long and sell winners too quickly, and are reluctant to sell their houses in a declining market, seeking to avoid

32.   BECKER, *supra* note 6, at 7 (footnote omitted).

33.   *See, e.g.,* Colin Camerer, *Individual Decision Making, in* THE HANDBOOK OF EXPERIMENTAL ECONOMICS 587 (John H. Kagel & Alvin E. Roth eds., 1995); Mark Kelman, *Consumption Theory, Production Theory, and Ideology in the Coase Theorem,* 52 S. CAL. L. REV. 669 (1979); Amos Tversky & Daniel Kahneman, *Judgment Under Uncertainty: Heuristics and Biases, in* JUDGMENT UNDER UNCERTAINTY, *supra* note 23, at 3–20 [hereinafter Tversky & Kahneman, *Uncertainty*].

34.   *See* Jolls et al., *supra* note 29, at 1477–85.

35.   This is the critical insight of the prospect theory work of Kahneman and Tversky. *See* Daniel Kahneman & Amos Tversky, *Prospect Theory: An Analysis of Decision Under Risk,* 47 ECONOMETRICA 263, 268–69 (1979).

36.   *See, e.g.,* Daniel Kahneman et al., *Experimental Tests of the Endowment Effect and the Coase Theorem,* 98 J. POL. ECON. 1325, 1341–46 (1990); George Loewenstein & Samuel Issacharoff, *Source Dependence in the Valuation of Objects,* 7 J. BEHAV. DECISIONMAKING 157 (1994).

37.   *See* Jolls et al., *supra* note 29, at 1482 (offering, as example, that individuals would not buy a Super Bowl ticket they held for $1000, but they would also refuse to sell at that price).

taking a loss.[38] Similarly, we know that individuals play the lottery, which clearly is irrational behavior in itself, and that they are loathe to sell a one dollar lottery ticket already in their possession even if offered a premium over the face value of the ticket, because it could be a winner! And even on the old Monty Hall game show, Let's Make a Deal, participants were typically reluctant to switch the door they initially picked (so as to avoid the dread feeling of regret should their initial choice have been correct), despite the fact that the structure of the game made accepting the offer to switch a significantly better strategy.

We also know that people integrate information oddly by responding to high salience cues rather than more circumscribed statistical inferences.[39] As a result, flood insurance sells quickly after a high profile, distant flood, as does earthquake insurance after a distant tremor. We know that people pour good money after bad, hoping to salvage investments gone sour, despite repeated admonitions from economists to disregard sunk costs in making investment decisions.[40]

While we may continue to debate the magnitude of these peculiar effects and the consequences of this type of decisionmaking,[41] there is little doubt about the existence of such behavioral phenomena. The important question is not to label these phenomena as being rational or otherwise. We live in a world so awash in information and data as to leave us incapacitated were we not to have some form of shorthand methods to conduct our lives. Attention to our holdings, aversion to losses, and awareness of significant events that imprint themselves on our consciousness are all mechanisms that allow us to survive in an increasingly complex world. Just as the eye evolved to focus on the salient effects of motion and change, so too we developed heuristics for capturing information that helps us deal with the problems of uncertainty. These heuristics are indispensable for ordering our lives. But as the effects described above indicate, they can distort our behavior in ways that lawyers should be aware of.

---

38. Issacharoff, *supra* note 31, at 1736 n.24. *See generally* RICHARD H. THALER, QUASI-RATIONAL ECONOMICS 11–13, 148–49 (1991) (providing examples of individuals' inability to disregard sunk costs in making market-related decisions).

39. This is often referred to as the "availability heuristic." *See* Jolls et al., *supra* note 29, at 1519; Tversky & Kahneman, *Uncertainty*, *supra* note 33, at 11.

40. *See* THALER, *supra* note 39, at 11–13, 148–49.

41. Robert E. Scott, for one, has argued that many of the models and studies described in this Chapter are flawed. *See* Robert E. Scott, *The Limits of Behavioral Theories of Law and Social Norms*, 86 VA. L. REV. 1603, 1639–46 (2000).

B.   *Examples in the Domain of Law.*

1.   *Following the Cues.*

Some examples should help us to understand the implications of behavioral insights for the legal system. The easiest to begin with is the problem of "framing"—the effect that presenting the same information as a matter of gains or losses has on the valuation. A fine example is presented in a study by Professors McCaffery, Kahneman, and Spitzer, which they describe as a problem of "Framing the Jury."[42] In this experiment, the authors asked individual subjects in an experimental setting to assume the role of jurors in a personal injury trial in which, following a determination of liability, an award had to be rendered for harms that consisted of extreme stiffness in the upper back and neck coupled with intermittent severe migraine headaches.[43] The subjects were all given identical information and an identical scale of possible awards to choose from.[44] The only difference between the two sets of subjects in the experiment was in the presentation of the question to be answered.[45] One group was asked how much should be awarded to make whole the victim of the accident.[46] The second group was asked how much they would have to be paid to accept the harm suffered by the victim.[47]

As should be evident, the answer to the two questions has to be the same if there were to be a coherent effort to provide compensation. If an individual were truly made whole, then that individual should be indifferent as to the occurrence or nonoccurrence of the accident. She will have been fully compensated for whatever harms she may have suffered and should therefore be in the same position whether or not the accident had occurred. The only difference in asking the question in one or another way is to pose the inquiry as backward-looking (*ex post* relief) or as forward-looking (*ex ante* valuation of the harm). In either case, the value should be the same.

Perhaps the values should be the same, but our intuition tells us that they are not. In many states, this intuition takes the form

---

42.   Edward J. McCaffery et al., *Framing the Jury: Cognitive Perspectives on Pain and Suffering Awards*, 81 Va. L. Rev. 1341 (1995).

43.   *Id.* at 1355–56.

44.   *Id.* at 1357.

45.   *Id.* at 1355–57.

46.   *Id.* at 1356.

47.   *Id.*

of a prohibition on lawyers asking jurors what they would accept to have the harm occur to them, a manifestation of the commonly observed disparity between willingness to accept and willingness to pay that is such a persistent bane to more formally inclined economists. True to form, this is precisely what the study by McCaffery and his collaborators found.[48]

When asked to make the victim whole, the subject jurors awarded an average of $290,000.[49] But when asked what they would have accepted ahead of time to suffer the victim's fate, the award jumped to $527,500.[50] The disparity from the mere framing of the question was almost 2–to–1.

Presentation of these experimental results is often met with skepticism. There must be something wrong with the pool from which subjects are drawn to allow such marked effects from how a question is framed. Such skepticism may be healthy, but I would hesitate to be so quickly dismissive of the results. By way of confirmation, I took the liberty of distributing some sample questions in presenting an earlier version of this material to a group much resembling the intended audience of this book. The sample questions were distributed among several hundred undoubtedly intelligent, rational, and sophisticated participants who should be expected to see through such cant: first-year law students, in this case a group at Florida State University.

To enlist the assistance of this admirable group, I distributed a question that asked students there to guess the population of Turkey. I did this by giving each student a questionnaire that gave an estimate of the population of Turkey, asked whether the student thought the estimate was true or false, asked the student to give a percentage estimate of how certain she was of her answer, and finally asked the student to give her own best estimate of what the actual population of Turkey might be. The only difference in the questions asked came with the initial population estimate: one-half of the students received a questionnaire that estimated the population at 34 million; the other half received a questionnaire with an estimate of 106 million.[51]

The interesting question is whether the final estimate of the two groups should be any different. Any rational calculus should

48. *Id.* at 1357–58.

49. *Id.* at 1372–73.

50. *Id.*

51. This is a variant on the initial studies of the anchoring effect done by Tversky and Kahneman. *See* Amos Tversky & Daniel Kahneman, *Judgment Under Uncertainty: Heuristics and Biases*, 185 Sci. 1124, 1128 (1974).

tell us that the two groups should converge in their final estimates. Since the distribution of the questionnaires was random within the classes, any actual knowledge of Turkey would likely be distributed randomly between the two groups. Similarly, any errors would also be likely to be randomly distributed. The only difference would come with the unverified and unsubstantiated number at the top of the questionnaire, something that shrewd and skeptical law students would quickly disregard as having no bearing on their informed judgments. Or so it would seem. As with the prospective jurors in the McCaffery study, however, the FSU students took their cues from the way the information was presented. The average estimate of the actual population of Turkey by those whose baseline was 34 million turned out to be 32.9 million. By contrast, the group whose baseline was 106 million turned in average estimates of 77.4 million. Again, a disparity of a little over 2–to–1, based solely on the way a question was asked.

2. *Being Led Astray.*

Other studies reveal just how powerful the framing effects are in overcoming logical structures in integrating information. For example, a study by Amos Tversky, Mark Kelman, and Yuval Rottenstreich[52] asked experimental subjects to figure out the appropriate remedy for an individual whose sense of peace and solitude had been disrupted by the sudden arrival of a loud weekend nightclub as a neighbor.[53] One set of subjects was presented with two choices: a payment that included weekend lodging to get away from the noise or an injunction to stop the high decibel activity.[54] Many will recognize this example as the familiar Coasean exchange from which emerges an assumption that, in the absence of transaction costs, parties will bargain to a mutually advantageous allocation of resources.[55] The twist in this experiment was to provide a second set of subjects with three rather than two options. Instead of allowing only a weekend lodging or an order diminishing the sound level, the second set of subjects were presented with a third option of a clearly inferior set of weekend choices for the afflicted neighbor, including free admission to the very sort of nightclub the burdened neighbor sought to escape.[56]

52. Mark Kelman et al., *Context–Dependence in Legal Decision Making*, 25 J. LEGAL STUD. 287 (1996).

53. *Id.* at 299.

54. *Id.* at 299–300.

55. The original work is R.H. Coase, *The Problem of Social Cost*, 3 J.L. & ECON. 1 (1960).

56. Kelman et al., *supra* note 52, at 299–300.

Among the group presented with two options, the participants split roughly in half.[57] A total of 53 percent chose the compelled decrease in sound and 47 percent accepted the alternative weekend lodging option.[58] If this roughly even division of choice were driven by the comparability of the two options, then the addition of a third inferior option should have no bearing on the results for the group of subjects presented with three options. Among the second set of subjects, everyone recognized that the weekend arrangements involving free nightclub passes were clearly inferior to the weekend arrangements involving alternative lodging. No subject chose the inferior weekend arrangement as the preferred outcome. So, in effect, the second set was choosing among the same two options as the first, save for the introduction of an undesirable, and hence irrelevant, bad choice. Yet the results were markedly different. Among the second set of subjects, 74 percent chose the initial weekend lodging option, while only 26 percent chose the diminution of sound from the offending nightclub.

	Percent Choosing Weekend Lodging	Percent Choosing Inferior Weekend Lodging	Percent Choosing Sound Decrease	N
Two–Option Group	47	. . .	53	32
Three–Option Group	74	0	26	31

Clearly, the presentation of two weekend options—one providing alternative lodging, the other unwanted entertainment—framed the subjects' approach to the question, even if in fact they were still choosing between the same two options as the first set.

Again, it is possible to detect the murmurs of skepticism arising from the sophisticated readers of this book. From where do these subjects come? Are they idiots? Dim–witted? Drunk? Well, these are fair questions and require that we compare these subjects to a group whose intellectual pedigree is beyond reproach. Of course, I refer again to the first-year class of Florida State law students who had the misfortune to invite me to lecture there. I decided to test the ability of this group to make the most logical of assessments of probability to see if the presentation of factual

57. *Id.* at 300.
58. *Id.*

information would cloud their judgment as it clearly did in the study by Kelman and his collaborators.

I presented a problem that turned on a very simple logical construct: the probability of two events both occurring can never be greater than the probability of either one of them occurring independently. This is simply the proposition that the conjunctive can never be more probable than the disjunctive: [A and B] can never be more likely than [A] or [B]. If two events are both possible, they can never be more likely to occur together than either one standing alone. So, if you had to bet on what are the chances of, say, the Texas Rangers or the Pittsburgh Pirates getting to the World Series, your odds would be better if you had to guess only that one of them would make it as opposed to guessing that they would both have to make it. No matter which you pick, you cannot improve your odds by picking both. The concept is simple enough and should be clear to all.[59]

But now, suppose we put this proposition to the test in a richer factual context, something a tad closer to the messy world in which facts present themselves in litigation. To do this, I turned to the famous pair of examples developed by Amos Tversky and Daniel Kahneman: Linda, the 31–year–old, bright and outspoken former philosophy student and student activist; and Bill, the 34–year–old, intelligent but unimaginative and lifeless former math major who showed little proclivity for social studies and the humanities.[60] For each of them, there is a series of eight options for which the subjects, here the FSU students, are asked to rank order what most likely characterizes the activities of Linda[61] and

59. If the question asks to assess the relative probabilities of the following:

1) A (alone)

2) B (alone)

3) A plus B

The answer cannot be that (3) is more probable. The conjunctive can never be more likely than the disjunctive.

60. Amos Tversky & Daniel Kahneman, *Judgments of and by Representativeness,* *in* JUDGMENT UNDER UNCERTAINTY, *supra* note 23, at 84–93 [hereinafter Tversky & Kahneman, *Representativeness*]. For additional examples of what is termed the "representativeness heuristic," *see* Korobkin & Ulen, *supra* note 31, at 1086.

61. Linda is thirty-one years old, single, outspoken, and very bright. She majored in philosophy. As a student, she was deeply concerned with issues of discrimination and social justice, and also participated in antinuclear demonstrations.

Please rank the following statements by their probability, using 1 for the most probable and 8 for the least probable.

— Linda is a teacher in elementary school.

— Linda works in a bookstore and takes Yoga classes.

— Linda is active in the feminist movement.

— Linda is a psychiatric social worker.

Bill[62] today. There are three choices that are of interest to us. For Linda, these are that she is active in the feminist movement, that she is a bank teller, or that she is a bank teller *and* is active in the feminist movement. For Bill, the choices of interest are that he is an accountant, that he plays jazz for a hobby, or that he is an accountant *and* plays jazz for a hobby.

It should be clear that these choices are nothing more than a factually rich rendition of the logical propositions set forth earlier. It may be that Linda is a bank teller, and it may be that she is active in the feminist movement, but it cannot be more likely that she is both a bank teller *and* active in the feminist movement than that she is either of the two standing alone. Similarly, it may be that Bill is an accountant, and it may be (however unlikely) that he plays jazz for a hobby, but it cannot be more probable that he is an accountant *and* plays jazz for a hobby than either one of those choices standing alone.

Yet the students of FSU, joining their brethren in numerous experimental settings,[63] would beg to differ. Applying a simple ordinal ranking to the choices, Linda is selected as being currently active in the feminist movement on average 2.22 among the 8 choices. The choice of her being a bank teller ranks at 6.37 out of the 8 choices. But Linda as a bank teller who is active in the feminist movement comes in at 5.1, significantly more likely, in the

---

— Linda is a member of the League of Women Voters.
— Linda is a bank teller.
— Linda is an insurance salesperson.
— Linda is a bank teller and is active in the feminist movement.

   62. Bill is thirty-four years old. He is intelligent but unimaginative, compulsive, and generally lifeless. In school, he was strong in mathematics but weak in social studies and the humanities.

   Please rank the following statements by their probability, using 1 for the most probable and 8 for the least probable.

— Bill is a physician who plays poker for a hobby.
— Bill is an architect.
— Bill is an accountant.
— Bill plays jazz for a hobby.
— Bill surfs for a hobby.
— Bill is a reporter.
— Bill is an accountant who plays jazz for a hobby.
— Bill climbs mountains for a hobby.

   63. Tversky & Kahneman, *Representativeness, supra* note 60, at 92–96.

view of hundreds of FSU students, than that she would be a bank teller with no additional requirement.[64]

Bill is treated no differently. The students here find it overwhelmingly likely that boring Bill is an accountant, with that choice receiving a scaled score of 1.68 (how cruel these students can be toward fraternal professions). By contrast, the prospect of Bill playing jazz for a hobby is deemed unlikely, receiving a score of 5.51. But the prospect of Bill being an accountant who plays jazz for a hobby receives a score of 4.0, as if the taint of being an accountant could overcome the apparent absence of sufficient creativity to play jazz.[65]

3. Believing in Yourself.

The examples I have just reviewed show just how central are our established frameworks for integrating information—what behavioral economists term our decisional heuristics. Even though there is no reason to trust an unsubstantiated statement on the population of Turkey, and even though we should all acknowledge as a formal matter that two events occurring together can never be more probable than one occurring alone, nonetheless we can easily fall prey to the way we look for cues to guide our behavior. These experimental observations do challenge the assumption of the formal economic model that information can be integrated in a cold, rational fashion. Whatever the full psychological pathways by which these decisions are made, there are evident departures from the predicted mechanisms for making decisions in light of new information.

64.

LINDA	1	2	3	4	5	6	7	8
A) Teacher	7	7	11	23	36	26	16	11
B) Bookstore/Yoga	19	15	24	35	16	5	9	12
C) Feminist	56	40	22	5	7	3	2	2
D) Psychiatric	19	24	28	24	24	11	3	3
E) League	26	40	28	18	13	4	3	3
F) Bank Teller	4	2	6	3	8	26	61	25
G) Insurance	3	4	3	5	4	16	26	76
H) Bank Teller/Feminist	3	4	14	25	25	44	16	5

65.

	1	2	3	4	5	6	7	8
A) Physician	16	37	36	27	9	7	3	11
B) Architect	7	36	31	20	16	22	8	6
C) Accountant	104	17	8	4	2	5	1	2
D) Jazz	0	7	12	16	33	34	24	20
E) Surfer	5	4	5	5	13	26	42	43
F) Reporter	3	14	14	27	30	19	16	19
G) Accountant/Jazz	5	18	28	31	24	11	18	3
H) Mountain Climber	2	6	10	11	19	19	34	38

Nonetheless, these observed behaviors alone are not enough to disrupt our confidence in the basic model of dispute resolution under American civil procedure. Whatever missteps may ensue from these heuristic biases appear to be random. There may be some efficiency losses when litigants fail to integrate information properly, but there is no systemic bias. The mistakes appear as likely as not to cancel each other out.

The same cannot be said for another set of studies that test whether the mistaken integration of information is truly random. I refer here to a series of studies undertaken by Linda Babcock, Colin Camerer, George Loewenstein, and me, which sought to assess a phenomenon we termed "self-serving bias."[66] In these studies subjects were presented with a rich set of factual materials taken from an actual case involving a motor vehicle accident. The materials included deposition excerpts, maps of the accident site, medical records, and witness statements. The key was that they were provided identical information and were informed of this and further told that there was no other private information available. The subjects were then placed in negotiation settings by pairs. One of the subjects was assigned the role of plaintiff, and the other was the defendant. The defendant was given a sum of money and the parties were instructed that they could settle as to the amount or else the matter would be assigned to a judge, and that they would be taxed the costs of the litigation. Every inducement was toward settlement.

These studies are somewhat extensive and cannot be fully represented in the course of an introduction to the field of civil procedure. But the key point can be readily summarized. If errors were random, there should be no particular bias to how the parties integrated information. Following the methodology of the Priest–Klein hypothesis, errors should wash out and the overall efficiency of the process should be maintained. Unfortunately, the results do not bear this out. Rather than finding a random distribution of error, we find a persistent tendency to integrate new information in a self-serving fashion.[67] Rather than bringing parties together,

---

66. Linda Babcock et al., *Biased Judgments of Fairness in Bargaining*, 85 Am. Econ. Rev. 1337 (1995) [hereinafter Babcock et al., *Biased Judgments*]; Linda Babcock et al., *Creating Convergence: Debiasing Biased Litigants*, 22 Law & Soc. Inquiry 913, 915–23 (1997) [hereinafter Babcock et al., *Creating Convergence*]; George Loewenstein et al., *Self–Serving Assessments of Fairness and Pretrial Bargaining*, 22 J. Legal Stud. 135 (1993).

67. *See* Issacharoff, *supra* note 31, at 1738; Korobkin & Ulen, *supra* note 31, at 1093.

sharing common information can provide a fertile environment for disagreement and inefficient impasses.[68]

Let me focus on just a subset of the findings that should illustrate the point, as set forth in the following table:

1 FAIR SETTLEMENT	PLAINTIFF $37,028	DEFENDANT $19,318
2 DIFFERENCE IN ESTIMATES OF FAIR SETTLEMENT	SETTLED $11,941	DID NOT SETTLE $33,915
3 DIFFERENCE IN FAIR SETTLEMENT VALUE ESTIMATES OF PLAINTIFF AND DEFENDANT	KNEW ROLES $19,756	DID NOT KNOW ROLES $6,275
4 SETTLEMENT RATE	KNEW ROLES 0.72	DID NOT KNOW ROLES 0.94

The first line shows the challenge to the hypothesized efficient convergence based on sharing information. In this scenario, subjects were given the exact same information and asked to assess what a fair value of the plaintiff's claim would be. There was no difference between the subject populations save that in each experimental setting the subjects were told that one was the plaintiff who was seeking some of the money given at the outset to the defendant and the other was the defendant who was in possession of the money. If parties could converge on the value of the claim, there should be no difference between the groups. Even if individuals made errors in judgment, so long as there was no systematic bias, the effect should wash out in the comparative aggregate valuations. As line 1 shows, however, the differences were hardly random. Plaintiffs valued the claim almost twice as greatly as did defendants. Out of a maximum value of $100,000, the plaintiffs thought the claim was worth roughly $37,000 to the defendants' $19,000.

That the parties differed in the valuations produced from identical sets of information is significant, but more significant is the impact that the difference in valuation has on the settlement prospects of the parties. As line 2 shows, the difference in valuation is directly correlated to the ability to settle. Among the subject pairs who settled, the average difference between plaintiff and defendant valuations was $12,000, while the nonsettling pairs differed in their valuations by almost $34,000. Line 3 establishes that the relation between the role of the parties and the valuations is not merely a matter of correlation but of causation. In a subsequent experiment, subjects were divided between those pairs who gave

68. *See* Babcock et al., *Biased Judgments, supra* note 66, at 1342; Loewenstein et al., *supra* note 66, at 157–59.

their estimates of fair value after being assigned a role as plaintiff or defendant and those who were not assigned a role until after they had formed an opinion of the value of the case. Not surprisingly, there is no systematic bias to the differences in value estimates in the group that did not have their roles assigned. Line 4 further establishes that the group that did not have roles assigned was able to settle more successfully than the group whose estimations were infected by what we term self-serving bias in the integration of information. Despite strong incentives to resolve the litigation, including penalties for each period of delay in negotiations, more than a quarter of the subject litigants assigned to a role were unable to settle despite basing their estimations on identical sets of information.

III. Conclusion.

The first generation of law and economics insights helped to systematize the understanding of law and to examine critically the regulatory ambitions of the law. Its insights largely buttressed the procedural system that emerged following the adoption of the Federal Rules in 1938. The next generation of this scholarship poses a direct challenge to the comfortable assumption that our legal system gets it pretty much right. The challenge is to understand the behavioral dynamics that drive the real people we encounter in our civil justice system. If our predictions rely on the narrow incentive structure admitted by law and economics, they will often fail. This impoverished model fails to capture a robust picture of human decisionmaking.

Our next challenge is to determine what use we can make of our understanding of these phenomena. How do they apply within the legal system in general? Are the effects robust? Are they substantively important? Do they suggest policy prescriptions?

Clearly we cannot remove from real world litigants knowledge of whether they are plaintiffs or defendants. Parties involved in a car accident know who was injured and who is the defendant. But there are debiasing techniques that may prove useful[69] in some circumstances, while there may be greater warrant for earlier judicial intervention in controlling the acceleration of discovery costs in others. Nonetheless, the challenge persists. The task is to adapt the system of dispute resolution to the world in which real humans exist, imperfections and all. It is the task to which the law must turn to define its success, as future disputants will engage our

---

69. *See* Babcock et al., *Creating Convergence, supra* note 66.

evolved but still evolving litigation system. Presumably, it is a system that may even catch the attention of the 71 million inhabitants of Turkey (at the time of the FSU lecture).

TABLE OF CASES

References are to pages

223

INDEX

References are to pages